AF352710

# INDIGENOUS INTELLECTUAL PROPERTY

## An Interrupted Intergenerational Conversation

*Val Napoleon, Rebecca Johnson, Richard Overstall,
and Debra McKenzie*

Historically, Indigenous artistic, cultural, and societal expression has been identified and examined within Canadian or international legal regimes. This book identifies Indigenous intellectual property concerns as an Indigenous legal issue to be taken seriously within specific Indigenous legal orders. *Indigenous Intellectual Property* opens up complex discussions about existing Indigenous intellectual property law, and avoids the tendency to pigeonhole Indigenous intellectual property into a Western legal model.

Drawing on diverse case studies, this book considers the existing laws in the Gitxsan, Secwepemc, and Hupacasath (Nuu-chah-nulth) legal orders, as well as from the Solomon Islands and Hawai'i. The case studies are grounded in their respective legal and oral histories, and contextualized within a broader discussion of Indigenous law, addressing issues of colonial myths, shrinking conceptions of Indigenous law, common resistances to Indigenous property and law, and important connections between Indigenous law and governance and citizenship.

The book carefully considers how the governance and civic value of intellectual property points to the unsuitability of the current state and international intellectual property legal regimes to many Indigenous intellectual property concerns. Ultimately, *Indigenous Intellectual Property* reveals the various ways in which to identify and understand law within Indigenous societies – through narrative and story analysis, observations of practices and ceremonies, and political and legal ordering.

VAL NAPOLEON is a professor, the director of the Indigenous Law Research Unit, and the Law Foundation Chair of Indigenous Justice and Governance in the Faculty of Law at the University of Victoria.

REBECCA JOHNSON is a professor of law and the associate director of the Indigenous Law Research Unit in the Faculty of Law at the University of Victoria.

RICHARD OVERSTALL is a lawyer with a particular interest acting for Indigenous groups constituted under their own laws.

DEBRA McKENZIE is a research coordinator in the Faculty of Law at the University of Victoria.

# Indigenous Intellectual Property

## An Interrupted Intergenerational Conversation

VAL NAPOLEON, REBECCA JOHNSON,
RICHARD OVERSTALL, AND DEBRA McKENZIE

UNIVERSITY OF TORONTO PRESS
Toronto Buffalo London

ISBN 978-1-4875-5821-5 (cloth)    ISBN 978-1-4875-6066-9 (EPUB)
ISBN 978-1-4875-5822-2 (paper)    ISBN 978-1-4875-5823-9 (PDF)

---

**Library and Archives Canada Cataloguing in Publication**

Title: Indigenous intellectual property : an interrupted intergenerational
    conversation / Val Napoleon, Rebecca Johnson, Richard Overstall, and Debra
    McKenzie.
Names: Napoleon, Val, 1956– author | Johnson, Rebecca, 1963– author | Overstall,
    Richard, author. McKenzie, Debra, author.
Description: Includes bibliographical references and index.
Identifiers: Canadiana (print) 20240443004 | Canadiana (ebook) 20240443659 |
    ISBN 9781487558215 (hardcover) | ISBN 9781487558222 (softcover) |
    ISBN 9781487560669 (EPUB) | ISBN 9781487558239 (PDF)
Subjects: LCSH: Intellectual property – Canada. | LCSH: Customary law – Canada. |
    CSH: First Nations – Legal status, laws, etc.
Classification: LCC KIB1200 .N37 2024 | LCC KF8210.I57 N37 2024 kfmod |
    DDC 346.7104/8 – dc23

---

Cover design: John Beadle
Cover image: *Knowledge from the Deep* by James Crawford

We wish to acknowledge the land on which the University of Toronto Press
operates. This land is the traditional territory of the Wendat, the Anishnaabeg, the
Haudenosaunee, the Métis, and the Mississaugas of the Credit First Nation.

This book has been published with the help of a grant from the Federation for the
Humanities and Social Sciences, through the Awards to Scholarly Publications Program,
using funds provided by the Social Sciences and Humanities Research Council of
Canada.

University of Toronto Press acknowledges the financial support of the Government of
Canada, the Canada Council for the Arts, and the Ontario Arts Council, an agency of the
Government of Ontario, for its publishing activities.

# About the Cover Artist

James Crawford was born in and raised all over northern British Columbia. He spent ten years working in the Gwaii Haanas National Park Reserve on Haida Gwaii as a Watchman. Living and working in the old Haida village sites inspired him to attend classes at the Freda Diesing School of Northwest Coast Art, where he completed his diploma in First Nations Fine Art in 2010. A member of the NaiKun KilGaaway Clan of Haida Gwaii, he now resides in Lekwungen Territory in Victoria, BC, with his wife and fellow artist Kristy and their two children.

jamescrawford.haida@gmail.com
www.ravenstealsthelightbulb.com

# Contents

# INDIGENOUS INTELLECTUAL PROPERTY

# Introduction

The premise of this book is that the articulation, restatement, and development of Indigenous intellectual property law must derive, at least in part, from the existing relevant Indigenous legal order, an integral part of the governance of an Indigenous society.[1] Specifically, the orientation and approach of this initiative is that tangible and intangible intellectual property concerns be identified as Indigenous legal issues, and that they be taken seriously and comprehensively as legal problems within a specific Indigenous legal order. This is in contrast to the more usual approach of focusing on the state and industry, as well as domestic and international law.

The vast literature in this field reflects the seemingly intractable problem of merging the precepts of Indigenous intellectual property with the prevailing Western notion of intellectual property law. Much has been written about the development of an international intellectual property legal regime,[2] and a major subset of this category comprises

---

1 For the purposes of this book, Indigenous societies are those that originate in Canada and Indigenous peoples are those who are Indigenous according to specific laws of an Indigenous society. Arguably, a people cannot be a people without law, and a society, state, or non-state cannot govern without law.

2 For example, see S von Lewnski, ed, *Indigenous Heritage and Intellectual Property: Genetic Resources: Traditional Knowledge and Folklore* (The Hague: Kluwer, 2004); World Intellectual Property Organization, *Intellectual Property Needs and Expectations of Traditional Holders* (Geneva: WIPO, 2001); Terri Janke, *Minding Culture: Case Studies on Intellectual Property and Traditional Cultural Expression* (Geneva: WIPO, 2003); Government of Canada, *Introduction to Intellectual Property and the Protection of Indigenous Knowledge and Cultural Expressions in Canada* (Ottawa: Government of Canada, n/d), online: <https://www.ic.gc.ca/eic/site/108.nsf/eng/00007.html>; Kathy Bowrey, *Emerging Challenges in Intellectual Property* (Oxford: Oxford University Press, 2011); Tony Simpson, *Indigenous Heritage and Self-Determination: The Cultural and Intellectual Property Rights of Indigenous Peoples* (n/p: Forest Peoples Programme/International Work Group for Indigenous Affairs, 1997).

an enormous literature that addresses the poor fit between Western regimes of intellectual property rights and the safeguarding of Indigenous knowledge. For example, Jane E. Anderson detailed the difficult positioning of Indigenous knowledge in the existing intellectual property legal regime,[3] Madhavi Sunder explored Indigenous intellectual property in the context of global justice,[4] and Christophe Geiger examined the intersection between human rights and intellectual property law.[5]

A second category at the state level is an immense literature that chronicles the development of an Indigenous intellectual property law through common law, state legislation, and national initiatives. For example, Jessica C. Lai[6] considered the impact of the New Zealand Waitangi Tribunal's report, referenced as the Wai 262 report;[7] Christoph Antons explored intellectual property government initiatives and case law in the Asia-Pacific region;[8] and McGill University considered the federal government's intellectual property strategy, whose main objective was to better understand the issues of Indigenous intellectual property.[9] Again the problem addressed is the poor fit between Western intellectual property legal regimes and Indigenous knowledge.

The third category of literature considers systems of customary law[10] that protect local knowledge. Chidi Ogumanam maintains that "virtually all

---

3   Jane E Anderson, *Law, Knowledge, Culture: The Production of Indigenous Knowledge in Intellectual Property Law* (Cheltenham, UK: Edward Elgar, 2009).

4   Madhavi Sunder, *From Goods to a Good Life: Intellectual Property and Global Justice* (New Haven: Yale University Press, 2012).

5   Christophe Geiger, *Research Handbook on Human Rights and Intellectual Property* (Cheltenham, UK: Edward Elgar, 2015).

6   Jessica C Lai, *Indigenous Cultural Heritage and Intellectual Property Rights: Learning from the New Zealand Experience?* (Cham, Switzerland: Springer, 2014).

7   The Waitangi Tribunal authored the Wai 262 report concerning ownership and use of Māori knowledge, cultural expressions, and Indigenous species of flora and fauna. The report found that the government had failed to comply with its obligations, under the Treaty of Waitangi, to ensure that guardian relationships between Māori and their *taonga* (their traditional knowledge and artistic works, and their culturally significant species of flora and fauna) were acknowledged and protected, and recommended that future laws, policies, and practices do acknowledge and respect those relationships. See: <https://forms. justice.govt.nz/search/WT/reports/reportSummary.html?reportId=wt_DOC_68356606>

8   Christoph Antons, *Traditional Knowledge, Traditional Cultural Expressions, and Intellectual Property Law in the Asia-Pacific Region* (Austin: Wolters Kluwer, 2009).

9   McGill University, Centre for Intellectual Property Policy, *Report of the Workshop on Indigenous Traditional Knowledge, Traditional Cultural Expressions, and Intellectual Property* (Montreal: Centre for Intellectual Property Policy/Faculty of Law, McGill University, 2020).

10   The term *customary law* is used rather than *Indigenous law* in a number of countries, for example in South Africa and in the South Pacific.

cultures have their own knowledge-protection protocols or conventions."[11] In fact, the TRIPs agreement[12] worked to integrate Indigenous knowledge-protection protocols into intellectual property discourse. Rosemary J. Coombe has suggested that Indigenous stakeholders must participate as "equitable stakeholders" in any dialogue regarding commodification of their resources.[13] Paul Kuruk recently published a book examining the role of customary law in the control of exploitation of genetic resources.[14]

Here we are closing in on where this volume is situated. It necessarily emerges from the first two categories where the unsuitability of fit of Western intellectual property law models with Indigenous knowledge was widely canvassed. However, the solution sought is not in a modified Western model of intellectual property law, but in each Indigenous people reaffirming legal control over its Indigenous knowledge. We look to Indigenous legal orders as Kuruk and Ogumanam did, but for the purposes of this book we focus on cultural, societal, and artistic purposes rather than patents and trademarks. The approach taken here is grounded in an understanding of the history, ethics, and governance of particular Indigenous peoples,[15] and the special nature of societal, cultural, and artistic expressions.

Fiona Macmillan[16] and Joseph R. Slaughter[17] have written about the problems wrought by the characterization of Indigenous intellectual property

---

11    Chidi Ogumanam, "Localizing Intellectual Property in the Globalization Epoch: The Integration of Indigenous Knowledge" (2004) 11:2 Indiana J of Global Legal Studies 135 at 136. Ogumanam contends that this fact was made evident from the results of the WIPO report *Intellectual Property Needs and Expectations of Traditional Knowledge Holders* (Geneva: WIPO, 2001), 26.

12    See WTO *Agreement on Trade-Related Aspects of Intellectual Property Rights* (TRIPS), 15 April 1994, reprinted in (1994) ILM 1197.

13    Rosemary J Coombe, "The Recognition of Indigenous Peoples' and Community Traditional Knowledge in International Law" (2001) 14 St Thomas L Rev 275 at 285.

14    Paul Kuruk, *Traditional Knowledge, Genetic Resources, Customary Law and Intellectual Property: A Global Primer* (Cheltenham, UK: Edward Elgar, 2020).

15    A similar approach was taken in Angela Cameron, Sari Graben & Val Napoleon, eds, *Creating Indigenous Property: Power, Rights and Relationships* (Toronto: University of Toronto Press, 2020); Cathy Bell & Val Napoleon, eds, *First Nations Cultural Heritage and Law: Case Studies, Voices and Perspectives* (Vancouver: UBC Press, 2008); and Catherine Bell & Robert Paterson, eds, *Intercultural Dispute Resolution in Aboriginal Contexts* (Vancouver: UBC Press, 2008).

16    Fiona Macmillan, *Intellectual and Cultural Property: Between Market and Community* (Abingdon, UK: Routledge, 2021).

17    Joseph R Slaughter, "Form & Informality: An Unliterary Look at World Literature" in R Warhol, ed, *The Work of Genre: Selected Essays from the English Institute* (Cambridge, MA: English Institute in collaboration with American Council of Learned Societies, 2011) at 177, online: <http://quod.lib.umich.edu/cgi/t/text/text-idx?c=acls;idno=heb90055>.

as "cultural property" within the international property legal regime. This is a point central to our discussion, but our focus is on the overuse and misuse of a "cultural" characterization that ignores crucial governance roles of forms of property fundamental to Indigenous legal orders.

The formulation of Indigenous intellectual property law must start with a consideration of the existing control of Indigenous knowledge in that specific Indigenous society. At a minimum, as chapter 1 notes, the following questions must be answered: What is the tangible or intangible property? Who, if anyone, has ownership rights? Who has a fiduciary duty to ensure the property is maintained and used for an appropriate purpose? What is the underlying purpose of the property in governance structuring, in the economy, in debt and compensation, as art, and so on? What is the legal harm or injury being caused, for example undermining of legitimacy, insult to authority, loss, or misrepresentation? What is the range of historic and present-day remedies and sanctions? The bottom line is that the system of legal control for Indigenous knowledge must be situated in the particular Indigenous society, just as the Western intellectual property regime arises from and reflects the liberal economic model.

We consider two disparate Indigenous societies here to show how Indigenous intellectual property may arise, its value to the community, and how its use is controlled within that society: Richard Overstall reveals art's important role as law in Gitxsan society, and Debra McKenzie finds evidence of intellectual property law in Secwepemc stories passed down through generations. Our proposition is that should a problem or concern arise regarding Gitxsan or Secwepemc intellectual property, this issue must be explored within the respective legal order to determine its legality or illegality from that legal perspective. What will become obvious when reading the case studies is that Secwepemc society and law are different from Gitxsan society and law. These are two distinct groups[18] with different languages, different social structuring, and different economic and political ordering. This diversity adds to the richness, the depth, and the scope of this initiative – and to its challenges. Both case studies have lessons that may be helpfully compared to and extrapolated to other Indigenous societies – as long as care is taken to fully appreciate the differences and contexts. Both chapters begin with descriptive "primers" of Gitxsan and Secwepemc societies. The intention of these primers is to assist the researcher and reader to

---

18  Secwepemc is part of the Salishan linguistic group and Gitxsan is part of the Tsimshian linguistic group. Each language has at least several dialects across its respective territory.

contextualize the law of each society so that its specific logics, histories, aspirations, and structures transparently inform the legal interpretive strategies and analysis through the research.[19]

The exploration of the treatment of existing intellectual property in these two Indigenous societies makes it clear that language such as "cultural expression" and "traditional knowledge"[20] is problematic and limiting in scope. These phrases connote a subset of knowledge defined within a broader context of Western intellectual property. This language fails to acknowledge the depth and dynamism of Indigenous legal systems, and consequently serves to stunt legal meaning and practice today.

As well, unless a new student of Indigenous law, whether Indigenous or non-Indigenous, has some grasp of the depth, scope, and complexity of that law, there is often a powerful tendency to either search for "rule book" descriptions full of prescriptions and proscriptions or to settle into the comfort of overarching philosophical statements. Such efforts usually result in oversimplification, conflation of norms with behaviour,[21] or decontextualization of Indigenous legal practices from their societal moorings.

There is no doubt that consideration of the treatment of Indigenous knowledge from the perspective of Indigenous societal and legal systems is a complicated process. Rebecca Johnson confronts this reality in a concluding chapter dealing with the theft of a pair of Hupacasath masks in British Columbia. The masks were more than works of art: they also held an important governance role in the community. Here a harm arose that was not recognized by the prevailing Western intellectual property regime that is grounded in liberal economic theory.

It is important to keep in mind that the theory underlying Western intellectual property law is economic. The rationale behind this

---

19  For more information on this methodology, see Hadley Friedland & Val Napoleon, "Gathering the Threads: Developing a Methodology for Researching and Rebuilding Indigenous Legal Traditions" (2015) 1:1 Lakehead Law J 17; and Val Napoleon & Hadley Friedland, "An Inside Job: Engaging with Indigenous Legal Traditions through Stories" (2016) 61:4 McGill Law J 725.

20  Article 31 of the United Nations Declaration on the Rights of Indigenous Peoples (UNDRIP) uses this language: "the right to maintain, control, protect and develop their cultural heritage, traditional knowledge and traditional cultural expressions."

21  For example, according to Julie Cruikshank, *The Social Life of Stories: Narrative and Knowledge in the Yukon* (Vancouver: UBC Press, 1998) at 60, "The pitfall of both axioms – one linking hunters with harmony, the other of conflating norms with behaviour – is that each so easily becomes a weapon when Indigenous people fail to pass arbitrary tests of authenticity."

constructed legal regime is to stimulate originality by awarding exclusive rights in a product, and to reward the labour that goes into creation and/or development. The so-called public domain is part of this regime, whereby general ideas are available to anyone to develop, and thereby to reap economic benefits from an original expression of that idea. For example, in the Western regime, a dance movement is considered an idea and in the public domain, while a choreographed production made up of dance movements would be subject to copyright law. In a non-Western society where different legal rules apply, the idea of a public domain of unprotected creative materials may not be appropriate. As Debra McKenzie points out in a chapter on the Hawaiian *hula*, dance movements may be imbued with meaning in themselves and are thus never freely available for appropriation.

It is also important, when we consider Indigenous intellectual property, to understand that Indigenous law is not static. That is why it is a misnomer to label Indigenous knowledge as "traditional" or "cultural." Like Western legal systems, Indigenous law is a process. Law may change, and the underlying societal structures and belief systems will largely determine the direction of that change. Val Napoleon's chapter examines such change in the Solomon Islands. In spite of colonialism and accompanying pressures to adopt liberalism and Christianity, societies do not change overnight. Indigenous knowledge and the control of that knowledge is grounded in that society. The law is there, and the aim of this volume is to make Indigenous intellectual property legal regimes visible.

We hope to provide a starting point for other Indigenous peoples' inquiries into their intellectual property laws. For instance, the forms of analysis and ways of conceptualizing multiple purposes of intellectual property employed here are important and necessary elements for future research. This identification of distinct purposes of property – governance versus artistic expression – will assist in structuring and conceptualizing research for other peoples. Several future research possibilities include examining the critical pedagogical questions of interiority and internalization of Indigenous law; exploring useful comparative points between various Indigenous remedies, sanctions, and political strategies; and deconstructing Canadian examples such the *Flag Act* or the nation's coats of arms.[22]

---

22  See CST Mackie, "The Reception of England's Armorial Law into Canada" (2008) 4 (3rd series) J Heraldry Society 137.

Indigenous societies were not culturally homogenous in the past, nor are they today – and an appreciation of time depth and the fullness of legal histories is critical here. The oral histories of Indigenous societies contain examples of the taking in and incorporation of other peoples as well as extensive intersocietal marriage arrangements, agreements, and trade. For example, in one author's own community, Saulteau First Nation, there are three historic languages – Dane-zaa, Cree, and Saulteaux (and, arguably, now English). In chapter 3, Richard Overstall writes about the Gitxsan who over time adopted people of a differing linguistic group from the north into their kinship groups and communities.[23] Another example is the Dene in the very far north, who took in other peoples to form a larger political and legal collectivity.[24] Given such examples, Indigenous law, again as with much other law, is already to a large extent plural, but legal fictions today perpetuate notions of small hermetically sealed and static culturally homogenous groups existing "as is" over thousands of years.

Law is a societal phenomenon that is capable of internal diversity of cultures and languages within societies. According to the 2021 census by Statistics Canada there are 634 First Nations communities (formerly called bands)[25] in Canada, speaking more than fifty distinct languages.[26] Historically, each Indigenous society's territory was the area they could defend both physically as well as legally according to their Indigenous legal orders. Colonially imposed reserve boundaries created by the

---

23  Solomon Marsden (Gamlaxyeltxw) 9 May 1988, BCSC trial transcript, 5932 at 5959, evidence for *Delgamuukw v The Queen*, [1991] BCJ No. 525, 79 DLR (4th) 185.

24  Factoring in time depth is critical in appreciating the historical dynamics, formations, and changing of peoples, according to June Helm, *The People of the Denendeh: Ethnohistory of the Indians of Canada's Northwest Territories* (Iowa City: University of Iowa Press, 2000). Helm described two groups of Hare Dene who lived on the northern shores of Great Bear Lake in the 1860s. By the early 1900s, these two groups were no longer identifiable as Hare, and instead had become part of a people who identified as Sahtu Dene or Bearlake Dene. In fact, the Bearlake Dene were a historical amalgamation of Hare, Tli Cho, Slavey, and Mountain Dene – these were formerly disparate linguistic groups. Helm's work also refers to other major territorial shifts and what she calls "intertribal" amalgamations that occurred through time, such as joint land occupancy by the Gwichin and Hare, the merging of the Yellowknives into the Chipewyan, and the submersion of the eastern Dogribs into the Chipewyan.

25  Canada, Royal Commission on Aboriginal Peoples, *Restructuring the Relationship*, vol. 2 (Ottawa: Supply and Services Canada, 1996) at 235.

26  Statistics Canada, *Indigenous Peoples Reference Guide, Census of Population, 2021*, online: https://www12.statcan.gc.ca/census-recensement/2021/ref/98-500/009 /98-500-x2021009-eng.cfm.

*Indian Act*[27] divided and grouped Indigenous peoples into small bands by slicing across their societal Indigenous legal orders.

This division of Indigenous peoples and imposed hierarchical governance severely undermined the efficacy of the larger legal orders and the operation of Indigenous laws that had jurisdiction over all territories and villages with essential cross-cutting ties and systems of accountability. For the Gitxsan, as for many other Indigenous peoples, the historic primary political orientation consisted of horizontal relationships within and between communities of matrilineal kinship groups.[28] With the advent of the *Indian Act*, the political orientation shifted from multiple meaningful horizontal relationships to a vertical relationship between the state and the bands while simultaneously internally reconfiguring the bands into state-determined patrilineal memberships.[29]

> A keystone of Aboriginal law jurisprudence is the Crown's recognition that organized societies pre-existed within the territorial limits of what is now Canada. It is artificial to separate the concept of pre-existing societies from that of pre-existing legal orders. No bright-line distinction exists between a normative principle and an identifiable law, much less in the case of societies which do not frame their own legal orders around the idea of written common law or statutes. Canada was, and remains, a multi-jural nation, in fact if not in law.[30]

Deep learning and engagement are required to enable one to "see" the Indigenous law in the world so that the depth and scope of Indigenous lawscapes[31] become visible. This collection is written to assist making

---

27  *Indian Act*, RSC 1985, c 1-5.

28  Val Napoleon, "Legal Pluralism and Reconciliation" (Nov. 2019) Māori Law Review 1.

29  The state does so through the *Constitution Act, 1867* (UK), 30 and 31 Vict, c 3, reprinted in RSC 1985, App 11, No 5, and the *Indian Act*, which recognizes bands as legal and political entities and provides bands with funding for housing and so on. For further discussion on questions of Indigenous democracy, see Val Napoleon, "Gitxsan Democracy: On Its Own Terms," in James Tully et al, eds., *Democracy Multiplicity: Perceiving, Enacting, and Integrating Democratic Diversity* (Cambridge: Cambridge University Press, 2022) 195.

30  Honourable Chief Justice Lance Finch, BCCA, "The Duty to Learn: Taking Account of Indigenous Legal Orders in Practice," presented at the Indigenous Legal Orders and the Common Law Conference for the Continuing Legal Education Society of British Columbia, November 2012 [unpublished; on file with author].

31  Nicole Graham employs the term *lawscape* to examine how law transforms environments, and how law relates to land and resources through its property regime. See Graham, *Lawscape: Property, Environment, Law* (Abingdon, UK: Routledge-Cavendish, 2011).

visible the Indigenous lawscape. It is intentionally broad so that it can examine some of the larger questions that surround Indigenous intellectual property, including legal histories, definitions and operation of law, theoretical perspectives, the nexus of law and governance, legalities, legal processes, and the current rebuilding of Indigenous legal orders.

This type of backgrounding is not necessary when discussing an area of Canadian law because Canadian law practitioners and most Canadians possess at least a basic understanding of the Canadian state and its institutions, such as law enforcement, legislation, and the courts. For the most part, they are also familiar with the implicit and explicit narratives that animate Canadian law, hold it together with some degree of coherence, and give Canadian law meaning – even if they disagree with it. An analogous widespread knowledge about and experience with Indigenous law has not yet been restored to Canada.

## BIBLIOGRAPHY


Anderson, Jane E. *Law, Knowledge, Culture: The Production of Indigenous Knowledge in Intellectual Property Law* (Cheltenham, UK: Edward Elgar, 2009).

Antons, Christoph. *Traditional Knowledge, Traditional Cultural Expressions, and Intellectual Property Law in the Asia-Pacific region* (Austin: Wolters Kluwer, 2009).

Bell, Catherine & Val Napoleon, eds. *First Nations Cultural Heritage and Law: Case Studies, Voices and Perspectives* (Vancouver: UBC Press, 2008).

Bell, Catherine and Robert Paterson, eds. *Intercultural Dispute Resolution in Aboriginal Contexts* (Vancouver: UBC Press, 2008).

Bowrey, Kathy. *Emerging Challenges in Intellectual Property* (Oxford: Oxford University Press, 2011).

Cameron, Angela, Sari Graben & Val Napoleon, eds. *Creating Indigenous Property: Power, Rights and Relationships* (Toronto: University of Toronto Press, 2020).

Canada, Royal Commission on Aboriginal Peoples. *Restructuring the Relationship*, vol 2 (Ottawa: Supply and Services Canada, 1996).

Coombe, Rosemary J. "The Recognition of Indigenous Peoples' and Community Traditional Knowledge in International Law" (2001) 14 St Thomas L Rev 275.

Cruikshank, Julie. *The Social Life of Stories: Narrative and Knowledge in the Yukon* (Vancouver: UBC Press, 1998).

Friedland, Hadley & Val Napoleon. "Gathering the Threads: Developing a Methodology for Researching and Rebuilding Indigenous Legal Traditions" (2015) 1:1 Lakehead L J 17.

Geiger, Christophe. *Research Handbook on Human Rights and Intellectual Property* (Cheltenham, UK: Edward Elgar, 2015).

Government of Canada. *Introduction to Intellectual Property and the Protection of Indigenous Knowledge and Cultural Expressions in Canada* (Ottawa: Government of Canada, n.d.), online: <https://www.ic.gc.ca/eic/site/108.nsf/eng/00007.html>.

Graham, Nicole. *Lawscape: Property, Environment, Law* (Abingdon, UK: Routledge-Cavendish, 2011).

Helm, June. *The People of the Denendeh: Ethnohistory of the Indians of Canada's Northwest Territories* (Iowa City: University of Iowa Press, 2000).

Janke, Terri. *Minding Culture: Case Studies on Intellectual Property and Traditional Cultural Expression* (Geneva: WIPO, 2003).

Kuruk, Paul. *Traditional Knowledge, Genetic Resources, Customary Law and Intellectual Property: A Global Primer* (Cheltenham, UK: Edward Elgar, 2020).

Lai, Jessica C. *Indigenous Cultural Heritage and Intellectual Property Rights: Learning from the New Zealand Experience?* (Cham, Switzerland: Springer, 2014).

Lewnski, S von, ed. *Indigenous Heritage and Intellectual Property: Genetic Resources: Traditional Knowledge and Folklore* (The Hague: Kluwer, 2004).

Mackie, CST. "The Reception of England's Armorial Law into Canada" (2008) 4 (3rd series) J Heraldry Soc 137.

Macmillan, Fiona. *Intellectual and Cultural Property: Between Market and Community* (Abingdon, UK: Routledge, 2021).

Marsden, Solomon (Gamlaxyetxw). 9 May 1988, BCSC trial transcript, 5932 at 5959, evidence for *Delgamuukw v The Queen*, [1991] BCJ No 525, 79 DLR (4th) 185.

McGill University, Centre for Intellectual Property Policy. *Report of the Workshop on Indigenous Traditional Knowledge, Traditional Cultural Expressions, and Intellectual Property* (Montreal: Centre for Intellectual Property Policy, Faculty of Law, McGill University, 2020).

Napoleon, Val. "Gitxsan Democracy: On Its Own Terms" in James Tully et al, eds., *Democracy Multiplicity: Perceiving, Enacting, and Integrating Democratic Diversity* (Cambridge: Cambridge University Press, 2022) 195.

Napoleon, Val. "Legal Pluralism and Reconciliation" (Nov. 2019) Māori L Rev 1.

Napoleon, Val & Hadley Friedland. "An Inside Job: Engaging with Indigenous Legal Traditions through Stories" (2016) 61:4 McGill L J 725.

Ogumanam, Chidi. "Localizing Intellectual Property in the Globalization Epoch: The Integration of Indigenous Knowledge" (2004) 11:2 Indiana J of Global Legal Studies 135.

Simpson, Tony. *Indigenous Heritage and Self-Determination: The Cultural and Intellectual Property Rights of Indigenous Peoples* (Copenhagen: Forest Peoples Programme/International Work Group for Indigenous Affairs, 1997).

Slaughter, Joseph R. "Form & Informality: An Uniliterary Look at World Literature" in R Warhol, ed, *The Work of Genre: Selected Essays from the*

*English Institute* (English Institute in collaboration with American Council of
Learned Societies, 2011) at 177, online: <http://quod.lib.umich.edu/cgi/t
/text/text-idx?c=acls;idno=heb90055>.
Statistics Canada. *Indigenous Peoples Reference Guide, Census of Population, 2021,*
online: <https://www12.statcan.gc.ca/census-recensement/2021/ref
/98-500/009/98-500-x2021009-eng.cfm>.
Sunder, Madhavi. *From Goods to a Good Life: Intellectual Property and Global
Justice* (New Haven: Yale University Press, 2012).
UN General Assembly. *United Nations Declaration on the Rights of Indigenous
Peoples: resolution / adopted by the General Assembly,* A/RES/61/295, 2
October 2007, online: https://www.refworld.org/legal/resolution/unga
/2007/en/49353.
World Intellectual Property Organization. *Intellectual Property Needs and
Expectations of Traditional Holders* (Geneva: WIPO, 2001).
World Trade Organization (WTO). *Agreement on Trade-Related Aspects of Intellectual
Property Rights* (TRIPS), 15 April 1994, reprinted in (1994) ILM 1197.

LEGISLATION CITED

*Constitution Act, 1867* (UK), 30 and 31 Vict, c 3, reprinted in RSC 1985, App 11,
No 5.
*Indian Act,* RSC 1985, c 1-5.

# 1 The Octopus: What Might Constitute Indigenous Intellectual Property?

VAL NAPOLEON

There is a troubling and conflicted story about an octopus from Lau, a lagoon at the northeastern tip of Malaita, Melanesia.[1] I am inviting the octopus herself into this chapter and am employing the octopus's story to explore and articulate some of the issues and questions of Indigenous intellectual property. What I am interested in is how people conceptualize intangible property or societal expressions, and its boundaries and control. What are the points of conflict and how do people manage conflict through their intellectual property laws?

One telling of the story begins like this:

> The Lau raised their children on the water, safe from the headhunters and mosquitoes that populated the bush. Fish filled their nets. Life was good. When the ancestors died, their spirits did not leave the lagoon. Instead, they inhabited the bodies of sharks and birds and, together with other spirit creatures, they were able to protect their descendants with their magic.
>
> …
>
> … Maranda tricked the priests into giving him the secret name of the ancestors. He used those words to beguile the octopus, lure it through the reefs and away across the Pacific. The creature did not go willingly. It used its power to strike Maranda with a terrible illness and it killed his wife. But still it did not return. The octopus had not been seen near its coral sanctuary in years. Now, with no spirit to protect them, the people of

---

1　Charles Montgomery, "The Octopus: Can the Myths of the Lau Lagoon Clan Survive Their Preservation?" (May 2006) 4:22 The Walrus, online: <https://thewalrus.ca/2006-05-anthropology/>. Montgomery wrote another version of this story in *Last Heathen: Encounters with Ghosts and Ancestors in Melanesia* (Vancouver: Douglas and McIntyre, 2004) at 238.

Foueda have become vulnerable, falling victim to mysterious diseases or drowning inexplicably in the empty and unforgiving sea.[2]

## Octopus Background

Foueda is a village on an island in the South Pacific archipelago of the Solomon Islands, just off the coast of Malaita. The people there understand that when their ancestors die, their spirits do not leave the vast Lau Lagoon, but rather return to inhabit the bodies of sharks, birds, and other creatures. In this way, the ancestors protected the people, and in turn the people honoured their ancestors with ceremonies and blood sacrifices.

Their strongest protector was the speckled octopus. The octopus took care of the people: "If they were lost at sea, he would bring them home. If they were drowning, he would save them."[3] Only the priests of the Rere clan knew the octopus's real name, but they kept it a secret so that "lay people, fools and enemies"[4] would not abuse its power.

In the mid-1960s, there arrived a newly minted anthropologist from Harvard, Pierre Maranda. He felt fortunate to have arrived ahead of the church and so found a people untainted by Christianity. By Maranda's account, the Rere priests allowed him to observe their rituals and record their stories, telling him to *"kede, kede, kede*: write, write, write!"[5] According to him, the priests allowed him to record their secrets and the sacred names of spirits and places, whispering all of these secrets to him, except the secret name of the speckled octopus.

In the conflicting story, the priests refused to let Maranda into their tabu hut, so he tied a tape recorder to a stick and poked it through the door of the tabu hut while the priests performed their sacrifices.[6] According to the men from Foueda, "That's how he stole all their secret incantations. That's why, when Maranda got on his boat and went back to Canada, the octopus followed him."[7] The next several decades were a period of colonial disruption: the church arrived, and when the people took up Christianity they disregarded the Rere priests and their ancient religious practices.

---

2   *Ibid* at 3.

3   *Ibid.*

4   *Ibid.*

5   *Ibid* at 7.

6   Montgomery, *Last Heathen, supra* note 1 at 239.

7   *Ibid.*

In Maranda's version, the priests told him that the religion of their ancestors was dying and that they could not find a non-Christian successor – not even their sons wanted their sacred knowledge. In 1975, the priests told him the secret name of the speckled octopus with the proviso that he could only tell the octopus's secrets to a non-Christian.[8] However, the alternative account, as we have seen, has Maranda tricking the priests by surreptitiously recording their closed gatherings.[9] In both versions of the story, the anthropologist went home to Canada, taking the octopus's secrets with him. The priests committed suicide (described as metaphysical transgression causing their death within weeks).[10]

And then arose another story from the South Pacific archipelago of Melanesia. It is this:

> A foreigner had stolen ... [the peoples'] octopus and was holding it captive in a swimming pool in his own faraway island, which was called Canada ... and [he] is using the magic power of our octopus to make himself rich and famous.[11]

When asked about this new story, Maranda was deeply hurt to be characterized as a thief. He loved the people that he had spent more than two decades with. To prove his innocence, Maranda showed his backyard to the bishop of Malaita, and later to the journalist Montgomery: "See, no swimming pool. No octopus."[12] The anthropologist wished all the people of Foueda could see his backyard.

---

8  Montgomery, "The Octopus," *supra* note 1 at 8.

9  Montgomery, *Last Heathen, supra* note 1 at 239.

10  *Ibid* at 240.

11  Montgomery, "The Octopus," *supra* note 1 at 2. As usual with any story, there are always conflicting stories so there is another account concerning the octopuses of the lagoon. According to Bennie Buga and Veikila Vuki, "The totem of the people of Foueda is the octopus. The Foueda people believe that octopus was a favourite food of their ancestors, who were brave warriors and gained victory over their enemies. It is believed that when these ancestors died they turned into octopuses. Octopuses have special protection on Foueda reefs, and because of these ancient beliefs the people will not eat octopus. Because of these restrictions, there is an abundance of octopus on reefs around the artificial island of Foueda." See Bennie Buga and Veikila Vuki, "The People of the Artificial Island of Foueda, Lau, Malaita, Solomon Islands: Traditional Fishing Methods, Fisheries Management and the Roles of Men and Women in Fishing" (July 2012) 22 Women Fisheries Information Bulletin 42 at 44. This means that the speckled octopus was not alone in that lagoon. Perhaps it also means that in spite of Christianity and liberalism the power of the octopus is alive.

12  *Montgomery*, "The Octopus," *supra* note 1 at 5.

Maranda said, "The knowledge is there. It's ready. It's available. But I'm not going to disclose it without a proper [non-Christian] recipient."[13] So there is truth to the myth of the stolen octopus, just as perhaps there is truth in all myth. From one perspective, the Lau's crisis "is grounded not so much in thievery as in loyalty. The Lau have pledged their allegiance to a competing god and a new set of myths. And Maranda, faced with a choice between fulfilling the aspirations of the dead or those of a new generation of Lau, has chosen the dead."[14]

Sadly, from Maranda's perspective, there was no Lau person qualified to hear the octopus's secrets. It seems that he became the last priest.

That is the end of the story. It is a complex story with hard edges, tensions, discomforts, and thorny questions, including: What are the speckled octopuses of today? Who are the priests of today? Who has access to the octopuses? How are octopuses created? Who controls the octopus? What is the constraining swimming pool comprised of? Why did the octopus leave? Does the octopus need to be freed? Different understandings of the octopus create very real material consequences in people's lives, and this is why we need to interrogate our interpretations of this conflicted little story.

The complicated speckled octopus is a useful metaphor for the complicated questions of Indigenous intellectual property. If one understands Indigenous intellectual property as being solely within the purview of the Canadian legislative regime (primarily copyright, patent, trademark, industrial designs[15]) or the World Intellectual Property Organization,[16] then those legal frameworks work to shape what intellectual property is and, obviously, also its protections. These national and international legal institutions and regimes are important for Indigenous peoples, who have employed them with varying degrees of success over the years.[17] These same regimes have also generated over

---

13   *Ibid* at 13.

14   *Ibid* at 15.

15   *Patent Act* RSC 1985 c P-4, *Trademarks Act* RSC 1985 c T-13, *Copyright Act* RSC 1985 c C-42, *Industrial Design Act* RSC 1985 c I-9, and the *Integrated Circuit Topography Act* SC 1990 c 37.

16   World Intellectual Property Organization, online: <https://www.wipo.int/portal/en/index.html.> See WIPO, *Intellectual Property and Traditional Cultural Expressions/Folklore* (Geneva: WIPO, n/d), online: <www.wipo.int>.

17   For examples see: Megan M Carpenter, "Intellectual Property Law and Indigenous Peoples: Adapting Copyright Law to the Needs of a Global Community" (2004) 7 Yale Hum Rts & Dev L J 51; WIPO, *Protect and Promote Your Culture: A Practical Guide to Intellectual Property for Indigenous Peoples and Local Communities* (Switzerland: WIPO, 2017), online: <https://www.wipo.int/edocs/pubdocs/en/wipo_pub_1048.

thirty years of frustrated critiques because of their failure to adequately meet the "protection needs" of Indigenous peoples.[18]

However, when one moves away from state or international law to instead locate intellectual property within Indigenous legal orders, one finds a very different understanding of intellectual property with different purposes and controls accordingly. As Debra McKenzie sets out in chapter 2, the establishment of domestic and international legal institutions and legal frameworks has shifted the legal treatment of Indigenous intellectual property away from that of *control* according to the Indigenous legal order, to that of *protection* within the external legal regime. This shift has profoundly reoriented the entire field of Indigenous intellectual property and its arising questions. In this way, the legal regimes of domestic and international intellectual property law seem to have become a swimming pool constraining the control and life of Indigenous intellectual property.

## Control of the Octopus: Indigenous Intellectual Property as Indigenous Legal Issue

The overarching tenet of this chapter is that Indigenous tangible and intangible intellectual property concerns can and should be identified as Indigenous legal problems so that they are taken seriously and integrally situated within specific Indigenous legal orders. This deliberate locating of intellectual property problems in a specific legal order requires, at a minimum, answering these questions: What is the tangible or intangible property? Who is the owner (i.e., kinship group, etc.)? How does law reflect and maintain the underlying purpose of the property (e.g., governance structuring, economic roles, art, compensation)? What is the legal harm or injury being caused (e.g., undermining of legitimacy, insult to authority, loss, misrepresentation)? What is the range of historic and present-day remedies and sanctions?

---

pdf>; Jada Boggs, "Protecting Indigenous Artists against Infringement and Appropriation" (17 November 2022), online (blog): Copyright Alliance https://copyrightalliance.org/protecting-indigenous-artists-infringement-appropriation/.

18  For examples see Molly Torsen & Jane Anderson, *Intellectual Property and the Safeguarding of Traditional Cultures: Legal Issues and Practical Options for Museums, Libraries and Archives* (Geneva: WIPO, 2010); Vandana Shiva, *Protect or Plunder: Understanding Intellectual Property Rights* (London: Zed Books, 2001); Jane Anderson, *Law, Knowledge, Culture: The Production of Indigenous Knowledge in Intellectual Property Law* (Cheltenham, UK: Edward Elgar, 2009).

The failure to articulate problems as Indigenous legal issues within a legal order is essentially a failure to harness and make available the legal resources, precedents, and principled reasoning so critically important to Indigenous peoples' self-government and self-determination today. Ultimately, it is a failure to comprehend the fullness of the octopus – her legal and governing purpose in the intellectual and economic life of the people of Lau.

Over almost four decades, a broad range of Indigenous intellectual property concerns have become increasingly prominent in national and international discourses and have generated an enormous literature.[19] Despite this, these issues continue to frustrate Indigenous artists, groups, and communities the world over. While there have been task forces and reports in many countries on intellectual property[20] topics, there has not yet been a focused and deliberate articulation of an Indigenous legal response developed from within an Indigenous legal order, as opposed to the typically unproductive focus on domestic and

---

19   Lindsay Nixon, *A Culture of Exploitation: "Reconciliation" and the Institutions of Canadian Art* (Toronto: Yellowhead Institute, 2020), online: <www.yellowheadinstitute.org>.

20   There are numerous reports, books, and articles on various aspects on Indigenous intellectual property worldwide, including from Canada. See, for example, Merle Alexander & James Struthers, "Squaring the Circle – Indigenous Intellectual Property and the Canadian Trademark System" (March 2020) Mondaq, online: <https://www.mondaq .com/canada/trademark/905606/squaring-the-circle-indigenous-intellectual-property -and-the-canadian-trademark-system>; Patricia Adjei, "Working Ethically with Indigenous Cultural and Intellectual Property: Australia Launches New Protocols" (2020) 4 Intellectual Property Magazine, online: <https://www.wipo.int/wipo_magazine /en/2020/04/article_0006.html>; Katy Ryley & Mary Moran, "Protecting Indigenous Intellectual Property Rights: Tools That Work" (Dec 2000) Cultural Survival Quarterly Magazine, online: <https://www.culturalsurvival.org/publications/cultural-survival -quarterly/protecting-indigenous-intellectual-property-rights-tools>; Terri Janke, *Minding Culture: Case Studies on Intellectual Property and Traditional Cultural Expression* (Geneva: WIPO, 2004); and Government of Canada, *Introduction to Intellectual Property and the Protection of Indigenous Knowledge and Cultural Expressions in Canada* (Ottawa: Government of Canada, n/d), online: <https://www.ic.gc.ca/eic/site/108.nsf/eng /00007.html>. For several examples of academic publications, see Jeremy de Beer and Daniel Dylan, "Traditional Knowledge and Governance Challenges in Canada" in Matthew Rimmer, ed, *Indigenous Intellectual Property: A Handbook of Contemporary Research* (Northampton, MA: Edward Elgar, 2015); and Reagan Seidler, "Constitutional Rights to Intellectual Property" (2020) 35 Intellectual Property Institute of Canada 37, online: <https://ipic.ca/cipr/constitutionalized-rights-to-indigenous-intellectual -property-2020-35-1.htm>; also see Cathy Bell and Val Napoleon, eds, *First Nations Cultural Heritage and Law: Case Studies, Voices and Perspectives*, companion vol (Vancouver: UBC Press, 2008); and Catherine Bell and Robert Paterson, eds, *Intercultural Dispute Resolution in Aboriginal Contexts* (Vancouver: UBC Press, 2008).

international law's treatment of Indigenous legal matters. The predominate state and international law orientation to the field has meant that perspectives from within Indigenous legal orders and their legalities remain largely unexamined. Instead, there is a continuing insistence or expectation that state and international legal processes can somehow be revised to deal with the range of intellectual property problems and conflicts experienced by Indigenous peoples.

## Learning to See the Whole Octopus

Every geographic space in Canada has more than one legal order occupying it – today, this is the common law and at least one Indigenous law, and in Quebec there is also civil law. We can see this overlapping of legal orders repeated in every country across the planet. For the most part, Indigenous legal orders, while still existing and operating, have been disrupted, displaced, and undermined by various colonial forces. Indigenous self-determination and self-governance require, first, the rebuilding of Indigenous legal orders, laws, and institutions, and second, the creation of legal and political arrangements for how Indigenous laws may interact with the respective state laws. Indigenous peoples in Canada and across the world are engaged in a kaleidoscope of activism and negotiations with states concerning all aspects of governance, political and arrangements, and jurisdiction.

Law is an essential and integral part of governance and of being a people – this is true for both Indigenous legal orders and nation state legal orders.[21]

> While there is no question that Indigenous laws have been passed on through the generations, we are not starting from a neutral spot, where Indigenous legal traditions are completely intact, left magically untouched by hundreds of years of colonialism. The task of greater recognition and use of Indigenous laws in Canada requires more than simply uncovering pristine laws in protective bubbles to isolate them from the damages of colonization. It is not an exercise in legal archaeology. Colonialism has disrupted Indigenous laws, legal pedagogies, and historic means of legitimization and promulgation. Today's work is about recovering and then

---

21  Val Napoleon, "Gitxsan Democracy: On Its Own Terms" in James Tully et al, eds, *Democracy Multiplicity: Perceiving, Enacting, and Integrating Democratic Diversity* (Cambridge: Cambridge University Press, 2022) 195. Also see the important work of Kristen Rundle, *Forms Liberate: Reclaiming the Jurisprudence of Lon L Fuller* (Oxford: Hart, 2012).

taking up an interrupted intergenerational conversation, with all its complexities and tensions.[22]

Rebuilding Indigenous law and reclaiming the language of law[23] is an immense undertaking, but absolutely doable and it is being done.[24] It means taking Indigenous law seriously as law, and includes understanding (1) how law is collaborative and legitimately ascertained, (2) when and how changes to laws are legitimately made, and (3) how law is applied and when it is broken.[25] As with every other legal order, Indigenous law takes time and intellectual effort to determine what the legal issues are, what the relevant laws are, whether laws have been broken, what precedents need to be analysed, and how to develop appropriate, principled, reasoned legal responses for application.

The articulation, restatement, and development of Indigenous intellectual property law and legal processes must derive, at least in part, from the relevant local/regional Indigenous legal order. Failure to locate Indigenous intellectual property law issues within an Indigenous legal order results in pan-Indigenous, general, simple, and often instrumental declarations of Indigenous law and of intellectual property problems.

## Approaching the Octopus

No society can properly be understood or explained without a coherent conception of its law and legal doctrine. The social, moral, and cultural

---

22   Hadley Friedland and Val Napoleon, "An Inside Job: Engaging with Indigenous Legal Traditions through Stories" (2016) special issue, McGill L J 725 at 740–1.

23   Hadley Friedland, *Reclaiming the Language of Law: Exploring the Contemporary Articulation and Application of Cree Legal Principles in Canada* (dissertation, University of Alberta, 2015) [unpublished, on file with author].

24   For examples, see University of Victoria, Faculty of Law, Indigenous Law Research Unit at <www.ilru.ca> and University of Alberta, Faculty of Law, Wahkowtowin Law and Governance Lodge at <https://www.ualberta.ca/wahkohtowin/index.html>.

25   HLA Hart, *The Concept of Law* (Oxford: Clarendon, 1961). For an application of Hart's theory in an American Indigenous jurist context, see Matthew Fletcher, "Rethinking Customary Law in Tribal Court Jurisprudence" (2006) 04 Indigenous Law & Policy Centre Working Paper. For an approach that disconnects Hart's theory from a centralized state, see Val Napoleon, *Ayook: Gitxsan Legal Order and Legal Theory* (dissertation, University of Victoria, 2009) [unpublished]. For an approach that connects Hart's theory to Indigenous linguistic methodologies, see Naiomi Metallic, "Five Linguistic Methods for Revitalizing Indigenous Laws" (2023) 68 McGill L J, online: <https://ssrn.com/abstract=4099156>.

foundations of the law, and the theories which both inform and account for them, are no less important than the law's "black letter."[26]

The law of every society must enable that society to collaboratively manage all aspects of messy collective life, including how it organizes relationships to the stuff (tangible and intangible) of the world. While the legal order of a society will be unique to that society, the kinds of problems that law must manage are of a universal nature.[27] At minimum, a legal order must include substantive and procedural law, legal processes, and legal institutions through which law operates to govern the full scope of its political ordering, economy, human relations with lands and resources, human relations with water and non-human life forms, families and children, international relations, harms and injuries, human rights, conflicts, and citizenship. Law, including Indigenous law, must be absolutely functional in order to do the reasoned, hard work of law in real and material ways. This is the depth and scope of Indigenous (and other) law that is necessary to enable stable societal-level management over the long term.

The application of Indigenous law begins with real legal problems; if those legal problems appear either unclear, minor, or simple, it is usually a sign that more research and thinking is necessary to make the law and legal resources visible in all their contextual complexity. In the conflicted stories of the speckled octopus, there is no mention of Lau law – instead, it remains invisible and the people appear to be lawless. Consequently, there is no intellectual frame or interpretative process that makes anything visible beyond a particular and very simplistic telling of a myth, and the people are also rendered simplistic, static and, worse, gullible.

### Don't Shrink the Octopus

Just as many Canadians have an anti-intellectual, instrumental, and impoverished understanding of Canadian law,[28] some Indigenous peoples have a limited understanding of their own law because it has been

---

26  Raymond Wacks, *Understanding Jurisprudence: An Introduction to Legal Theory* (Oxford: Oxford University Press, 2005) at 5.

27  Friedland & Napoleon, "Inside Job," *supra* note 23; Hadley Friedland & Val Napoleon, "Gathering the Threads: Indigenous Legal Methodology" (2015) 1:1 Lakehead L J 33 (translated into French for use in Quebec and Labrador).

28  This was recently demonstrated by the demands of the truckers' convoy organized in response to mandated vaccinations and restrictions. See, for example, Peter McLaren, "Some Thoughts on Canada's 'Freedom Convoy' and the Settler Colonial State" (2022) 54:7 Educational Philosophy and Theory 867; Alain Beauclair, "Freedom in the Age of Social Stupidity" (2023) 37(1) J Speculative Philosophy 117.

undermined through intrusive and oppressive state law, and by relentless neo-liberalism. The internalization of law and its essential lived interiority are crucial for the maintenance of reasoned lawfulness and the fullness of Indigenous legal worlds. Pedagogical questions of Indigenous legal interiority have not received enough critical attention, but must be incorporated into the rebuilding of Indigenous law if it is to be sustained beyond rhetoric or philosophy. Critical engagement with Indigenous law must include the processes of how its legalities are collaboratively conceived and sustained in Indigenous public discourse and around kitchen tables in everyday life.

We know that enforcement on its own is never adequate to ensuring societal lawfulness or adherence to law, whether intellectual property law or any other area of law.[29] It is necessary to expand the thinking of Indigenous law beyond the limiting notions of "law as enforcement" and "law as rules" towards "law as lived" to empower people to see themselves as legal agents and so act accordingly. Again, one of the future key pedagogical questions is how Indigenous peoples internalize the law from their legal order so that they can take part in its legal problem solving as effective, self-determining legal actors. Law, in its best sense, creates and enables healthy citizenries and communities. Indigenous law, legal processes, and institutions must explicitly centre citizenship and human dignity as core animating concepts.[30]

In the tellings of the conflicted octopus stories, the Rere priests appear to rigidly hold all the authority and associated knowledges such as the name of the octopus, which are not shared with the people. Consequently and, arguably, reasonably, the colonial experience and attendant hardships were simplistically interpreted by the people as being caused by the theft of the octopus. Because this authority and knowledge were withheld from them, the people were passive and unable to comprehend their situation as legal agents with any control.[31] They

---

29   Kristen Rundle, "Fuller's Relationships" in H Takikawa, ed, *The Rule of Law and Democracy: The 12th Kobe Lecture and the 1st IVR Japan International Conference, Kyoto, July 2018* (Stuttgart: Franz Steiner, 2020) 17; and Kristen Rundle, *Forms Liberate, supra* note 23.

30   *Forms Liberate, supra* note 23.

31   See Stefan Krieger's analyses of the writing of two rabbis, Rabbi Akiva and Rabbi Ishmael, and their opposing interpretations of the Torah. Rabbi Akiva interpreted the stories in such a way that the resulting laws were "mandatory, and people have no autonomy in their decision making." As a result, Rabbi Akiva's stories "portray a passive people given explicit commandments for all aspects of their lives ... Akiva gives no discretion [in decision making] either to the people or their leaders." In contrast, Rabbi Ishmael believes people have the ability to reason in

could only wait until the octopus returned of her own volition or was brought back by someone else; until then, there is a type of narrative paralysis within this colonial suffering.

Now imagine that the story of the speckled octopus was explicitly articulated as a legal construct that was part of a larger Lau legal order.[32] Arguably, the octopus would then be understood as an intangible property owned by, perhaps, the priests or the larger political collectivity of the people. If this were the case, the octopus couldn't be stolen, though there could still be related issues of cultural appropriation.[33] What happened within the story in terms of information, treatment, and legal response would be framed and collaboratively reasoned through Lau law concerning intellectual property (i.e., processes, precedent, range of legitimate legal responses, guiding legal principles, substantive and procedural rights, and legal obligations).

The story of the theft of the speckled octopus would itself become part of the repertoire of available Lau oral histories as a counter-story and precedent concerning what not to do in the solving of future intellectual property problems. Were this the telling of the speckled octopus, the Lau people would be an active citizenry with proactive narratives with the abilities to find their way through the tangle of colonial oppressions.

## Colonial Octopus Myths

The emerging field of Indigenous law is fraught with fears, critiques, and conflicts about how to work with and research Indigenous law. There are several exceptionally resilient and pervasive colonial myths that circulate and recirculate, often paralysing critical conversations about Indigenous law. One of these is a narrative of fragility, and another is a narrative of incommensurability.[34]

---

their decision-making processes and individuals have some independence in their own decisions. According to him, decisions "are to be made in the context of the everyday experience of the people and their rabbis, not based solely on some eternal command of Mount Sinai." Stefan H. Krieger, "The Place of Storytelling in Legal Reasoning: Abraham Joshua Heschel's Torah Min Hashamayim" (2010) 6 Storytelling, Self, Society 169, online: <http://ssrn.com/abstract=1010930>.

32  There is a parallel found in Hadley Friedland, *The Wetiko Legal Principles: Cree and Anishinabek Responses to Violence and Victimization* (Toronto: University of Toronto Press, 2018), where Indigenous legal principles are usefully applied to contemporary social issues.

33  See the discussion in Jesse Wente, *Unreconciled: Family, Truth and Indigenous Resistance* (New York: Penguin Canada, 2021).

34  Friedland and Napoleon, "Inside Job," *supra* note 24 at 753–4.

First, according to the narrative of fragility, if someone engages "improperly" or critically with Indigenous law, it will break or become somehow weakened. In other words, Indigenous law is so fragile that only the most delicate engagement with it is possible, usually from an idealizing distance with no touching and no critical questions. This is such a powerful and pervasive myth that I often have to tell my students or audiences that they will not break Gitxsan (or any other Indigenous) law by asking hard questions. In fact, the most respectful thing they can do is to treat it seriously as law and to ask tough questions – after all, Indigenous law, as with any other law, must do the hard work of law in Indigenous societies and locally in their communities.[35]

Second, the narrative of incommensurability holds that Indigenous peoples cannot tell non-Indigenous peoples (or sometimes other Indigenous peoples: urban, etc.) about Indigenous laws because they, the non-Indigenous (or other), are incapable of understanding it. Variations of this narrative are levelled at Indigenous peoples who do not speak their own language or were not raised in their own Indigenous community. It seems clear enough that this narrative is rooted in stereotypes and, often, fear. Again, when one looks at the oral histories of different Indigenous legal orders (e.g., Cree, Dene, Gitxsan, Tsilhqot'in), one finds ample examples of deliberate legal and political practices of Indigenous internationalism and communication across legal orders because, quite simply, no Indigenous society ever lived in isolation. Such intersocietal practices include the capacities to communicate across societal bounds, across language differences beyond word translations, and to explore patterns and differences in order to develop comparative conceptions, logics, and constructs.[36]

It should go without saying, but doesn't, that Indigenous peoples were and are intellectual beings (along with their emotional, spiritual, and physical selves, of course). Law is fundamentally a collaborative intellectual enterprise that is informed by cosmologies, deeply held ethics,[37] philosophies, and so on. Perhaps it is the extensive emphasis on healing in recent years combined with the ruthless colonial denial of Indigenous thought that has caused the emotional and spiritual to

---

35  For a discussion of the "hard work" of law see Jutta Brunnée & Stephen J Toope, *Legitimacy and Legality in International Law* (Cambridge: Cambridge University Press, 2010).

36  See the invaluable work of Naiomi Metallic, *supra* note 27. Also see Naiomi Metallic, "Six Examples Applying the Meta-principle Linguistic Method: Lessons for Indigenous Law Implementation" (2022) 73 UNB L J.

37  John Borrows, *Law's Indigenous Ethics* (Toronto: University of Toronto Press, 2019).

eclipse the intellectual in so much of the discourse. It is worth noting that the Cree medicine wheel, which represents, among other things, holism, comprises four elements: mental/intellectual, physical, emotional, and spiritual.

The stories, and the elders and communities, all demonstrate that Indigenous laws are made of stronger stuff than the limiting colonial narratives assume.[38] Today's challenge is for Indigenous legal scholarship to fully engage with Indigenous laws, and for scholars to be transparent about their methods and rigorous and critical in their own work.[39] Working critically with Indigenous law raises many more critical questions. These need to be embraced and taken on as an integral part of Indigenous legal work.[40]

> After all, such questions are a vital part of robust and respectful engagement with Indigenous legal traditions. For example, we need to acknowledge and directly address the fact that Indigenous laws are influenced by the power dynamics and politics around them (just as Canadian laws are). We need to be open and reflective about our own backgrounds, interests and influences as we approach this work. We need to be mindful of the questions around forms creating externally imposed or unexamined transformation of Indigenous legal traditions. What we do not want to do is let these critical questions paralyze us into inaction.[41]

---

38   Val Napoleon, "Did I Break It? Recording Indigenous (Customary) Law" (2019) 22 PER/PELJ 2019, online: <http://dx.doi.org/10.17159/1727-3781/2019/v22i0a7588>.

39   Some of the weaknesses that have undermined human rights in non-state justice initiatives throughout the world include the lack of a sound research base and poor scholarship, resulting in "inconsistent, incoherent or unrealistic policies." International Council on Human Rights, *When Legal Worlds Overlap: Human Rights, State and Non-State Law* (Geneva: ATAR Roto, 2009) at ix.

40   There are an increasing number of Indigenous legal scholars and allies engaging with Indigenous law around the world. Here are just a few: Antonio Pena Jumpa (Peru), Meghan Davis (Australia), Nicole Watson (Australia), Claire Charters (New Zealand), Carwyn Jones (New Zealand), Darcy Lindberg (Canada), Tracey Lindberg (Canada), Alan Hanna (Canada), Naiomi Metallic (Canada), Patricia Barkaskas (Canada), John Borrows (Canada), Hadley Friedland (Canada), Lindsay Borrows (Canada), Tamara Pearl (Canada), Rebecca Johnson (Canada), Richard Overstall (Canada), Janna Promislow (Canada), Fatima Osama (South Africa), Chuma Humonga (Zambia), Merle Alexander (Canada), Tamara Napoleon (Canada), Koren Lightning-Earle (Canada), Sarah Morales (Canada), Aaron Mills (Canada), Karen Drake (Canada), Ghislain Otis (Canada), Jean LeClair (Canada), Sophie Théiault (Canada), Jeremy Webber (Canada), Robert Clifford (Canada), and Lana Lowe (Canada).

41   Friedland & Napoleon, "Inside Job," *supra* note 24 at 753–4.

## The Octopus and the Stuff of the World

As has been argued above, every society has governed itself comprehensively, which has included legal and political ordering. Law is an integral part of how people organize themselves in their relationships with the stuff of the world – with all parts of their worlds – land, non-human life forms, water, air, art, and every tangible and non-tangible form of expression. Indigenous legal orders included property systems[42] or legal ways of relating to the stuff of the world.[43] We see Indigenous laws governing trespass (e.g., land and "chattels"), access, inheritance, liability, transfers, life interests, economic and political obligations (e.g., forms of taxation), and definitions of private and public.[44]

In English and in common law, this system of organizing is called property, a way to legally determine and manage the relationships between people and things. It is useful to note that there are many systems of property, one of which is private property, but even private[45] property is part of a public legal system, and arguably, all law – including Indigenous law – is public. While there is much important criticism about property writ large, and particularly about its instrumental role in colonial exploitation and theft and in ongoing economic and power disparities the world over, care must be taken not further displace Indigenous law or to create unnecessary dichotomies by erroneously characterizing Indigenous law as having been entirely communal and to further render Indigenous legal institutions and property invisible.[46]

---

42   There is resistance to property being a necessary part of how human societies govern themselves. See, for example, Rinaldo Walcott, *On Property* (Windsor, ON: Biblioasis, 2021).

43   Angela Cameron, Sari Graben & Val Napoleon, eds, *Creating Indigenous Property* (Toronto: University of Toronto Press, 2020. Also see CBC, "Rinaldo Walcott Calls for the Abolition of Property" (with Val Napoleon and Christopher Essert), *Ideas* (5 March 2021), online: <https://www.cbc.ca/radio/ideas/rinaldo-walcott-calls-for-the-abolition-of-property-1.5936800>.

44   Napoleon, *Ayook, supra* note 27. Also see Richard Overstall, "Encountering the Spirit in the Land: 'Property' in a Kinship-Based Legal Order" in John McLaren, AR Buck & Nancy E Wright, eds, *Despotic Dominion: Property Rights in British Settler Societies* (Vancouver: UBC Press, 2004).

45   Private law (property, torts, and contracts) concerns disputes that are between individuals rather than between an individual(s) and the state. Private property describes land that is owned by an individual or group, as opposed to public land such as parks, Crown land, or other form of public ownership.

46   See for instance, Walcott, *supra* note 44.

## Seeing the Octopus's Multiple Purposes

One way to examine and make visible the dual and multiple purposes of some Indigenous intellectual property is with an exploratory exercise:[47]

> Millie is an internationally renowned Gitxsan opera singer. She is unusual because she both writes opera music and sings in Gitsanimx. To date, most of her necessary artistic copyright protections fit within the existing Canadian *Copyright Act*. She belongs to the House of Luuxhon of the Frog Clan from Gitanyow. Millie recently launched a new opera. However, multiple concerns have been raised because this new opera is based almost entirely on an oral history that:
>
> *Scenario 1*: belongs to the House of Luuxhon, her matrilineal kinship group in the Frog Clan
>
> *Scenario 2*: belongs to another Gitxsan House in the Wolf Clan
>
> *Scenario 3*: is based on a Secwepemc oral history (a different people from a different linguistic group in the British Columbia interior)
>
> Millie has approached you for advice. For each scenario, consider what you need to know. What advice might you provide? Specifically, to answer Millie in the context of each scenario, what do you need to know about Gitxsan law and about Secwepemc law?

In Gitxsan law, formal oral histories, crests, names, and many songs form the decentralized governing institutions for Gitxsan people, and they are owned by the matrilineal kinship groups (called "Houses" in English).[48] However, they are also tangible and intangible property from both Gitxsan and Canadian legal perspectives. In other words, for the Gitxsan and many other Indigenous peoples, governance is the original purpose of the intellectual property law, as opposed to commodification.

For Millie, these are artistic and societal/cultural expressions that historically belonged to and are owned by either the Gitxsan or the Secwepemc people through their respective legal orders, and which fulfil numerous specific societal and economic functions in those societies. However, the songs, dances, crests, oral histories (*adaawk, antamahlaswx,* and other forms of oral histories) may also be understood as forms of Canadian intellectual property as they resemble, at least partially and superficially, the subject matter of the copyright.

---

47  Val Napoleon, a class exercise example of transsystemic property law (2021) JID/JD, University of Victoria.

48  For a more extensive applied treatment of Gitxsan intellectual property, see Richard Overstall's "A People of Themselves" at chapter 3 herein.

For the Gitxsan, the other purposes of intellectual property are manifestly societal and include compensation, gifts, debt payments, establishing international relations, and trade. Important questions for Millie include who owns the property (e.g., the House), how is the property owned (e.g., in trust, collective, or individual), and what is owned (e.g., formal oral/legal histories, shared oral histories). Part of the necessary research is to delve into the legal histories in order to establish the lineage of the oral history and whether there is an earlier shared history or historic political/legal amalgamation with another House. Millie might then move on to the next steps of exploring Gitxsan and Secwepemc dispute-management processes for intellectual properties and identifying past legal processes and precedents for analysis and application.

This example of Millie's legal difficulties demonstrates that there are present-day artistic expressions and creations that are individual and that, for the most part, may well be adequately dealt with through existing Canadian copyright legislation. However, the point where that legislation falls short generates the kind of questions that may be taken up nationally through larger Indigenous collaborations with the federal Department of Canadian Heritage and the Canada Council for the Arts[49] – in addition to the exploration of and engagement with Indigenous legal orders as advocated herein.

## We Live in the Worlds We Imagine

In Indigenous intellectual discourse, there are often expressions of grief and loss, and sometimes these expressions seem paralysing. For example, I have heard about Nisga'a songs being stolen and used in non-Indigenous musical productions, with the tale of theft often related with real grief and anger. While I am certainly not condoning this theft or unauthorized use of Nisga'a songs, it strikes me as a parallel to the octopus story, as told by the men from Foueda, at least in some ways.[50] To what extent does the narrative we tell trap us in despair by positioning us as powerless?[51] How does the narrative we tell shape our expectations of ourselves and our abilities to, for instance, change and free the

---

49  See, for example, Val Napoleon, Rebecca Johnson & Brooke Edmonds, *What We Heard: A Report from Consultations on the Arts and Societal/Cultural Expression of Indigenous Peoples* (31 May 2021), on file with the Indigenous Law Research Unit at <www.ilru.ca>.
50  Recall Montgomery, *Last Heathen, supra* note 1 at 239.
51  Ron Crenlinsten, "The World of Torture" (2003) 7:3 Theoretical Criminology 293 at 293. Crenlinsten begins his article with a 1928 quote by WI Thomas: "If people define their situations as real, they are real in their consequences."

sharing of the speckled octopus's name beyond the dead priests? The Nisga'a songs are still sung today in the Nass Valley by Nisga'a people at their pole-raising feasts. Of course, there remains the unauthorized use of the songs, but proactively approaching this as a legal issue according to Nisga'a law represents a reframing that recognizes Nisga'a people as legal agents, not simply victims.

## Gender and Power and the Speckled Octopus

All Indigenous legal questions arising from intellectual property problems require consideration of, and attending to, the animating dynamics of both gender and power. There is no gender neutrality in any legal order, and law does not exist outside the surrounding power relations; rather, law is always constitutive of society and is always being constituted by society.

If we turn back to the speckled octopus stories with a gender or LGBTQ+ lens, we can see that women and LGBTQ+ people are invisible. There are no women or LGBTQ+ priests, and is it men who are recounting the story. Given that all law is gendered, how does this shape our understanding of the speckled octopus and our interpretations?[52] How might this inform our expectations of and our ability to see Lau law, and the consequences of the practice of Lau law?

## What Might the Speckled Octopus See?

She wakes from a long sleep. Slowly she stretches out her tentacles one at a time, and says, "What the heck?" Suddenly, she feels like she is an octopus version of the Matrix, where Neo pokes his finger through the mirror in front of him. The mirror is not "real"! She discovers that the walls of the swimming pool that have restricted her movements and sight for so long disintegrate, simply vanish. She realizes that she has been sleeping in the Lau lagoon among all the other ancestors.

She watches the Lau people for a long time and learns how they have suffered because they have not been able to see her through the colonially constructed walls of the swimming pool. She sits quietly for a while considering what has caused her long sleep and led to her finally waking up. The beautiful speckled octopus begins to think about how to reintroduce herself to the Lau people.

_______________

52   Emily Snyder, "Queering Indigenous Legal Studies" (2015) 38 Dalhousie L J 591.

BIBLIOGRAPHY

Adjei, Patricia. "Working Ethically with Indigenous Cultural and Intellectual Property: Australia Launches New Protocols" (2020) 4 Intellectual Property Magazine, online: <https://www.wipo.int/wipo_magazine/en/2020/04/article_0006.html>.

Alexander, Merle & James Struthers. "Squaring the Circle – Indigenous Intellectual Property and the Canadian Trademark System" (March 2020) Mondaq, online: <https://www.mondaq.com/canada/trademark/905606/squaring-the-circle-indigenous-intellectual-property-and-the-canadian-trademark-system>.

Anderson, Jane. *Law, Knowledge, Culture: The Production of Indigenous Knowledge in Intellectual Property Law* (Cheltenham, UK: Edward Elgar, 2009).

Beauclair, Alain. "Freedom in the Age of Social Stupidity" (2023) 37(1) J Speculative Philosophy 117.

Bell, Catherine & Val Napoleon, eds. *First Nations Cultural Heritage and Law: Case Studies, Voices and Perspectives*, companion vol (Vancouver: UBC Press, 2008).

Bell, Catherine & Robert Paterson, eds. *Intercultural Dispute Resolution in Aboriginal Contexts* (Vancouver: UBC Press, 2008).

Boggs, Jada. "Protecting Indigenous Artists Against Infringement and Appropriation" (17 November 2022), online (blog): Copyright Alliance <https://copyrightalliance.org/protecting-indigenous-artists-infringement-appropriation/>.

Borrows, John. *Law's Indigenous Ethics* (Toronto: University of Toronto Press, 2019).

Brunnée, Jutta & Stephen J Toope. *Legitimacy and Legality in International Law* (Cambridge: Cambridge University Press, 2010).

Buga, Bennie & Veikila Vuki. "The People of the Artificial Island of Foueda, Lau, Malaita, Solomon Islands: Traditional Fishing Methods, Fisheries Management and the Roles of Men and Women in Fishing" (July 2012) 22 Women Fisheries Information Bulletin 42.

Cameron, Angela, Sari Graben & Val Napoleon, eds. *Creating Indigenous Property* (Toronto: University of Toronto Press, 2020).

Carpenter, Megan M. "Intellectual Property Law and Indigenous Peoples: Adapting Copyright Law to the Needs of a Global Community" (2004) 7 Yale Hum Rts & Dev L J 51.

CBC. "Rinaldo Walcott Calls for the Abolition of Property" (with Val Napoleon and Christopher Essert), *Ideas* (5 March 2021), online: <https://www.cbc.ca/radio/ideas/rinaldo-walcott-calls-for-the-abolition-of-property-1.5936800>.

Crenlinsten, Ron. "The World of Torture" (2003) 7:3 Theoretical Criminology 293.

de Beer, Jeremy & Daniel Dylan. "Traditional Knowledge and Governance Challenges in Canada" in Matthew Rimmer, ed, *Indigenous Intellectual*

*Property: A Handbook of Contemporary Research* (Northampton, MA: Edward Elgar, 2015).

Fletcher, Matthew. "Rethinking Customary Law in Tribal Court Jurisprudence" (2006) 04 Indigenous Law & Policy Centre Working Paper.

Friedland, Hadley. *Reclaiming the Language of Law: Exploring the Contemporary Articulation and Application of Cree Legal Principles in Canada* (dissertation, University of Alberta, 2015) [unpublished, on file with the author].

Friedland, Hadley. *The Wetiko Legal Principles: Cree and Anishinabek Responses to Violence and Victimization* (Toronto: University of Toronto Press, 2018).

Friedland, Hadley & Val Napoleon. "Gathering the Threads: Indigenous Legal Methodology" (2015) 1:1 Lakehead L J 33.

Friedland, Hadley & Val Napoleon. "An Inside Job: Engaging with Indigenous Legal Traditions through Stories" (2016) special issue, McGill L J 725.

Government of Canada. *Introduction to Intellectual Property and the Protection of Indigenous Knowledge and Cultural Expressions in Canada* (Ottawa: Government of Canada, n/d), online: <https://www.ic.gc.ca/eic/site/108.nsf/eng/00007.html>.

Hart, HLA. *The Concept of Law* (Oxford: Clarendon 1961).

International Council on Human Rights. *When Legal Worlds Overlap: Human Rights, State and Non-State Law* (Geneva: ATAR Roto, 2009).

Janke, Terri. *Minding Culture: Case Studies on Intellectual Property and Traditional Cultural Expression* (Geneva: WIPO, 2004).

Krieger, Stefan H. "The Place of Storytelling in Legal Reasoning: Abraham Joshua Heschel's Torah Min Hashamayim" (2010) 6 Storytelling, Self, Society 169, online: <http://ssrn.com/abstract=1010930>.

McLaren, Peter. "Some Thoughts on Canada's 'Freedom Convoy' and the Settler Colonial State" (2022) 54:7 Educational Philosophy and Theory 867.

Metallic, Naiomi. "Five Linguistic Methods for Revitalizing Indigenous Laws" (2023) 68 McGill L J, online: <https://ssrn.com/abstract=4099156>.

Metallic, Naiomi. "Six Examples Applying the Meta-principle Linguistic Method: Lessons for Indigenous Law Implementation" (2022) 73 University of New Brunswick L J.

Montgomery, Charles. *Last Heathen: Encounters with Ghosts and Ancestors in Melanesia* (Vancouver: Douglas and McIntyre, 2004).

Montgomery, Charles. "The Octopus: Can the Myths of the Lau Lagoon Clan Survive Their Preservation" (May 2006) 4:22 The Walrus, online: <https://thewalrus.ca/2006-05-anthropology/>.

Napoleon, Val. *Ayook: Gitxsan Legal Order and Legal Theory* (dissertation, University of Victoria, 2009) [unpublished].

Napoleon, Val. "Did I Break It? Recording Indigenous (Customary) Law" (2019) 22 PER/PELJ 2019, online: <http://dx.doi.org/10.17159/1727-3781/2019/v22i0a7588>.

Napoleon, Val. "Gitxsan Democracy: On Its Own Terms" in James Tully et al, eds, *Democracy Multiplicity: Perceiving, Enacting, and Integrating Democratic Diversity* (Cambridge: Cambridge University Press, 2022) 195.

Napoleon, Val, Rebecca Johnson & Brooke Edmonds. *What We Heard: A Report from Consultations on the Arts and Societal/Cultural Expression of Indigenous Peoples* (31 May 2021), on file with the Indigenous Law Research Unit at www .ilru.ca.

Nixon, Lindsay. *A Culture of Exploitation: "Reconciliation" and the Institutions of Canadian Art* (Toronto: Yellowhead Institute, 2020) online: <www .yellowheadinstitute.org>.

Overstall, Richard. "Encountering the Spirit in the Land: 'Property' in a Kinship-Based Legal Order" in John McLaren, AR Buck & Nancy E Wright, eds, *Despotic Dominion: Property Rights in British Settler Societies* (Vancouver: UBC Press, 2004).

Rundle, Kristen. *Forms Liberate: Reclaiming the Jurisprudence of Lon L Fuller* (Oxford: Hart, 2012).

Rundle, Kristen. "Fuller's Relationships" in H Takikawa, ed, *The Rule of Law and Democracy: The 12th Kobe Lecture and the 1st IVR Japan International Conference, Kyoto, July 2018* (Stuttgart: Franz Steiner, 2020) 17.

Ryley, Katy & Mary Moran. "Protecting Indigenous Intellectual Property Rights: Tools That Work" (Dec 2000) Cultural Survival Quarterly Magazine, online: <https://www.culturalsurvival.org/publications/cultural-survival-quarterly /protecting-indigenous-intellectual-property-rights-tools>.

Seidler, Reagan. "Constitutional Rights to Intellectual Property" (2020) 35 Intellectual Property Institute of Canada 37, online: <https://ipic.ca/cipr /constitutionalized-rights-to-indigenous-intellectual-property-2020-35-1.htm>.

Shiva, Vandana. *Protect or Plunder: Understanding Intellectual Property Rights* (London: Zed Books, 2001).

Snyder, Emily. "Queering Indigenous Legal Studies" (2015) 38 Dalhousie L J 591.

Torsen, Molly & Jane Anderson. *Intellectual Property and the Safeguarding of Traditional Cultures: Legal Issues and Practical Options for Museums, Libraries and Archives* (Geneva: WIPO, 2010).

Wacks, Raymond. *Understanding Jurisprudence: An Introduction to Legal Theory* (Oxford: Oxford University Press, 2005).

Walcott, Rinaldo. *On Property* (Windsor, ON: Biblioasis, 2021).

Wente, Jesse. *Unreconciled: Family, Truth and Indigenous Resistance* (New York: Penguin Canada, 2021).

WIPO. *Intellectual Property and Traditional Cultural Expressions/Folklore* (Geneva: WIPO, nd) online: <www.wipo.int>.

WIPO. *Protect and Promote Your Culture: A Practical guide to Intellectual Property for Indigenous Peoples and Local Communities* (Geneva: WIPO, 2017), online: <https://www.wipo.int/edocs/pubdocs/en/wipo_pub_1048.pdf>.

LEGISLATION CITED

*Copyright Act* RSC 1985 c C-42.
*Industrial Design Act* RSC 1985 c I-9.
*Integrated Circuit Topography Act* SC 1990 c 37.
*Patent Act* RSC 1985 c P-4.
*Trademarks Act* RSC 1985 c T-13.

# 2 Secwepemc Law of Intellectual Property

DEBRA McKENZIE

The discussion of Indigenous intellectual property commonly proceeds in one of two directions. First, it is argued that Indigenous intellectual property cannot fit into the existing intellectual property legal framework. This approach treats the Western legislative framework as the gold standard for intellectual property. The assumptions underlying the framework are grounded in capitalism and a market economy,[1] and Indigenous notions of communal ownership, perpetual time frames, and non-monetary value do not mesh well with this model. Second, it is argued that Indigenous intellectual property "transcend[s] purely commercial attributes" and must be protected in order to "ensure the survival of Indigenous identity and culture."[2] This approach treats Indigenous intellectual property as something fundamentally different from, and more fragile than, non-Indigenous intellectual property. It shifts the purpose of intellectual property law from the *control* of to the *protection* of Indigenous intellectual property.[3]

---

1  Dora Marinova & Margaret Raven, "Indigenous Knowledge and Intellectual Property: A Sustainability Agenda" (2006) 20:4 J of Economic Surveys 587 at 587.

2  Danielle M Conway, "Indigenizing Intellectual Property Law: Customary Law, Legal Pluralism, and the Protection of Indigenous Peoples' Rights, Identity, and Resources" (2009) 15 Tex Wesleyan L Rev 207 at 238.

3  For example, compare the titles of two Canadian government websites: "Intellectual Property: It's Yours. Own It," online: <https://www.ic.gc.ca/eic/site/cipointernet -internetopic.nsf/eng/wr04312.html#Who> and "Introduction to Intellectual Property Rights and the Protection of Indigenous Knowledge and Cultural Expressions in Canada," online: <https://www.ic.gc.ca/eic/site/108.nsf/eng/00007.html> [Canada].

These approaches are both problematic, as the starting point for each is how to manage Indigenous intellectual property in a post-colonial world given the Western legal system. Indigenous intellectual property is viewed through an external lens as the *other* intellectual property that only not does not fit into the Western model but also is a weaker version and in need of protection. What is lacking in both approaches is any rigorous enquiry, legal or otherwise, into Indigenous intellectual property in its own right. The starting point should be the fact that Indigenous communities have always had their own intellectual property legal framework. How else can one explain the survival of diverse systems of lifestyles, art, and societal/cultural expressions through millennia? If there had been a free-for-all where insiders and outsiders alike had free access to everyone else's particular resources and intangible property, then how did the many societies, distinct from one another, survive?

The discussion must go beyond the descriptive or anecdotal in order to understand the role that intellectual property plays in a community, and how that community is able to retain control over resources and intangible assets developed in the community. To start with the basics, "intellectual property" is defined as "a category of intangible rights protecting commercially valuable products of the human intellect."[4] "Commercially valuable" connotes that the products are valuable to others, and it can be argued that intellectual property can exist outside of a marketplace. The products that attract these rights are those created by human intellect, or knowledge. In an Indigenous community, this may include the ways and means developed to sustain an ecosystem, to prepare foods or medicines, or to organize a community. It also includes the artwork, songs, dances, and ceremonies created and perpetuated by the community. The crux of intellectual property law is that rights of ownership and control of knowledge may be created when something of value is created or developed, and those rights are held by those who created or developed that value.

The enquiry into Secwepemc intellectual property legal traditions follows an approach informed by legal analysis. Here, the method developed by Napoleon and Friedland is utilized whereby legal principles are drawn out from publicly available Indigenous stories.[5] Secwepemc

---

4   *Black's Law Dictionary*, 11th ed, *sub verbo* "intellectual property."

5   Val Napoleon and Hadley Friedland, "An Inside Job: Engaging with Indigenous Legal Traditions through Stories" (2016) 61:4 McGill L J 725 at 734.

stories collected by James Teit[6] are analysed in order to elucidate the principles of intellectual property law that have always been a part of the Secwepemc legal order. The stories, which Ignace and Ignace called "ancient stories" or "oral traditions," have been told and retold for countless generations[7] and provide a window into the long-standing legal world of the Secwepemculecw, or Secwepeme nation.[8] The stories are many layered, and the interpretation of the stories may generate broad principles about Secwepemc society, or a well-lived Secwepemc life. These interpretations often come from a deep personal knowledge of Secwepemc history and storytelling. Here, the approach to the stories takes a narrower and legal interpretation.

In the report *Secwepemc Lands and Resources*,[9] members of the Indigenous Law Research Unit (ILRU) and Shuswap Nation Tribal Council worked with versions of these *stsptekwll* (ancient stories), which were recorded in the Teit collection mentioned above. As published and publicly available versions of the stories, they are available as resources for both learning about and visualizing Secwemepc legal principles. In the context of the ILRU project, the legal question was focused on land use and resource sharing. The stories, like other rich resources, can be turned to for exploration of other questions. We focus on questions about "intangible" dimensions, about the ways the Secwepemc legal order addressed issues about control (or protection) of intellectual knowledge production.

There was no central authority or system of codified laws to regulate behaviour in the Secwepamec legal order. Legal reasoning was deeply internalized,[10] and the long-standing stories repeated through

6   James Teit, "The Shuswap" in Franz Boas, ed, *The Jesup North Pacific Expedition: Memoir of the American Museum of Natural History*, vol 2, pt 4 (Leiden: EJ Brill /New York: GE Stechert, 1909) 621.

7   Marianne Ignace & Ronald Ignace, *Secwepemc People, Land, and Laws: Yeri7 re Stsq'eys-kucw* (Montreal: McGill University Press, 2017) at 57 [Ignace & Ignace].

8   John Borrows has suggested that Indigenous stories are similar to common law cases in that they relate disputes and their resolutions; they are regarded as authoritative by their listeners; there are natural and social consequences that result from the violations of the instructions contained in them; and the interpretation of the stories promotes personal and collective adherence to the consequences that result. See John Borrows, "With or Without You: First Nations Law (in Canada)" (1966) 41 McGill L J 629 at 647.

9   Jessica Asch et al, directed by Val Napoleon, "Secwépemc Lands and Resources Law Research Project," Indigenous Law Research Unit and Shuswap Nation Tribal Council (Tk'emlúps: Shuswap Nation Tribal Council, 2016) [Asch].

10   See Hadley Friedland et al, "Porcupine and Other Stories: Legal Relations in Secwepemculecw" (2018) 48:1 Revue générale de doit 153 at 162.

generations provided a way to communicate and reinforce proper behaviour.[11] An analysis of the stories, with a focus on these questions, provides insight into how intellectual property was legally considered outside of, and before, the imposition of a Western legal order. This information may be used as part of a starting point in the revitalization of a Secwepemc intellectual property legal regime grounded in the Indigenous legal order.[12]

## Secwepemculecw

Before turning to a legal analysis of the stories, I provide a brief primer on Secwepemc society in order to contextualize the discussion that follows.[13] The Secwepemc nation covers a vast stretch of land, from near the Alberta border west of Jasper to the plateau west of the Fraser River and southeast to the Arrow Lakes and the Columbia River.[14] On this land, the Secwepemc peoples have lived as a self-governing nation composed of independent communities united by common culture, language, and law for thousands of years.[15]

Fishing was a dietary mainstay,[16] and in the winter dried salmon became a staple of trade.[17] As a result, many means of fish harvesting were devised.[18] Salmon was caught by dip-nets in the Fraser River, by gaffs, and by two- or three-pronged spears in the Thompson River. The individuals or families who built and maintained platforms on the banks to access fishing grounds were the first to harvest fish there. Gill nets and conical fish traps were utilized in the calmer waters. Annual fish dams were also set up in river mouths as the salmon migrated upstream.

Hunting was also an important activity to secure food.[19] Hunting grounds were considered communal property, but deer fences and

---

11  *Ibid.*

12  *Ibid* at 160.

13  For a comprehensive ethnography of the Secwepemc People see Ignace & Ignace, *supra* note 7.

14  Marianne Ignace & Ronald Ignace, "The Secwepemc: Traditional Resource Use and Right to Land" in R Bruce & C Roderick Wilson, eds, *Native Peoples: The Canadian Experience* (Don Mills: Oxford University Press, 2004) 377 at 380.

15  See Ron Ignace, *Our Oral Histories Are Our Iron Posts: Secwepemc Stories and the Historical Consciousness* (dissertation, Simon Fraser University, 2008) [unpublished] 129 [Ignace].

16  *Ibid* at 133.

17  Teit, *supra* note 6 at 535.

18  For detailed explanation of fishing methods see Ignace, *supra* note 15 at 132–3.

19  *Ibid* at 135.

eagle-cliffs thereon were considered inheritable family property.[20] Hunters went out in groups accompanied by their families. The men tracked and killed large game while the wives and families stayed at the camp to snare small game and gather plants, and to smoke the meat brought in by the hunters. Ignace reported that hunting, gathering and fishing activities kept families on the move travelling and camping for two-thirds of the year.[21]

Diets were supplemented by fruits and vegetables collected throughout the spring and summer, much of which was prepared and stored for winter. Berry patches were communal property with picking under local control.[22] The cambium of the pine tree was harvested for its sweet taste and medicinal qualities, and black tree lichen was raked off fir trees to be pit-cooked and dried for future use.

The right to live in the Secwepemc land and to reap the benefits of its resources was found in family connections.[23] The core unit of the Secwepemc economy was the extended family, and the community of interrelated families was led by chiefs.[24] There were chiefs to manage resources, war chiefs, and chiefs of dances. These positions were filled by those most capable, elected by the community. There were also hereditary chiefs in each community. These chiefs held no special privileges, but they played an important leadership role in looking after the band welfare, regulating the harvest of the food supply, advising on important matters, and acting as agents of the band in dealing with strangers.[25]

## Strangers on the Land

Indeed, the stranger or outsider who visited the Secwepemc nation must figure prominently in any early consideration of Indigenous knowledge, societal/cultural expressions, and the governing intellectual property law. The control of outsiders' access to local knowledge or intellectual property by local peoples may be viewed as an integral part

---

20  Teit, *supra* note 6 at 573.

21  Ronald E Ignace & Nancy B Ignace, *"Re tsuwet.s-kucw ne Secwepemcúlecw:*
Secwepemc Resource Use and Sense of Place" in Marianne B Ignace, Nancy J Turner
& Sandra L Peacock, eds, *Secwepemc People and Plants: Research Papers in Shuswap
Ethnobotany* (Tacoma, WA: Society of Ethnobiology, 2016) 31.

22  *Ibid.*

23  Ignace, *supra* note 15 at 187.

24  *Ibid* at 206.

25  Teit, *supra* note 6 at 570.

of territorial authority.[26] As Indigenous knowledge is so heavily tied up in land, resources, and place, it follows that access to that knowledge must be subject to the laws and jurisdiction that govern that land.[27]

There is documented evidence of Secwepemc chiefs' treatment of strangers in the early twentieth century. In 1910 the chiefs of the Shuswap (Secwepemc) along with the chiefs from the Okanagan and Thompson "tribes" (*sic*) sent a letter to Sir Wilfrid Laurier, the prime minister of Canada at that time,[28] conveying their concerns over poor treatment by the British Columbia government. In that letter, the chiefs referred to the fur traders as the "good whites" who had come to the country prior to the gold rush and the settlers that followed. Here, the chiefs explained their concept of a good guest:

> The "real whites" we found to be good people. We could depend on their word, and we trusted and respected them. They did not interfere with us nor attempt to break up our tribal organization, laws, and customs. They did not try to force their conceptions of things on us to our harm. Nor did they stop us from catching fish, hunting, etc.[,] they never tried to steal or appropriate our country, nor take our food and life from us … We never asked them to come here, but nevertheless we treated them kindly and hospitably and helped all we could. They made themselves (as it were) our guests.[29]

In this document, the chiefs asserted a right to their own customs and way of life. Guests were treated kindly but were not allowed to appropriate their food, country, or life. It appears that guests were held at arm's length, kept on the outside so as not to disrupt the existing well-organized society. There clearly was no openness to criticism or appropriation from guests, and there was an interest in the maintenance of the differences in lifestyles and "conceptions of things" that distinguished the guest from the host, the outsider from the insider.

There is a recurring motif of the "bungling host" in North American Indigenous stories.[30] It is repeated in stories from the Canadian

---

26   For an explanation of this approach see IPinCH, "Secwepemc Territorial Authority – Honoring Ownership of Tangible/Intangible Culture," Intellectual Property Issues in Cultural Heritage: Theory, Practice, Policy, Ethics (SFU), online: <https:// www.sfu.ca/ipinch/project-components/community-based-initiatives/secwepemc -territorial-authority-honoring-ownership-ta/>.

27   *Ibid.*

28   Chiefs of the Shuswap, Okanagan and Couteau Tribes of British Columbia, *Memorial to Sir Wilfrid Laurier, Premier of the Dominion of Canada* (Ottawa: National Archives MG 26-G, vol. 641, 174,070-174,077, 1910).

29   *Ibid* at 3.

30   See Daniel Clément, *The Bungling Host: The Nature of Indigenous Oral Literature* (Lincoln: University of Nebraska Press, 2018).

Subarctic to the American Southwest.[31] In every instance a trickster arrives as a hungry traveller and by magical means is fed by their hosts. Later, the trickster becomes the "bungling host" when they try to imitate the food preparation of the hosts, always with disastrous results. The prevalence of the stories as a far-flung genre indicates travel between nations, as the form of the story must have been shared. It also speaks to the treatment of strangers: they were well treated as guests, but were not permitted to carry the host's magic away with them, just as we see in the Laurier letter above.

The trickster found in Secwepemc stories is Coyote. Like many tricksters, Coyote is a transformer figure with magical powers. As Coyote travelled through the land he often defied the norms of acceptable behaviour, and it is through these travails that the proper (or lawful) behaviour, rights, and remedies are illuminated.[32] Borrows said that "Indigenous legal traditions manifest themselves through social experiences that involve people communicating with one another about how best to conduct relationships and resolve disputes."[33] Coyote, as trickster, manipulates situations to mimic these relationships, and thus the often humorous and always memorable teaching stories are devised.

In the stories, Coyote often seems silly, naughty, or devious, but it is well established that Coyote brings a message with that folly. The position of the Coyote stories as a source of Secwepemc knowledge and as an important teaching tool is ongoing and well recognized. There are a number of contemporary examples. You can find a metal sculpture of Coyote atop the House of Learning at the Kamloops campus of Thomson Rivers University (TRU), which is located on the traditional grounds of the Tk'emlups te Secwepemc. When TRU instituted a program to create a campus that was welcoming and supporting to Indigenous students and staff in response to the Truth and Reconciliation Commission's calls to action, that undertaking was called the Coyote

---

31  *Ibid.*

32  For more readings on Coyote's role as trickster see Sylvia Moore, "A Trickster Tale about Integrating Indigenous Knowledge in University-Based Programs" (2012) J of Environmental Studies and Sciences 324; Jo-ann Archibald (Q'um Qum Xiiem), "An Indigenous Storywork Methodology" in J Gary Knowles and Ardra L Cole, eds, *Handbook of the Arts in Qualitative Research* (Thousand Oaks: Sage, 2008); Kathryn A Michel, *Trickster's Path to Language Transformation: Stories of Secwepemc Immersion from Chief Atahm School* (dissertation, University of British Columbia, 2012); John Borrows, "Heroes, Tricksters, Monsters, and Caretakers: Indigenous Law and Legal Education" (2016) 61–4 McGill L J 795; Ignace, *supra* note 15.

33  John Borrows, *Canada's Indigenous Constitution* (Toronto: University of Toronto Press, 2010) at 10.

Project.[34] The name has its basis in the Secwepemc story *Coyote Brings Food from the Upper World*.[35] Finally, in 1999 an anthology of Indigenous stories was created to mark the tenth anniversary celebration of a successful partnership between the Secwepemc Cultural Education Society and Simon Fraser University; the anthology was entitled *Coyote U*.[36]

We now turn to follow the trickster Coyote on a journey through Secwepemc in a seven-part story entitled *Coyote and the Hosts*.[37] Here Coyote travels through seven communities in Secwepemc lands. Throughout the journey Coyote is portrayed as a visitor or guest, which means that he is distinguished from all others who are relatives.[38] Throughout these stories, Coyote relentlessly tries to access and appropriate the knowledge of his hosts.

## Secwepemc Intellectual Property in the Stories

The first four stories are of the "bungling host" genre. Coyote pauses in his travels because he is hungry, and in each story he is fed by his hosts. Later, Coyote is injured in his unsuccessful attempts to replicate his hosts' magical cooking skills. These stories have been considered elsewhere,[39] and their overall message has been described as "the importance of recognizing the authority and integrity behind other people's practices."[40] Ron Ignace tells us that in addition these stories remind one of cultural autonomy and being true to one's own ways.[41] In the legal analysis of the story, the actions, rights, and responsibilities of the parties are also considered. The focus is shifted from the Trickster to the host, from the bungling host to the good host, and the issues of the host's knowledge and control of that knowledge are drawn out.

---

34   For more information on the Coyote Project, see Thompson Rivers University, "Coyote Project," online: <https://www.tru.ca/indigenous/coyote.html>

35   This story tells how Coyote brought plants that the Secwepemc use for food and medicine, and how animals and fish got their shape and features. It reminds the Secwepemc peoples that they are the caretakers of the land and living things.

36   PJ Murphy, George P Nicholas & Marianne Ignace, eds, *Coyote U: Stories and Teachings from the Secwepemc Education Institute* (Penticton: Theytus Books, 1999).

37   Teit, *supra* note 6 at 627.

38   Ignace, *supra* note 15 at 232.

39   For a comprehensive discussion of these stories as they relate to Secwepemc lands and resources law, see Asch, *supra* note 9.

40   *Ibid* at 19.

41   Ignace, *supra* note 15 at 351.

In the first story Coyote meets Fat-Man, who offers Coyote part of his own body as a meal. Fat-man offers a slice of his back fat, which was considered the best fat of an animal.[42]

Coyote was travelling over the earth. He felt hungry. He saw a house, entered, and found it inhabited by an old man called Fat-Man (Skia'uz-kelesti'mt). There was nothing to eat in the house, and he thought, "What will this old man give me to eat?" The man knew his thoughts and, making the fire blaze brightly, he sat with his bare back close in front of it. His back became soft and greasy, and he asked Coyote to eat. "Eat what?" said Coyote. And the man answered, "My back, of course." Coyote refused at first; but the man invited him to eat his back. Coyote said to himself, "I will bite his back right to the bone, and kill him." Going up to the man, he took a big bite; but the piece came away in his mouth, and no mark was left on the man's body. He found the food was very good.

Now he thought he could do the same thing: so, making a big blaze, he turned his back to the fire. But his back burned; and the smell of burning hair made the man angry, who threw him outside, saying, "You try to imitate me, but you cannot do it. You fool! Don't you know it is I only who can do that?"[43]

Here there is no question who has the rights over or ownership of the method and ingredients of the shared meal. As a good host, Fat-Man shares the best part of himself with Coyote. Coyote does not have permission to use this knowledge that he has witnessed. In fact, Coyote is told that he cannot imitate Fat-Man. The rights to the knowledge rest with the host, as that knowledge is (literally) part of who he is. The host controls the knowledge, and thus Coyote is unable to recreate the meal preparation without permission.

Next, Coyote enters the home of Fish-Oil-Man, who has a special method for preparing drippings. Teit reported that the Secwepemc utilized trays made of spruce and pine bark to catch fat-drippings before the fire,[44] and this appears to be Fish-Oil-Man's practice here.

Continuing his journey, Coyote came to another house, which he entered. It was inhabited by an old man called Fish-Oil-Man (Stiauzka'instimt). Feeling hungry, and seeing nothing in the shape of food, he wondered what

---

42   Teit, *supra* note 6 at 672.
43   *Ibid* at 627.
44   *Ibid* at 501.

this man could give him to eat. The man made the fire blaze, and placed a wooden dish for catching drippings in front of it. He held his hands over it, with the fingers turned down, and the grease dropped from his finger-ends. When the dish was full, he placed it before Coyote, and asked him to eat. Coyote said, "I can't eat that." And the man answered, "Try it. It is good." Coyote then ate some and, liking it, he finished the contents of the dish.

Coyote thought, "I will show this fellow that I can do the same thing." So, making the fire blaze, he took the wooden dish, and held his hands above it, in the same way the man had done. His hands shrivelled up with the heat, but no grease dropped from them. This is the reason why the coyote has short paws. He cried with pain; and the man threw him outside, saying, "You fool! That method belongs to me only."[45]

In this story Fish-Oil-Man produces a meal for his guest with his hands. Once again Coyote is told that he cannot use this knowledge. I suggest that the production of the meal from the hands refers to knowledge added to local resources to produce something useful. Once again, the host makes it clear to the guest that the knowledge of the method belongs to him.

Next, Coyote stops at the home of Beaver-Man. Here, Coyote is given the bark of the alder tree to eat. This is an unfamiliar food for Coyote, but cambium of tree bark was harvested as a food and medicine by the Secwepemc.[46] In this story Coyote is not injured, but is admonished by his host.

Again Coyote was travelling, and, coming to the house of a man called Beaver-Man (Skala'uztimt), he entered. He felt hungry, but saw nothing to eat. He wondered what the old man would give him. The man took a sap-scraper and a bark dish, went outside to an alder-tree, and scraped off the cambium layer. When the dish was full, he brought it in and gave it to Coyote, who had been watching him meanwhile. Coyote said, "I cannot eat sticks." And the man assured him it was good, and that it was sap, and not sticks. Coyote ate, and found it very good.

Now he tried to imitate Beaver-Man. He took a sap-scraper and bark dish, went to an alder-tree, and scraped off the bark, which he offered to the old man, saying, "Eat some of my food." The man, seeing it was only bark, threw it away, and said, "Why do you try to imitate the methods which you ought to know belong to me only?"[47]

---

45   *Ibid* at 627.
46   *Ibid* at 515.
47   *Ibid* at 627–8.

Once again, the host declares that Coyote cannot imitate methods that belong to him only. In this case the host served Coyote sap, but Coyote served him bark. Coyote is ignorant of the method when he goes out and scrapes a tree, as he observed the host had done. He does so incorrectly because he is not privy to local ways, and again the host does not want to share that knowledge with him. This story concerns the correct use of local plants, but it could also pertain to rules and protocol that regulated usage.

Lastly, Coyote visits the home of Kingfisher-Man. The kingfisher is a bird common to the area, known for its ability to dive down from a perch in order to catch fish in its long beak. Coyote is not physically capable of recreating his meal here. This story may speak to local fishing access and knowledge.

Coyote continued his journey, and reached the abode of an old man called Kingfisher-Man (Tsalasti'mt), who lived in an underground house near the water's edge. He entered the house, feeling hungry, and looked around for food, but could see none. He thought, "What can this fellow give me to eat?" The man stripped the bark off a willow-bush and made a string of it, which he put around his waist. Then he ascended to the top of a ladder, gave a cry, and dived down into the water through a hole between some driftwood. Coyote watched; but, as he did not see him reappear, he thought he must be dead. At last, however, the man came up bringing a string of fish, which he cooked and placed in a dish in front of Coyote. The latter refused to eat, saying that it was bad food. He was, however, assured that it was good, and ate it all.

Then Coyote made a bark string, went to the top of the ladder, and cried like a kingfisher. Then he dived into the hole. But his head stuck fast, and he would have been drowned had not the man pulled him out, saying, "You fool! Why try to imitate the method that belongs to me alone?"[48]

Again, Coyote tried and failed to imitate his host. Kingfisher-Man was able to access the fish in a difficult manoeuvre through a hole in some driftwood, and he appeared to stay under water for an extended period of time. Again, Coyote is told that the method belonged to the host alone.

In each of the "bungling host" stories the host used local knowledge and/or resources in order to prepare food for Coyote. The Bear-Man gave of himself, Fish-Oil-Man used his hands, Beaver-Man harvested

---

48   *Ibid* at 627.

local resources, and Kingfisher-Man made a daring dive into waters he knew well. In every case, the host represented a local society. This is a reasonable assumption to make even though the hosts appear as individuals because, as discussed above, Secwepemc resources were utilized communally. I suggest that the individual representative hosts were the chiefs who controlled resource use, and dealt with guests as mentioned above. It is clear that the use of distinctive local knowledge, controlled by the chiefs for the local society, was restricted to local use only. This certainly parallels the information in the letter from the chiefs to Laurier discussed above. These stories do not indicate how Coyote might have been able to access the knowledge. He unsuccessfully copied what he saw, but he was not aware of the local ecology, environment, or possible rules and protocols, and thus he was denied access to this knowledge.

### Stories about the Control of Valued Intangible Assets

The knowledge of the community, which may be collectively defined as the community's "resources and intangible assets,"[49] are the societal/cultural expressions that form the basis for the identification of the community and community values.[50] Observance of protocol and ceremony by members of the community often reinforces rules of social standing and leadership roles. Community members' participation in ceremonies, dances, and songs serves to bond the members to one another and to reinforce the social order. It bolsters a shared understanding of community goals and authority within the community[51] and thereby plays an important governance role.

Participation in the production and performance of this knowledge serves to define who is and who is not a member of that society. If dissemination of this knowledge is not controlled and is freely accessible to members and non-members alike, then the essence of belonging to that particular society may be lost, along with the existing society. This rationale for control of the dissemination of knowledge is applicable to the bungling hosts stories above, but is particularly relevant to the next story. Here, Coyote is denied access to view or to participate in a

---

49   Conway, *supra* note 2 at 238.
50   *Ibid* at 210.
51   See Harvey Whitehouse & Jonathan A Lanman, "The Ties That Bind Us: Ritual, Fusion and Identification" (2014) 55:6 Current Anthropology 674; Elizabeth Bott & Edmund Leach, "The Significance of Kava in Tongan Myth and Ritual" in JS LaFontaine, ed, *The Interpretation of Ritual* (London: Routledge, 1972) 204.

dance. In fact, he is punished by the community for attempting to force his way in:

> Coyote travelled along, and came to an underground house in which people were dancing. He looked in, but saw only a row of different kinds of snowshoes, which were standing on their ends all around the house. As soon as he left, the dancing commenced again; and when he looked in, it stopped. Then he entered and seized one of the snowshoes; and the others at once attacked him, striking him all over the body. He threw down the snowshoe he had seized, and ran out.[52]

Coyote once again suffered injury after attempting to access knowledge that was not available to him as a stranger. Coyote was aware that a cultural event was happening, but not only is he denied entry, he is denied any knowledge of the goings on. This indicates a different and greater level of control by the hosts compared to the first four stories, because in those scenarios Coyote was allowed to witness the preparation of the food.

In this story, however, certain further qualifications are required for participation. In his 1909 report on the Secwepemc peoples, James Teit described a social grouping with a snowshoe or snow as protector.[53] The Snow group could form a larger group with the Moose, Caribou, Elk, and Deer groups, which were usually made up of hunters. Each group had their own songs and dances, but members of the larger unit had the right to perform the dances and songs of the others. A community member could join a group by passing a course of training and fasting in the woods, and a son generally joined his father's group.[54]

Thus, Coyote could not access the dance because he did not qualify to join in any capacity. He was not a hunter in the community, his father was not in the group, and he had not undergone the community training. Further, Coyote was not only forbidden to observe the dance, he was punished when he tried to take a snowshoe. This was more than simply a dance performance. Controlled membership in the group served to define not only membership in the community but also one's role and family relationship within that community. The ceremony of performing your group's dances and songs reinforced a sense of belonging and allegiance to your community. This, in turn, sustained the community. The knowledge of the dance was held as intellectual

---

52  Teit, *supra* note 6 at 628.
53  *Ibid* at 577.
54  *Ibid*.

property by the community, and access to and participation in that knowledge was controlled by rules restricting membership.

## Perpetuity of Community Knowledge

The next story in this series explores the very nature of Indigenous knowledge. Recall the first four stories where Coyote witnessed the local magic but was warned not to try and reproduce it. In the next story, Coyote was denied even a view of the cultural spectacle he wished to see, and his attempt to steal a part of the dance earned him a beating at the hands of the members participating in the dance.

Coyote continued on his journey. At his next stop he does not try to access knowledge, but his antics uncover the resilience of local knowledge.

[Coyote] continued his journey, and soon he came to another underground house, which was quite full of small children. He said to himself, "I will play a trick on them," went in, took off his moccasins, and showed the children some cracks in the heel of his foot. He said, "My shoes are full of holes, and my feet have become very sore." Then all the children went out and brought in gum, which they gave to Coyote. That night, when they were all asleep, he daubed their eyes with gum, and then left the house.

The mothers of these children were Blue (or Dusky) Grouse, Willow (or Ruffed) Grouse, Prairie-Chicken (or Sharp-Tailed Grouse), and Fool-Hen (or Franklin's Grouse). When the children awoke in the morning, they could not open their eyes, and, wandering around, lost one another, and could not find their way back to the house. Their mothers arrived, and after some difficulty found them all and cleaned their eyes.

The children told them that Coyote had played them this trick: therefore, the Grouse mothers followed his tracks until they caught sight of him. The trail followed along the brink of a precipice. They passed Coyote unobserved and hid themselves near the precipice, at considerable distances apart. As Coyote came along, he sang, "They will never find their children, I have tricked them!" While he was thus singing, Fool-Hen arose suddenly from cover and startled him. When he saw who it was, he said, "Oh, it is you! I suppose you are going home. Well, you will find your children all well." Going on, he commenced to sing again, and forgot all about meeting Fool-Hen, when suddenly Prairie-Chicken arose and startled him as he leaned over backwards. He said to Prairie-Chicken, "You will find your children all well," and continued his journey, and again commenced to sing, when Willow-Grouse flew out and startled him so that he nearly fell back over the cliff. He recognized the Grouse, and said, "You are going home. You will find your children all well." He kept on his way and sang his song, when suddenly Blue-Grouse arose in front of him with a loud noise, and startled him so much that he lost his balance and fell right over the cliff into the river below.[55]

Again, Coyote proved to be a terrible guest, tricking the children into coming close to him and then glueing their eyes shut. The children could not observe the world around them; they lost one another and could not find their way home. However, this youngest generation of potential knowledge holders was found and restored by their mothers. It is clear in the story that it was a difficult task to find the children. However, the mothers not only found the children and cleaned their eyes, but were also able to catch up to Coyote and eventually cause him to fall into the river. Coming on the heels of the stories of Coyote's attempts to access local knowledge, one can presume that this story is also about knowledge, and the control of that knowledge by the local Indigenous society. Whereas Coyote attempted to steal the knowledge in the first five stories, here he attempts to prevent the perpetuation of knowledge. The mothers, of course, ensure that their children will continue to have their eyes open to their surroundings, their families, and their homes, because these are the sources of their knowledge. Here, knowledge is revealed as a valuable resource that these mothers will go to great lengths to preserve and defend.

## Becoming a Member of the Community

In Coyote's next and last stop in this narrative, he illustrates how he could legally gain access to a community's knowledge and ways. This part of the story begins with Coyote floating in the river after the mothers caused him to tumble off the cliff.

Here he was in danger of drowning, and transformed himself into one thing after another; but as none of them floated satisfactorily, he at last changed himself into a piece of plank. Thus he drifted down the stream until he came beyond the Lower Thompson region, where he was stopped by a weir belonging to two sisters who inhabited that country, and who were noted for their magic. On the next morning, when the women came to their weir to catch salmon, they saw the piece of plank, which they picked up, saying, "We will take this piece of wood home. It will make a nice dish." They made a plate of it; but each time they ate off it, the food would diminish so quickly that it disappeared before they had taken

---

55    *Ibid* at 629.

many mouthfuls. At last they became angry and threw it into the fire, saying, "There is too much magic about that dish."

Coyote immediately transformed himself into a little baby boy, and cried from the centre of the fire. The women said, "Quick! Pull it out! We will rear it as our child"; for they had no husbands or children. They made a carrier for him, and when they went to bed they placed him between them. When they were both asleep, Coyote arose and had connection with them, returning again to his cradle. Next morning, when they went to wash themselves, one of them said, "I feel queerly. My abdomen is all wet." And the other replied, "I also feel strange. There is blood between my legs." "How can this be," said they, "when no men are around?"

Soon Coyote outgrew his carrier, and the women alternated in carrying him on their backs when they travelled about. He annoyed them very much, however, for he would constantly slip down lower and lower on their backs until he managed to have connection with them.

Thus the women kept him for a time, until one morning he arose early and, going to the weir, broke it in the middle, and crossed to the opposite side of the river. When the women awoke, they searched for him, went to the weir, and found that it was broken and the salmon were passing through in great numbers. Then they noticed Coyote walking up the other side of the river; and he called to them, "I am going back to my country ..." The women said, "It is the dog of a coyote who has been fooling us, and playing tricks on us." They were unable to mend the break in their weir, for Coyote had beaten them in magic. They said, "Coyote has stolen our salmon, and has left us pregnant." Coyote now conducted the salmon up the Fraser River to its source, and afterwards up the Thompson River. This is the reason why the Fraser River is a superior salmon stream to the Thompson River. He said, "Henceforth every year, this season, salmon shall run up the rivers, and the people of the interior shall fish, and eat them. They shall no longer be kept at the mouth of the river, nor shall the people there have a monopoly of fishing and eating them."

As he went along, he cleared the waters of the rivers of obstructions, and arranged the banks so that it should be easy for people to fish for salmon as they ascended. The people were grateful for this great work of Coyote.[56]

Teit observed fish weirs on many rivers and lakes throughout the Secwepemc lands. He also noted that although every "band" (*sic*) had its common recognized fishing places, any member of the broader Secwepemc community could use them without restriction.[57] Teit noted

---

56   *Ibid* at 630.
57   *Ibid* at 572.

that where salmon were plentiful, lower weirs were generally not built right across the river, or they were opened regularly by the owners to allow fish to reach the weirs erected by families upriver.[58]

In this story two sisters appear to be custodians of a fish weir that spans the river. Coyote gained access to their magic by becoming a relation. In fact, Coyote the Trickster transformer becomes both child and husband to the women. In the end, Coyote improved the lives of the broader Secwepemc society when he outpowered the women's magic to break their weir. Teit described Coyote's actions in this story as the Trickster's "greatest work."[59]

How does this story fit into, and conclude, the series about Coyote's quest for access to the knowledge he is always denied? Coyote tricked the sisters into sharing their magic by transforming into a family member. However, he was always a stranger, and at the end of the story Coyote returned to his country. It may be that strangers sometimes have something of value to offer. Early fur traders in the region were invited to welcome dances that "represent[ed] notions of respect and good will towards people who are not kin," and those dances expressed an invitation to a "reciprocal relationship."[60] The legal key here is "reciprocity." Knowledge was never given up freely to those outside of the community. Just as Coyote paid for his sojourn in their land and access to their knowledge by opening the weir and releasing the salmon, the fur traders paid their hosts for local knowledge with ammunition and metal tools.

## Holistic View of Intellectual Property

The next two stories illustrate how intellectual property and resources do not necessarily stand alone. Intangible property such as ceremony, dance, songs, and images may all be part of a protocol intertwined and inseparable from a resource or activity. In these stories, the effectiveness of the magic of the intellectual property is tied to proper resource use. In other words, some songs and dance, like those of the hula discussed elsewhere in this volume, are not simply entertainment. They play a greater societal role, and this must be a consideration in the development of an Indigenous intellectual property legal regime.

---

58  *Ibid* at 573.
59  *Ibid* at 595–6.
60  Duane Thomson & Marianne Ignace, "'They Made Themselves Our Guests': Power Relationships in the Interior Plateau Region of the Cordillera in the Fur Trade Era" (2005) 146 Summer BC Studies, 3 at 8.

In the first story, Coyote appears to know the song and dance that subdues the swans. However, once again, he is a guest in the land. The hunting grounds were only open to Secwepemc peoples,[61] and further, meat was usually brought home and distributed among the hunter's neighbours.[62]

> Coyote, while travelling with his son Kalle'llst, passed a lake, on the grassy shores of which they saw four swans. Coyote sang and danced, and thus brought it about that the swans lost their power of flight, and fell prey to his son, who clubbed them and tied them together. Coyote said to his son, "We will cook and eat them. You must watch them while I gather fire-wood. I will cut off the dry top of that tree yonder." Coyote climbed the tree, and was standing on a branch, busily engaged cutting the tree-top, when his son cried to him, "Come quickly, father! The swans have come to life, and I cannot hold them." Coyote got excited, and cried, "Catch them! Hold them!" As he hurriedly descended the tree, the sharp point of a broken limb penetrated his scrotum, and he yelled with pain. Meanwhile the swans all got loose and flew away, and, although Coyote danced and sang, they kept on their way, and alighted far out on the lake.[63]

Although Coyote knew the incantations to bewitch the swans, he did not know that the incantations were just one part of a bigger picture. The swans seemed to awaken and fly off when it became evident that Coyote was a stranger on the land. As he sought firewood in the tops of nearby trees, it was clear he was not preparing to take the swans home to share with his neighbours. Compare Coyote's story with the story where Sna'naz also bewitches swans:

> The swans were sitting near the edge of the ice, and Sna'naz approached them, as a shaman would, with incantations. They became so heavy that they were unable to fly; and Sna'naz clubbed them all, and killed them. He tied them together, carried them home, and the people ate their fill.[64]

Here, Sna'naz shared the swans with his neighbours. The magic of the songs was available to those who lived there and knew how to use the resource properly.

---

61   Teit, *supra* note 6 at 572.
62   *Ibid* at 573.
63   *Ibid* at 638.
64   *Ibid* at 703.

In the next story Coyote loses his salmon catch as he prepares to give a feast in order that he be considered a "great man." Teit reported that aside from the hereditary and elected chiefs mentioned above, there were a few other people called chiefs "because of their influence obtained through excellence of oratory, wise counsels, wealth, or liberality."[65] These were known to give frequent large feasts and gifts to the people, and it appears that Coyote aimed to be counted among these special individuals.

> Some time after Coyote had introduced the salmon, he said, "I have never given a feast yet. Why should I not feast the people?" He caught and dried great numbers of sockeye and king salmon, and also made much salmon-oil, and buried much salmon-roe. Then he sent out messengers to invite all the people. He said to himself, "I will sing a great song, and perform a dance, when the people assemble. They will think me a great man."
>
> Then he practised his dance, and sang, going out and in between the poles where the salmon were drying. While doing so, his hair was caught in the gills of one of the salmon, and he could not free himself. He got angry, pulled the whole fish down, and threw it into the river. Immediately all the salmon came to life and, jumping off the poles, ran to the river. Then Coyote tried to stop them, but in vain. As he was endeavoring to catch the last one, he noticed that the oil had also come to life, and was running to the river. He ran to stop it, but too late. The salmon-roe he had buried also came out and jumped into the river. When the people arrived, they found nothing to eat, and were very angry, for they thought Coyote had played a trick on them.[66]

The Secwepemc people practise careful and respectful management of resources. They are careful not to over-harvest animals, they do not waste any part of the animal, and they treat the animals with respect.[67] Coyote assumed that he could become a great man simply by providing the feast, singing the songs, and dancing the dance. However, when he threw the whole fish out in anger, he did not demonstrate the qualities and behaviour expected from a great Secwepemc person. The song and dance did not give him that respectability, as they did not have any power to make him a great man. Rather, he had to be a great man to sing those songs.

---

65   *Ibid* at 569.
66   *Ibid* at 637.
67   Ignace & Ignace, *supra* note 7 at 203.

In terms of law, these last two stories illustrate the importance of context in a consideration of intellectual property. The value of intangible property may be found in a greater whole. Societal/cultural expressions may have a societal value far beyond their entertainment value, and this is an important feature of Indigenous intellectual property. Some such property may be inextricably bound to a society. In other cases, it may be important to know how an Indigenous societal/cultural expression will be used once it leaves a society so that important intangible property is not denigrated.

## Losing Control of Intellectual Property

The important role of an intellectual property law regime is to protect intellectual property rights, or to control access to those rights. The right to control or protect access to intellectual property resides with the owner and/or inventor of the property. The rationale for the protection and/or control is that there is value in that intangible property. In the case of Indigenous legal orders, where the intangible property is communally owned, loss of intangible property is a loss to the whole society. These legal principles of ownership, control, and value are evidenced in the stories that follow.

In the first story, *The Mammals Steal Fire from the Fishes*, it appears that the fishes have control over the idea of fire but have lost interest in controlling that ownership.

> The Fish people had all gone to bed, and their fire had burned low. The Mammals crept stealthily up in the darkness and took some of the embers. The Fishes knew what had happened, but were not inclined to rise. Their chief said, "Call out in a loud voice, 'Our fire has been stolen!'" Then the TsokEmu's fish called out, but his voice was very weak. Next Tcoktci'tcen called; but his voice was not much stronger. Then Ma'melt called out, but not loud enough. Now Kwa'ak called, and his voice sounded very far; but by this time the Mammals were far away.[68]

The Fishes had a valued resource in the idea of fire, but their control of the fire embers appears to have become lackadaisical. The chief asked the Fishes to raise the alarm, but the Fishes were inclined neither to get up nor to call out in loud voices. For some reason, the Fishes had become less vigilant about the control and protection of their valuable

---

68   Teit, *supra* note 6 at 669.

resource, and so it was taken away without compensation. It was a communal resource as the chief refers to "our" fire, and the text implies that there were many who held some responsibility for the safeguarding and safekeeping of the knowledge. One can assume that the Fishes were worse off after their fire embers were taken.

In the next story a man obtained a wolf as a guardian spirit, which gave him instructions to ensure a successful hunt.[69] Note that the man kept this information to himself, and this ultimately led to calamity at the hands of Coyote.

There was a famine in the land, and a certain family of people were moving from place to place, trying to find game. Among them was a man called Little-Leader (Tcotcu'lca), who was noted as an indifferent hunter; and, being in a very weak and starving condition, he could not keep up with the other people when they moved camp.

On the following day he was travelling behind the people, as usual, and again he noticed the tracks of a deer and a wolf which had just crossed his path. He followed them, and came to where the wolf had eaten the deer. There he found a number of bones with more or less meat on them, put them in his pack, and ate the meat when he reached camp. On the third day the same thing happened, and he found more meat on the bones than before. On the fourth day, tracks crossed his path as before, and, following them, he came to where a large wolf was sitting beside the carcass of a deer that he had just killed.

The Wolf said, "Come here! What are you doing?" And the man answered, "I have followed your tracks, thinking that I might get some of the meat you might leave, as I am a poor hunter, and I am weak and starving." The Wolf said, "It is well. You have been poor and hungry a long time. Now I will help you." He took two long feathers from the centre of the tail of a chicken-hawk and a small bag of red paint, and gave them to the man, saying, "When you hunt, tie up your hair behind your head and stick these feathers in the knot. Take this paint, and draw with it one stripe on each side of your face, from the eyebrow down over the eye to the jaw. This deer that I have killed is of no use to me, for its entrails are torn. Take the carcass home with you and feed your people."

The man carried the deer home, and when he gained strength, he began to hunt, and was so successful that he soon filled all the lodges with meat, and the people had plenty to eat. He was very careful to follow closely all

---

69  For a discussion on guardian spirits as reported by Teit in 1909 see Teit, *supra* note 6 at 605–11.

the instructions the Wolf had given him. He never ate any meat himself, but only the marrow of old deer-bones, which he roasted. This made him fleet of foot. Although the people pressed him to marry, he always refused, saying, "If I take a wife, I shall lose all my power, and I shall not be able to run fast."

The people did not know that the Wolf had helped him and had become his guardian, and they wondered how such a poor hunter had suddenly become far superior to all the other people. Coyote said, "He has become a shaman, and has obtained some great guardian spirit."

One day, when the man was sweat-bathing alone, Coyote noticed that he had left his clothes and his quiver lying near his bed; and he said to himself, "I will examine them, and see if I can find out what his guardian spirit is." He searched the man's bed, and underneath his pillow, but could find no trace of any medicine-bag. The people told Coyote to desist, saying that he had no right to search another man's bed; but he paid no attention, and looked through Little-Leader's clothes. Now, the Wolf had told the man to hide the paint and feathers at the bottom of his quiver, and never to let anyone see or touch them. Coyote, having looked in vain everywhere else, took Little-Leader's quiver and emptied out the arrows. At the bottom he found the paint and feathers, and said to the people, "Look here! These are his guardians. He paints his face and ties these feathers to his hair when he hunts, and thus he is successful. I will do likewise and go hunting."

The man in the sweat-house knew at once what had happened, and began to howl like a wolf. The wolves also knew, and came around the camp, howling. The man left the sweat-house, assumed the form of a wolf, and ran off and joined the wolves, with whom he disappeared, howling loudly. Then all the fat and meat, and even the bones and skins, in camp, came to life, assumed the forms of deer, ran away, and also disappeared, with the wolves baying behind them. Thus the people were left starving as before, and could not find game, for the wolves drove it all away. The man never returned; and it is said that thereafter he lived with the wolves, and became as one of them.[70]

Teit reported that most Secwepemc men acquired guardian spirits, and the guardian often gave the man particular objects to wear or behaviours to follow,[71] as is the case in this story. However, it is unusual that "the people did not know that the Wolf had helped him and had become his guardian." Teit reported that at least once every winter the

---

70   *Ibid* at 718.
71   *Ibid* at 605.

people gathered and each man sang his mystery-song obtained from his guardian.[72] This was done "for the purpose of discovering whether any sickness were approaching, whether anyone had been bewitched, or if any other evil were threatening … Each man, in his song, told whatever was wonderful or important that had happened to his spirit since last they sang the mystery-songs."[73] Apparently another object of the ceremony was to train the youths in the singing of the songs, to give them self-confidence and see how they were progressing in their training, and to find out who their guardians were and who among them was likely to become the best.[74]

This suggests that the guardians or, more importantly, the having of a guardian played an important governance role. The men, through the guardian songs, shared news of their accomplishments throughout the year and predicted what might happen in the coming year. The progress of the young men was recorded, and future leaders emerged.

In this story the hunter was told not to let anyone see or touch his paint or feathers, but he was not told by the Wolf to keep his guardian a secret. Had the hunter shared his mystery-song Coyote would not have been driven to search the hunter's belongings for the source of his powers, with disastrous results for the community.

Again, the songs were not just songs; they played an important role in informing the society about the activities of the men and what the future might hold. The society was made stronger in the long run by the sharing of this knowledge. The hunter, who held himself apart from the society, did not sing the songs, and even refused to be married, was made vulnerable to Coyote's tricks.

## Conclusion

Legal analysis of the stories above provides a starting point for the development of an intellectual property framework for the Secwepemc nation. The stories show that the value of the special knowledge and ways of the people, as well as societal/cultural expressions, were known and controlled. Not only did the shared knowledge sustain the environment and people, it provided a bond of a communal knowing that separated the insiders from those looking in. Although there

---

72   *Ibid* at 610.
73   *Ibid.*
74   *Ibid.*

was no hierarchical social order, certain societal/cultural expressions in dance and ceremony cemented bonds and clarified roles of those in attendance.

The stories considered both resources and intangible assets to be of value and of interest to outsiders. There was a sense of ownership in that one could not gain access to those assets unless one was, or became, a member of that society. In most cases, the value was created by and found in the community. This flowed not only from the fact that physical assets and land were held communally, but also because the society managed their environment as a group, and maintenance of the group was necessary for survival.

There was no time limit to the communal intellectual property held. The societal intangible assets were passed from generation to generation, as was the right to protect and control those assets. If the special knowledge belonging to the society was lost, the social group could be weakened and might face amalgamation with or assimilation to another society. The stories evidence an awareness of rights in intellectual property, and their importance to the survival of the society.

When the Secwepemc stories were first told and retold, the nation was in firm control of its land and resources. The stories reinforced the notion that their societies and shared knowledge were something of value to be controlled and kept intact. Threats may have come from communities or individuals outside the Secwepemc community, but mainly the stories are about celebrating the strength and cohesion gained from the shared knowledge. Rights in intellectual property were held by those societies who had created that value in their lives and livelihoods, and the stories illustrate the concomitant right to control access to that communally held knowledge.

The control of access to community-created resources and intangible assets took on a new urgency with the advent of colonialism. In recent years the Secwepemc community in Kamloops has sought to control access to the archaeological information extracted from their community through research contracts between the community and outside researchers.[75] For the past thirty years there has been a collaborative, interdisciplinary research program focused on Secwepemc plants, language, and culture supported by, and often in consultation with, the Shuswap Nation Tribal Council, the Secwepemc Cultural Education

---

75   See George P Nicholas & Kelly P Bannister, "Copyrighting the Past? Emerging Intellectual Property Rights Issues in Archaeology" (2004) 45:3 Current Anthropology 327 at 340.

Society, and elders and researchers. An agreement governs control over the traditional plant knowledge and any potential development of marketable products.[76]

Such agreements control access to community assets between parties, but they do not provide the wider protection and control offered by a comprehensive intellectual property framework. Further, the government of Canada has identified various "potential gaps and barriers"[77] that impact Indigenous knowledge within the existing state intellectual property system. The potential gaps and barriers relevant to this discussion include the requirement for a known individual creator or inventor, meeting a standard of originality, the fixed form requirement that does not cover oral expressions or knowledge itself, and the limited term of protection or the requirement of a date of creation.

These technical requirements, part of the constructed Western legal intellectual property regime, are geared to the commodification of expressions of knowledge. The purpose of the proprietary interest in intangible assets may be very different in an Indigenous society, as illustrated by the Secwepemc stories, where the existing intellectual property legal regime worked to control access to and use of societal/cultural expressions that held important value in the society. Given these fundamental differences, it is a far better approach to develop a modern Indigenous intellectual property regime with a basis in Indigenous law, rather than try to figure out how Indigenous societal/cultural expressions can somehow fit within the prevailing Western model.

BIBLIOGRAPHY

Alexiades, Miquel N & Sarah A Laird. "Laying the Foundation: Equitable Biodiversity Research Relationships" in Sarah A Laird, ed, *Biodiversity and Traditional Knowledge: Equitable Partnerships in Practice* (London: Earthscan, 2002) 3.

Archibald (Q'um Q'um Xiiem), Jo-ann. "An Indigenous Storywork Methodology" in J Gary Knowles & Ardra L Cole, eds, *Handbook of the Arts in Qualitative Research* (Thousand Oaks: Sage, 2008).

Asch, Jessica et al, directed by Val Napoleon. "Secwépemc Lands and Resources Law Research Project." Indigenous Law Research Unit &

---

76   Miquel N Alexiades & Sarah A Laird, "Laying the Foundation: Equitable Biodiversity Research Relationships" in Sarah A Laird, ed, *Biodiversity and traditional Knowledge: Equitable Partnerships in Practice* (London: Earthscan, 2002) 3 at 11.

77   See Canada, *supra* note 3.

Shuswap Nation Tribal Council (Tk'emlúps: Shuswap Nation Tribal Council, 2016).

Borrows, John. *Canada's Indigenous Constitution* (Toronto: University of Toronto Press, 2010).

Borrows, John. "Heroes, Tricksters, Monsters, and Caretakers: Indigenous Law and Legal Education" (2016) 61:4 McGill L J 795.

Borrows, John. "With or Without You: First Nations Law (in Canada)" (1966) 41 McGill L J 629.

Bott, Elizabeth & Edmund Leach. "The Significance of Kava in Tongan Myth and Ritual" in JS LaFontaine, ed, *The Interpretation of Ritual* (London: Routledge, 1972) 204.

Chiefs of the Shuswap, Okanagan and Couteau Tribes of British Columbia. *Memorial to Sir Wilfrid Laurier, Premier of the Dominion of Canada.* National Archives MG 26-G, vol. 641, 174,070-174,077, Ottawa, 1910.

Clément, Daniel. *The Bungling Host: The Nature of Indigenous Oral Literature* (Lincoln: University of Nebraska Press, 2018).

Conway, Danielle M. "Indigenizing Intellectual Property Law: Customary Law, Legal Pluralism, and the Protection of Indigenous Peoples' Rights, Identity, and Resources" (2009) 15 Tex Wesleyan L Rev 207.

Friedland, Hadley et al. "Porcupine and Other Stories: Legal Relations in Secwepemculecw" (2018) 48:1 Revue générale de doit 153.

Government of Canada. "Intellectual Property: It's Yours. Own It," online: <https://www.ic.gc.ca/eic/site/cipointernet-internetopic.nsf/eng /wr04312.html#Who>.

Government of Canada. "Introduction to Intellectual Property Rights and the Protection of Indigenous Knowledge and Cultural Expressions in Canada," online: <https://www.ic.gc.ca/eic/site/108.nsf/eng/00007.html>.

Ignace, Marianne & Ronald Ignace. *Secwepemc People, Land, and Laws=Yeri7 re Stsq'ey s-kucw* (Montreal: McGill University Press, 2017).

Ignace, Marianne & Ronald Ignace. "The Secwepemc: Traditional Resource Use and Right to Land" in R Bruce & C Roderick Wilson, eds, *Native Peoples: The Canadian Experience* (Don Mills: Oxford University Press, 2004) 377.

Ignace, Ron. *Our Oral Histories Are Our Iron Posts: Secwepemc Stories and the Historical Consciousness* (dissertation, Simon Fraser University, 2008) [unpublished].

IPinCH. "Secwepemc Territorial Authority – Honoring Ownership of Tangible/ Intangible Culture." Project in Intellectual Property Issues in Cultural Heritage (IPinCH): Theory, Practice, Policy, Ethics (SFU), online: <https:// www.sfu.ca/ipinch/project-components/community-based-initiatives /secwepemc-territorial-authority-honoring-ownership-ta/>.

Marinova, Dora & Margaret Raven. "Indigenous Knowledge and Intellectual Property: A Sustainability Agenda" (2006) 20:4 Journal of Economic Surveys 587.

Michel, Kathryn A. *Trickster's Path to Language Transformation: Stories of Secwepemc Immersion from Chief Atahm School* (dissertation, University of British Columbia, 2012) [unpublished].

Moore, Sylvia. "A Trickster Tale about Integrating Indigenous Knowledge in University-Based Programs" (2012) J of Environmental Studies and Sciences 324.

Murphy, PJ, George P Nicholas & Marianne Ignace, eds. *Coyote U: Stories and Teachings from the Secwepemc Education Institute* (Penticton: Theytus Books, 1999).

Napoleon, Val & Hadley Friedland. "An Inside Job: Engaging with Indigenous Legal Traditions through Stories" (2016) 61:4 McGill L J 725.

Nicholas, George P & Kelly P Bannister. "Copyrighting the Past? Emerging Intellectual Property Rights Issues in Archaeology" (2004) 45:3 Current Anthropology 327.

Teit, James. "The Shuswap" in Franz Boas, ed, *The Jesup North Pacific Expedition: Memoir of the American Museum of Natural History*, vol 2, pt 4 (Leiden: EJ Brill/New York: GE Stechert, 1909).

Thompson Rivers University. "Coyote Project," online: <https://www.tru.ca/indigenous/coyote.html>.

Thomson, Duane & Marianne Ignace. "'They Made Themselves Our Guests': Power Relationships in the Interior Plateau Region of the Cordillera in the Fur Trade Era" (2005) 146 Summer BC Studies 3.

Whitehouse, Harvey & Jonathan A Lanman. "The Ties That Bind Us: Ritual, Fusion and Identification" (2014) 55:6 Current Anthropology 674.

# 3 A People of Themselves: Some Field Notes on Gitxsan Law

RICHARD OVERSTALL

In his scholarly and artful account of the cultural and legal clashes on the upper Skeena River in the five decades or so spanning the turn of the twentieth century, Hamar Foster focuses on the 1927 arrest and conviction of five Gitxsan men from Kitwancool for obstructing dominion surveyors intent on laying out *Indian Act* reserves within their territories.[1] He contrasts the police and court reports of the men's actions with the observations of the artist Emily Carr, who visited the village the following year to paint and, by chance, lodged with the family that played a leading role in the community's resistance to the settler encroachment onto their lands.

Foster frames his account in terms of three legal narratives. One of them emerges from the stumbling intrusion of European colonists into the region – the nervously aggressive British Columbia settler narrative. Another and more distant narrative took place among the few lawyers attempting to find a legal bridge, a reconciliation if you like, between that seemingly unstoppable wave of colonial arrogance and the third legal narrative, the one arising out of millennia of indigenous peoples' interactions with each other and with the spirit in the land. In the Upper Skeena, the indigenous people are the Gitxsan who practise within a legal order that allows resolution of conflicts within their territories and beyond – across what is now northwest British Columbia and southeast Alaska.

In this chapter, I traverse the same ground as Foster but in doing so observe as best I can the indigenous legal narrative – the relevant Gitxsan law and legal processes people followed as they dealt with

---

1 Hamar Foster, "Two 'White' Perspectives on Indigenous Resistance: Emily Carr's *Klee Wyck*, the RCMP, and Title to the Kitwancool Valley in 1927" (2021) 43:1 Manitoba L J 1 ["Two White Perspectives"].

their internal disputes and their disputes with the largely ignorant colonists. Aside from the 1927 Kitwancool arrests, Foster also relates four other late-nineteenth-century incidents in the region. I had originally planned to take one of them, the 1888 police shooting of "Kitwancool Jim,"[2] to draw out some particulars of dispute resolution within the Gitxsan legal narrative. But as in many stories, especially indigenous ones, this one could not be so neatly contained. It overflowed back into the past and forward into the future. In the end, it covered most of the incidents discussed by Foster, including the 1927 Kitwancool clash between the indigenous legal narrative and the aggressive settler legal narrative. These incidents all took place within that short turn-of-the-century window before colonial powers were able to effectively suppress many indigenous legal practices and while there were enough ethnologists, police, judges, and other government officials around to record the details of those practices. On a broader perspective, the story overflows into the present along the continuum of indigenous resistance to the Crown's attempts to suppress their societies and legal orders. This resistance in recent times has often been manifested as the push to get section 35 into the Canadian Constitution, and the subsequent aboriginal rights and title claims under that section.

To construe the relevant Gitxsan law, I rely on witness accounts of the legal processes that people followed and of the decisions that arose from them. I took notes of events, stories, performances, and images related by witnesses, primarily for the legal meaning participants derived from them. This semiotic approach is distinct from seeing Northwest Coast artefacts and histories as purely artistic, decorative, or entertainment objects. I tend to discount participants' declarations of the law and specifically identify where a witness appears to have inserted such declarations into their accounts. This chapter thus records the law of what people did, not of what they said ought to have been done. It does not test any particular theory of law, but rather takes field notes of people's decisions and observes their consequences, much as a naturalist records biological interactions she observes on a forest transect.

Because the account relies on records of a century ago, I use the past tense when drawing conclusions about the Gitxsan legal order. This should not be taken to indicate that the order no longer exists. Rather, it should be taken to acknowledge that the order has likely evolved since then and that its later forms, including those of the present, are not covered by the evidence surveyed here.

---

2 *Ibid* at 15 and 16.

The witness evidence of the relevant legal processes is problematic. The Gitxsan accounts of the events surrounding the 1888 shooting of the Kitwancool chief, known to the settlers as Kitwancool Jim and to his community as Gamgaxmilmuxw, are contained in a series of interviews the ethnologist Marius Barbeau of the then National Museum of Canada conducted with Gitxsan chiefs in 1923 and 1924, more than three decades after the events they describe. The interviews appear to be one-on-one sessions with each interviewee, with no apparent attempt to clarify differences among them. For example, there is nothing in the records to distinguish between events that the interviewee witnessed and events that she or he subsequently heard about. In some cases, both the context and the details of an incident give some confidence that the informant is providing a first-hand account; in others, the circumstances of a reported action or conversation are such that the interviewee could not possibly have known what was done or said.

The process used to record the interviewees' information is also fraught with possibilities for error. The interviews were conducted in Gitxsanimx, the language spoken by Gitxsan people, with interpreters whose verbal English translations were recorded by Barbeau in shorthand in his field notebooks. The shorthand notes were in turn transcribed into a series of typescripts by stenographers who exhibit no knowledge of the region's geography, peoples, or indeed, at times, English spelling and syntax. Barbeau does not appear to have corrected or edited the archived typescripts to any great extent.

The dozen or so interviews that I rely upon as the principal sources for this chapter are listed in the appendix.

This body of evidence is deficient in one important respect: it does not include interviews with any Kitwancool residents[3] or with members of the Wolf Clan. In common with settlers, surveyors, and other government officials, Barbeau was given limited access to the village during his 1920s fieldwork. He records his difficulty in getting information on some Kitwancool poles "owing to the avowed hostility of the Wolf clan of Kitwancool against white intruders."[4] The source of this hostility will become apparent as the events central to this chapter unfold. I create a core narrative from Barbeau's interviews based on a consensus of the

---

3 The interviews with the Kitwancool Frog Clan chiefs, Luuxhon and Gwinuu, were apparently obtained in Gitwangak.

4 Marius Barbeau, *Totem Poles of the Gitksan, Upper Skeena River, British Columbia* (Ottawa: Department of Mines, National Museum of Canada, 1929) at 122 [*Totem Poles*].

events being recorded, with greater weight given to accounts where an interviewee had apparent first-hand knowledge and discounting those where an interviewee is more obviously inserting his or her own view of what might have occurred or ought to have occurred. The sources of the consensus are not referenced for each segment of the chapter except where there are significantly conflicting accounts.

Along with the Barbeau interviews, I frequently refer to William Beynon's account of a two-week series of pole-raising feasts held in Gitsegukla in 1945.[5] Beynon was a Tsimshian ethnographer, trained and employed by Barbeau as well as by other Northwest Coast anthropologists. His detailed notes of the 1945 feasts are unique in that they are the only complete, published record of all the transactions that take place in a Northwest Coast feast series.[6] By cross-referencing the records of some salient events, it is possible to confidently say that the legal processes and transactions of the 1888 Gitxsan feasts were very similar to those of the 1945 feasts. As well as Foster's analysis of indigenous peoples' attempts to have their land claims adjudicated in provincial, dominion, and imperial courts and his exposition of the police records of the 1927 arrests, I rely on Robert Galois's equally detailed examination of government archives and of the Barbeau/Beynon notes that also looks at the Kitwancool Jim story, labelled by provincial sources as the "Skeena Uprising."[7] Galois focuses on the settler intervention in an internal Gitxsan dispute and the appropriate legal process and remedy when one person has killed another. There have been many other popular and academic articles about this incident, including a fictionalized history by Barbeau based on his mid-1920s interviews.[8]

While my methodology is to use the recorded events surrounding the shooting of Gamgaxmilmuxw to draw out aspects of the Gitxsan law, some basic information about the legal order may help those unfamiliar with Northwest Coast societies. This might best be done by putting the reader in the position of a somewhat inattentive Gitxsan youth living in one of the Upper Skeena villages where most of the action to be described took place. As such, you would also have been aware that you were a member of a *wilp* or House – a kinship group that included

---

5  William Beynon, *Potlatch at Gitsegukla: William Beynon's 1945 Field Notebooks*, ed M Anderson and M Halpin (Vancouver: UBC Press, 2000).

6  *Ibid* at 11.

7  RM Galois, "Gitxsan Law and Settler Disorder: The Skeena 'Uprising' of 1888" in Theodore Binnema & Susan Neylan, eds, *New Histories for Old: Changing Perspectives on Canada's Native Pasts* (Vancouver: UBC Press, 1992) 220 ["Gitxsan Law"].

8  CM Barbeau, *The Downfall of Temlaham* (Edmonton: Hurtig, 1973 [1928]).

your siblings, your mother, her siblings, and her maternal ancestors. Within your House, you would have heard there are a couple of distinct lineages, each of which could form its own House if it could generate enough wealth to be independent. You would have experienced the efforts of your father and his House members to educate you, train you, and establish your standing within the society. You would also have been aware that your House and its members belonged to one of four *pdeek* or clans: the Lax Gibuu (Wolves), the Lax Ganeda or Lax Se'el (Frogs), the Lax Xskiik (Eagles), and the Gisk'aast (Fireweeds), and that you were strictly forbidden to marry, or indeed to have a relationship, with a member of your own clan. Your parents would have pointed to themselves as coming from different Houses and clans. One of your mother's siblings would have taken you to the *gangan*[9] or poles in the village. The carved *dzepk* or images on those erected by your House, it would have been explained, were of the *ayuks* or crests that capture events from your lineage's *adaawk* or histories. These crests could be used to identify your lineage relatives in an unfamiliar village in the Skeena watershed and up and down the coast. That same uncle or aunt might have taken you out to camps on your House territories, naming many of their geographical features, showing you their territory boundaries, and sternly warning you of the consequences of hunting or trapping beyond those boundaries. You were suitably impressed by their warnings, although you would have to be reminded of some of the place names and boundary markers another time. You would also have been aware of the *yukw* or feast at which chiefs from all Houses and clans came together to conduct business considered to be important by senior family members but which you have yet to attend.

Finally, a note on the orthography used in the chapter. I have tried to use modern spellings for Gitxsan names and terms, although there are probably inconsistences. For further simplicity, no diacritics have been used. Gitxsan terms are written in italics followed by an approximate English translation. Gitxsan names may be harder for the reader to keep straight. As in a Russian novel, there are so many of them and the language is so unfamiliar. For the main protagonists in the story, I provide a genealogical chart (Figure 1) by which the reader can be reminded of their relationships, House memberships, and clan identities. An added source of confusion is that a Gitxsan person will pass through several feast-names as they mature and assume greater responsibilities in the society. Informants tend to refer to a person by the

---

9 Singular, *gan*.

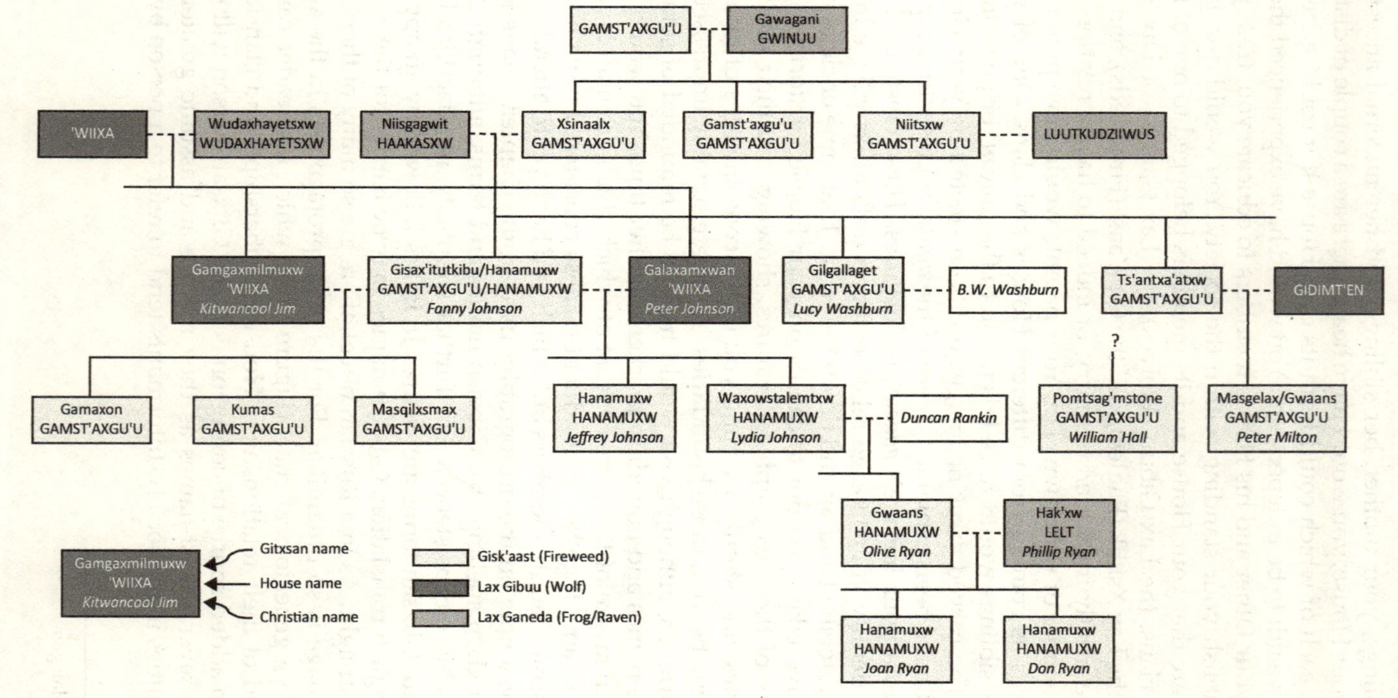

Figure 1. Genealogical connections of some participants in the story

feast-name or chief-name they held at the time of an interview rather than the name they held at the time of the event being recounted. In most cases, I attempt to consistently use the name an individual would have held at the time of the event and provide their Christian names when they had one.

To reduce the plethora of Gitxsan names and terms on a page, I refer to the *pdeek* or clans in English translation. The names of the villages are given in their most commonly used forms: Kispiox, Gitanmaax, Gitsegukla, Gitwangak, and Kitwancool. This latter village has been called Gitanyow for most of its history. By the mid-nineteenth century, however, wars with the Tsetsaut people in the Meziadin Lake area had so reduced the village's population that the community renamed itself Kitwancool, an anglicized spelling that refers to the smaller number of people then remaining.[10] In the early 1990s, the name reverted to Gitanyow as the community's population recovered to its former strength.

As for the English orthography, I do not capitalize the words now commonly designated as proper nouns used to lump together indigenous societies in Canada, such as "indigenous," "aboriginal," "native," and so on.[11]

The legal processes encountered in this chapter were precipitated by a number of premature deaths, beginning with that of Gamaxon, the son of Gamgaxmilmuxw and his wife, Gisax'itutkibu, in the winter of 1887–88.

## Deaths

### Gamaxon

The accounts of the lives and deaths at the heart of this chapter begin with the *halayt* performances[12] that preceded a December 1887 *yukw* or feast held in Gitwangak. The invited guests included the chiefs and members of the Houses from the closest villages, Gitsegukla to the east

---

10  Wilson Duff, ed, *Histories, Territories and Laws of the Kitwancool* (Victoria: Royal British Columbia Museum, 959) at 31.

11  It seems to me to be the ultimate colonial arrogance to attempt to take away peoples' lands, governance, and children and in return put capital letters on the collective nouns employed to classify them. I attempt to show my respect by using the same grammatical rules as I do with all other legal orders. Similarly, and contrary to provincial and federal government style guides, I also italicize all *Gitksanemx* terms as I find it makes the text easier to read – in much the same way as lawyers and judges italicize Latin words and phrases.

12  The word *halayt* has the same lexical root as *halhal*, a spinning top or spindle whorl, reflecting the twirling dances integral to the performances.

and Kitwancool to the north. As the ceremonies were to take place over several days, the visitors camped in village groups, each a short distance from Gitwangak.

Each Gitwangak House hosted a *halayt* in the home of its leading chief. These performances dramatize spiritual aspects of each host's *daxgyet*, or bundle of powers,[13] with costume, dance, and song, as well as other theatrical props and effects. The power and its theatrical depictions, both called *naxnox*, were acquired by the performer's ancestor from spirits that had assumed earthly forms. The host performs a charade of his or her *naxnox* name in the centre of the room, a performance that requires reciprocity between the host and each guest. Full-face carved masks and shape-shifting, gender-shifting costumes hide the performer's corporeal identity and emphasize the timelessness and other-worldliness of *halayt* theatre.

*Halayt* performances often dramatize one of three basic aspects of the Gitxsan legal order. *Halayt* participants are both entertained and reminded of the immortality of *naxnox* names and hence of the lineages they embody by the recuring motif of the host chief acting out death while each guest chief attempts to revive him or her by performing their own *halayt* power. Ultimately, they succeed. The lineage lives on. Secondly, some *naxnox* masks allow the performer to switch from a blind being to a seeing one. The seeing being is one who is aware of the interrelatedness of life, the land and the spirit. Lastly, a *halayt* performance may dramatize the normative standards that each chief strives to maintain. The holder of the highest name in a lineage, the House chief, is called a *wiihalayt*, a "great dancer" at a *halayt*, and a *simoogit*, literally a "real person," in the feast hall. As such, the holder of the name is required to maintain the society's highest ideals. These standards are examined in *halayt* performances by the host acting out the exact opposite of the required behaviour – being a liar, a thief, indifferent, uncaring, and so on – until the actor is ushered out of the room by his or her attendants.[14] The frailties that beguile and torment us as humans are thus paraded and vanquished.

---

13  *Daxgyet*, literally a "firmly bound person," is a concept not easily translated although the English term "powers" is often used. Two of its many elements are crucial: a chief's initial marriage with the spirit of particular territories, and his successors' and his lineage's subsequent duty to respect both the human and supernatural partners of the marriage.

14  Beynon's notes of the 1945 Gitsegukla pole-raising feasts record twenty-seven *halayt* performances, thirteen of which showed revivals of comatose persons and twelve of which portrayed undesirable human traits. The other dramatizations were of animals or supernatural beings: Beynon, *supra* note 5 at 26 and 27.

After sunset in Gitwangak, a messenger called the guests from their camps to the village. To the sound of whistles and bugles, members of the House hosting the *halayt* – about forty strong – ushered each visiting chief into the building while his family remained outside singing. Once inside, the guests were seated around three sides of the room with the fourth side facing the door reserved for the House hosting the *halayt*. In the middle of the room was a large open fire radiating heat and light for the performances due to take place around it. Guests were grouped by village and within each village grouped by clan. Each chief sat in the front row so he or she could step forward at the appropriate time to dance in response to his or her host's *halayt*. Immediately behind sat the likely successor to the chief's name, and behind him or her sat the next in line.[15] Thus, the room acted as a matrix of the participants' legal relationships. Each person's village, clan, and House kinship and their role within their House were put on public record for all to see. Timing added a further dimension to the algorithm. The order in which each chief was announced and admitted reflected the hosts' assessment of the chief's rank, and thus of his or her House, among the invited guests. Rank was assessed by consideration of a House's wealth in resources and members, as well as its chief's charisma, moral behaviour, modesty, and skills at resource management and dispute resolution. Unlike a lineage's identity, its rank was subject to change as its fortunes waxed and waned relative to those of others.

At the first of those late-1887 *halayt* performances in Gitwangak, the established order was challenged. The highest-ranked Gitsegukla chief, Wiigyet of the Fireweed Clan, was seated first, followed by the other Fireweed chiefs, Guuxsan, Xsgogmlaxha, Txatguml, and Tsa'waals. The next Fireweed House chief to be called to take his seat was Gamst'axgu'u,[16] who had recently died, and the House appeared to have not yet chosen a successor.[17] A member of the House, Gisax'itutkibu, had dressed her young son, Gamaxon, in chief's regalia and placed him in the Gamst'axgu'u seat.[18] At that point, Gisax'itutkibu's uncle,[19] Niitsxw,

---

15 Beynon, *supra* note 5 at 57.

16 The House of Gamst'axgu'u is now known as the House of Hanamuxw.

17 A pole raised in Gitsegukla around the time of these events was said by Guuxsan, Fireweed, Gitsegukla (Dan Guxsan) to commemorate a holder of the Gamst'axgu'u name: *Totem Poles, supra* note 4 at 82.

18 According to Dan Guxsan, Gamaxon would have been the same age as he was at the time, about thirteen. It is very unusual for someone so young to succeed to a House chief's name. Most chiefs are not chosen for this role until they have the wisdom and experience of late middle age. None of Barbeau's interviewees, however, comment on this.

19 Some accounts say that Niitsxw was Gisax'itutkibu's brother.

also in chief's regalia, entered the room. He too considered himself a successor to the Gamst'axgu'u name and attempted to take the boy's seat, saying, "Not many times will you sit there." As Niitsxw was a *swansk* or shaman with the reputed power to harm as well as to cure people, Gisax'itutkibu took his words as a threat to her son. The boy, supported by his mother, refused to move.

Niitsxw left the *halayt* house. Someone went after him and shook *mixk'aax*, eagle down, over him, saying, "I think that the chiefs will settle that trouble for you." The shaking of eagle down was itself a *halayt* performance signifying respect for the recipient and imposing a cooling off during which disputes can be safely settled. In this case, the host of that evening's *halayt* performances, Giilawaw', a Gitwangak Eagle chief, placed a chair near the house door for Niitsxw, which then became his seat in the subsequent Gitwangak *halayt* performances and feast.[20] Throughout the Northwest, the placement of a chief's seat in a location outside of the established feast-hall matrix could signal a particular honour. Similarly, an unusual order of entering the feast-hall, for example always being the first or the last to come in, was also used to show specific regard. So there was a peace of sorts afterwards, although Niitsxw was said to "never had a very good heart for that woman and the child."[21]

Later that same winter, the Wolf Houses of Kitwancool also held a feast.[22] Again, people from the two nearest villages, Gitwangak and Gitsegukla, as well as from Gitanmaax, travelled to camp near the host village to participate in the feast and its *halayt* performances. While they were there, a measles epidemic struck the region, killing many children, including Gamaxon and a younger brother. Gisax'itutkibu recalled Niitsxw's earlier threats and blamed him for using his *swansk* powers to cause Gamaxon's death. She would have been well primed to have a strong belief in shamanic skills. While a girl, she had become blind and lost the use of one foot. She told Barbeau in 1924 that her husband, Gamgaxmilmuxw, called the shamans from the neighbouring

---

20 Another account states that the seat was a blanket-covered trunk that Niitsxw subsequently took away as his own.

21 This account of the seating dispute at the Gitwangak *halayt* performances is based on interviews with Gamayam (Charles Mark), Gwinuu (Lucy Lagaxnits), and Laganitsxw/Hlengwax (Jim Lagaxnits). These recorded more details of the incident and were more or less consistent with each other, more so than were other accounts, which conflated the occasion of the initial dispute with subsequent feasts that winter.

22 Some interviewees said the Wolf House was 'Wiixa, others say it was Malii.

villages who identified a song that was haunting her. On their instructions, she sang the song wearing a grizzly claw headdress and holding an owl rattle.[23] She then walked around the house in the direction of the sun before collapsing unconscious. When she awoke, her disabilities were gone. Gamgaxmilmuxw had paid the shamans well in food, regalia, and blankets for his young wife's cure.[24]

Nevertheless, Gisax'itutkibu must have been aware that Gamaxon died in the middle of an epidemic. The resident Methodist missionary at Gitsegukla, William Pierce, reported that over two hundred Gitxsan, mainly children, died from measles that winter. There were so many deaths at Kispiox that the dead could not be buried, and had to be cremated on an open fire in the middle of the village. Between Gitsegukla and Hazelton, Pierce "passed two or three women lying under the trees, their babies strapped to their backs ... frozen stiff."[25] Perhaps Gisax'itutkibu's rivalry with Niitsxw blinded her to the more likely cause of her sons' deaths.

*Niitsxw*

This is the point at which Gamgaxmilmuxw assumes more of a role in the story. When he and Gisax'itutkibu returned to their home in Gitsegukla after the 1888 Wolf feasts in Kitwancool, she began harassing him to avenge their boy's death. Although they were unlikely to have been privy to the couple's conversations, Barbeau's interviewees record that Gisax'itutkibu told her husband, "Go out and shoot grouse," meaning he was to kill Niitsxw.[26] When he did not do so, she said, "If you do not kill Niitsxw, I will kill you." Gamgaxmilmuxw didn't like that his wife troubled him all the time. He eventually took his gun and told Gisax'itutkibu, "Prepare the kettle before I come back, I am maybe going to kill a grouse for you." All the accounts are clear that Gisax'itutkibu was responsible for goading Gamgaxmilmuxw into pursuing Niitsxw.

---

23 The grizzly claw headdress and rattle were standard items of shamanic paraphernalia: Joanne MacDonald, *Gitwangak Village Life: A Museum Collection* (Ottawa: Minister of Environment, Parks Canada, 1984) at 65 [*Gitwangak Village Life*].

24 Gisax'itutkibu's account of her cure is reproduced in *ibid* at 65.

25 WH Pierce, *From Potlatch to Pulpit* (Vancouver: Vancouver Bindery, 1933) at 57.

26 The Grouse is a Fireweed *ayuks* or crest. *Ayuks* are represented as *dzepk* or emblems on members' poles, house fronts, and regalia encapsulating their lineage's history and identity. The Grouse crest, however, is not reported to be specifically linked to Niitsxw or other lineages in the Gamst'axgu'u House: *Totem Poles, supra* note 4 at 163 and Beynon, *supra* note 5 at 179.

Because Gamgaxmilmuxw was of the House of 'Wiixa, a Kitwan-cool Wolf House, and Niitsxw was of the House of Gamst'axgu'u, a Gitsegukla Fireweed House, their dispute was subject to the laws of compensation. There is no record, however, of either Gisax'itutkibu or Gamgaxmilmuxw seeking any compensation from Niitsxw. None of Barbeau's interviewees comment on this omission. An additional point of Gitxsan law may have come into play here. While death, injuries, or other wrongs to an adult are taken up by the victim's maternal relatives and House, harms to a child are taken up by the child's paternal rela-tives, and by extension, the father's House. When a Gitanmaax youth accidentally drowned in 1884 while he worked for a white trader, it was the boy's father who required acknowledgment and compensation from the trader and, when they weren't forthcoming, killed him.[27] This incident also shows that under Gitxsan law and throughout the North-west Coast, it is immaterial whether a harm was intentional or acciden-tal. In either case, the rule of strict liability applies to the obligation to both acknowledge and compensate for the harm. Subsequent events played out in 1888 on the same basis.

As Gamgaxmilmuxw set out from Gitsegukla with his gun, Niitsxw was in Kitwancool preparing to return home from a *tets*, an inviting party to a *yukw* or feast. He was one of five or six high-ranking Gitsegukla Fireweed men who had travelled to Gitwangak and then to Kitwancool to invite the people there to the funeral feast of Tse'oyimx, an uncle of Wiigyet, the leading Fireweed chief in Gitsegukla. Wiigyet had waited three weeks for the measles epidemic to subside before sending out his messengers. Niitsxw appears to have been the *galdim'algax*,[28] the chief's speaker, of behalf of Wiigyet. In a *tets* invitation, the *galdim'algax* explains to the invited Houses the purpose of the forthcoming feast and the reason why the invited chiefs' attendance is required. The date, time, and place of the *yukw* are also given. The host House would have already had an internal feast (*li'liget*), likely with other Houses of its clan in its village, to fix the date and, more importantly, discuss and reach consensus on the matter to be announced at the *yukw* – the suc-cessor to the Tse'oyimx name. The *yukw* invitees respond to the invita-tion with *halayt* songs and performances, scattering eagle down on the messengers to signify their acceptance.

---

27  For a full account of this incident based on Barbeau's 1924 interviews with Gamayam, House of Guuxsan, Fireweed, Gitsegukla (Charles Mark) and Ts'igwii, House of Wiigyet, Fireweed, Gitsegukla (Isaac Tens), see Neil J Sterritt, *Mapping My Way Home: A Gitxsan History* (Smithers: Creekstone, 2016) at 276–9 [*Mapping*].

28  Literally, a "box of words".

A House hosting a feast took care that the invitees included all the chiefs and other high-ranking members of those Houses that had a legal interest in the host's decision. In each village there would have been one chief, the *nidinsxwit*, who would have responded first to the hosts' announcement.[29] The *nidinsxwit* would usually have been the chief of the House with the strongest marriage connections and thus alliances with the host House. At the feast, these chiefs will validate that the host's proposed actions are being carried out in accordance with Gitxsan law.[30] The plural term, *nidinsx*, has been translated as "the ones who approve."[31] This point was clearly made in 1945 when Wiiseeks spoke first on behalf of the *nidinsxwit* in response to host Gaxsbgabaxs's telling of his House's history and crests at his Gitsegukla pole-raising feast. Wiiseeks validated his host's assertions: "Yes, Chief Gaxsbgagaxs, what you said is true. I myself attended a former feast of your uncle, where he narrated the same story that you now tell, and everything is as you now tell. And you have done the proper thing in showing this to your fellow chiefs, who know that what you say is true."[32] A *yukw* feast, then, was less a process of debating or legislating issues and more a judicial review of the legality of a House's decision by the other Houses directly affected by it.

The Wiigyet *tets* party in Kitwancool was winding up its business. The Frog chiefs there had indicated their acceptance of the invitation and the Wolves were making ready to reply. Some of the messengers had already returned to Gitsegukla, leaving Niitsxw, Mark Wiget,[33] and a young boy, Peter Mark,[34] in Kitwancool. Mark Wiget thought they should stay there until they had a definite response from the Wolves,

---

29  Richard Daly, *Our Box Was Full: An Ethnography for the Delgamuukw Plaintiffs* (Vancouver: UBC Press, 2005) at 75.

30  Fuller descriptions of the Gitxsan *tets* inviting procedure can be found in *ibid* at 74–7 and Beynon, *supra* note 5 at 57–66.

31  Gwaans, House of Hanamuxw, Fireweed, Gitsegukla (Olive Ryan): Beynon, *supra* note 5 at 254.

32  Beynon, *supra* note 5 at 140. Wiiseeks, House of Wiigyet, Fireweed, Gitsegukla (Steven Morgan) was obliquely referring to a dispute between Gaxsbgabaxs, Frog, Gitsegukla (Simon Turner), and Hlengwax, Frog, Gitwangak (Mathius Bright) over which of their Houses had the right to display a particular crest: see Beynon, *supra* note 5 at 65–6, 77–81, 129–30, 136–9, and 150–1.

33  Mark Wiget held the name Wiigyet when Barbeau interviewed him in 1924. However, as Steven Morgan is known to have held Wiigyet in 1910, Mark Wiget would not have held it in 1888. Further, a House chief was not usually a member of a *tets* party for a *yukw* feast his House would be hosting.

34  In 1945, Peter Mark held the chief name Guuxsan: Beynon, *supra* note 5 at 45.

but Niitsxw thought otherwise. He left alone early the next morning with a large pack containing bags of eulachon grease that he had received at an earlier feast. This was the same morning that Gamgaxmilmuxw left Gitsegukla.

The two men met at Wints'ihlniilitxw, a steep hill on the trail[35] about two miles south of Kitwancool. From the top of the hill, Gamgaxmilmuxw loaded his flint-lock musket with steel balls and shot Niitsxw in the stomach and into his backbone. The wounded Niitsxw is reported to have said to Gamgaxmilmuxw, "Who is that? Did I shoot your grandfather? Shall you shoot me if I did not shoot one of your family? If you know I kill your family, all right, kill me."[36] Here, Niitsxw was said to be invoking the rules of the feud under Gitxsan law. As already mentioned, when someone was killed or otherwise wronged, either accidently or intentionally, the offender's House was required to pay compensation to the victim's House. If compensation was not forthcoming or was too little in the victim's family's opinion, they could legally take the life of a person in the offender's House. Moreover, that person must not be of lower status to the first victim. Niitsxw was reminding Gamgaxmilmuxw of this when he allegedly asked if he had shot Gamgaxmilmuxw's grandfather, who would have been the Kitwancool House chief 'Wiixa and presumably a person Niitsxw would have considered to be of comparable rank to himself.

Niitsxw continued to the summit of Wints'ihlniilitxw, where he took off his pack and lay down out of the snow beside the roots of an upturned tree. Gamgaxmilmuxw ran past him to Kitwancool to the home of 'Wiixa, his House chief. There, he announced that he had shot Niitsxw. 'Wiixa responded angrily, "Who told you to do this? You kill Niitsxw when I order you to do it. Go outside and don't come in here. That chief was the highest chief." Here, we get a glimpse of the internal machinations within a House when faced with a serious wrong by one of

---

35  The trail between Kitwancool, Gitwangak, and Gitsegukla on which Niitsxw set off and on which later events took place was a section of a much wider network, the grease trails, that linked the vital eulachon fishery at the mouth of the Nass River with numerous villages in the interior. See George F MacDonald & John J Cove, eds., *Tsimshian Narratives*, vol. 2: *Trade and Warfare* (Ottawa: Canadian Museum of Civilisation, 1987) at x–xvii.

36  The quote is from an account by Gamayam, House of Guuxsan, Fireweed, Gitsegukla (Charles Mark). Another of Barbeau's interviewees, Simediik, Eagle, Gitwangak, reported Niitsxw's words as: "Who is it among your family that I have shot before, that you shoot me now?" These statements may have been attributed to Niitsxw as the interviewees' conceptualization of the appropriate Gitxsan law rather than their knowledge of what, if anything, was actually said.

its members. First, 'Wiixa appears to have been reminding Gamgax-milmuxw that since the consequences of a killing are to be borne by all the House members, the act should be decided by all of them and conveyed by the head chief to the person chosen to carry out the deed. Second, by pointing out that Niitsxw was "the highest chief," 'Wiixa may have been indicating that any compensation negotiated with Niitsxw's House would be costly, as it increased with the status and rank of the person harmed.

Word quickly spread through the village, resulting in much agitation. One account indicates that "a relative of Niitsxw" in Kitwancool heard the news and prepared for revenge.[37] Gamgaxmilmuxw sent for Mark Wiget, who cautioned him to say nothing. Gamgaxmilmuxw immediately set off for Gitsegukla. By his own account, Wiget set off to find Niitsxw. When he did, Niitsxw was still alive and asked him to not let the rest of the family retaliate and to carry on with the planned feast of his uncle, Tse'oyimx.[38]

In the meantime, a member of the House of Gwinuu[39] went to her house and asked her family to go out and look for Niitsxw's body. This would have been the House's duty, as Niitsxw's father had been Gawagani, a member of the House of Gwinuu. While a Gitxsan person takes the lineage, House, and clan identity of his or her mother, the father's House has responsibilities at the beginning and the end of that person's life. The father is responsible for protecting and educating the child and for enhancing their rank by distributing wealth at a series of feasts on their behalf. One of the last in this series is the *halayt* performance that precedes the feast at which the child is given a name for the first time in their mother's House.[40] From then on, the person's role and rank within the Gitxsan legal order is determined within their House. What is known as the *wilksiwitxw* or "father's side" has some subsequent roles, such as being responsible for the tree selection and carving of an offspring chief's pole, but further significant duties occur at the end of the person's life. On an adult child's death, the *wilksiwitxw* will help its House deal with its bereavement and will finance the funeral. These duties are undertaken by the father's side even if the father is long dead himself.

---

37  The account of Ts'igwii, House of Wiigyet, Fireweed, Gitsegukla (Isaac Tens).

38  The account of Mark Wiget. This incident may be more Wiget editorializing what should have been done rather than what Niisxw actually said.

39  This was the mother of Barbeau's 1924 interviewee, Gwinuu, Frog, Kitwancool (Lucy Lagaxnits). In 1888, Lucy was a child. She and her mother were present in 'Wiixa's house when Gamgaxmilmuxw arrived there after he shot Niitsxw.

40  Beynon, *supra* note 5 at 100.

So it was that as Niitsxw lay dying in the shelter of the uprooted tree, four or five young men from his *wilksiwitxw*, the House of Gwinuu, took a lantern and set out from Kitwancool to find him.[41] They discovered him still alive. They stayed with him for the rest of the night, wrapping him in blankets and making a box to carry him. At daybreak, they started on their journey to bring him back to Gitsegukla. Some time later, they were joined by Lulak and Niiswagaye from the House of Lelt, a Frog Clan House from Gitwangak that is closely related to Gwinuu.[42] The wives of the men bearing Niitsxw made them food, which was relayed to them on the trail. The next night, they camped at Gasalaxlo'obit, where there was a good supply of firewood. There, Lulak was able to remove some of the shot from Niitsxw's back.

While at Gasalaxlo'obit, the party also met up with Ukslax'a'mks, a young woman of the House of Gamlaxyeltxw (Frog, Kitwancool) who was travelling from Gitsegukla to Kitwancool. Because she was Gamgaxmilmuxw's cousin,[43] some in the party wanted to shoot her. In the end, she was allowed to continue. Simediik, later Ukslax'a'mks' husband, told Barbeau that if she had been killed, "there would have been a big war."[44]

In the meantime, Gamgaxmilmuxw had arrived in Gitsegukla after midnight. He quickly told his wife, "I have shot the grouse that you wished for." Apparently, she did not at first believe him. He then went

41  The number and names of the people in this party vary from interviewee to interviewee. A consensus of the evidence is that the party from Kitwancool was made up of Guugak, Gawagani, and Gwildeda'o from the House of Gwinuu, and Hodumuxw and Ga'khl from the closely related Frog House of Hodumuxw.

42  *Totem Poles, supra* note 4 at 41.

43  Generally, in English translations from Gitxsan, "nephews" refers to lateral relatives on a person's mother's side, that is, the person's own House, and "cousins" refers to lateral relatives on the person's father's side. In this case, the House of Gamlaxyeltxw is closely related to the House of Wudaxhayetsxw, Gamgaxmilmuxw's father's House.

44  Simediik refers to his wife as Lisee'iw, a name in the House of Gamlaxyeltxw. A comparison of the captions for the same 1910 photograph in George MacDonald, *The Totem Poles and Monuments of Gitwangak Village* (Ottawa: Environment Canada, Parks Canada, 1984) at 18 and in Neil Sterritt et al, *Tribal Boundaries in the Nass Watershed* (Vancouver: UBC Press, 1998) at front and back covers [*Tribal Boundaries*] indicates that Simediik's wife later held the chief name Gamlaxyeltxw and the Christian name Miriam Douse. Others of Barbeau's interviewees refer to the future chief Gamlaxyeltxw by the name Ukslax'a'mks. She therefore likely held the names Ukslax'a'mks, Lisee'iw, and Gamlaxyeltxw in succession at various points in her life. In this chapter, she will be identified by the name she was likely holding at the time of the events being described.

to his father, Wudaxhayetsxw (Frog, Kitwancool), who at that time lived in Gitsegukla.[45] On hearing of Niitsxw's shooting, the father asked, "Is that what your father taught you? I never told you to kill a man. Every time I told you: Don't kill! Don't kill!" Wudaxhayetsxw here recounts his legal duty as a father to educate his children and to raise them to be restrained, ethical individuals. He laments that Gamgaxmilmuxw failed to abide by those lessons.

Gamgaxmilmuxw feared that the Gitsegukla Fireweed people would kill his father to revenge Niitsxw's shooting. He was able to persuade his brother, Galaxamx'wan (Peter Johnson) and his father to return with him to Kitwancool. They left that night. Along the way, they met the party carrying Niitsxw to Gitsegukla. They asked if Niitsxw had died and were told, "No, he still lives." Gwildedao took a gun and wanted to shoot Gamgaxmilmuxw but others in his party restrained him, saying, "No, don't do that!" The family was allowed to proceed to Kitwancool. Gamgaxmilmuxw, however, stopped now and then to let his slower-moving father get ahead and to wait and see if anyone was following them. In fact, by noon in Gitsegukla everyone knew that Niitsxw had been shot, and immediately three young nephews from his House, Masgelax (Peter Milton), Pomtsag'mstone (William Hall), and Axtiwigenox,[46] started after Gamgaxmilmuxw. However, when they met the group bearing Niitsxw, they returned to Gitsegukla with them. Niitsxw died on the trail eight miles out of Gitwangak.

Gamgaxmilmuxw's actions following his shooting of Niitsxw demonstrate an important point of Gitxsan dispute law. He immediately set off to tell his House chief in Kitwancool and then his father in Gitsegukla what had he had done. As the accounts show, the news thus became public very quickly in both communities, setting off a cascade of events that subjected Gamgaxmilmuxw to severe dressing down by both his mother's side and his father's side as well as putting him in some danger from his victim's House members. This immediate public revelation of a wrong is necessary, however, for the public process for its compensation and the restoration of relations between the wrongdoer's and the victim's lineages to begin.

The legal consequences of hiding a death, whether accidental or intentional, are shown by the previously mentioned incident at Gitanmaax.

---

45 Gamgaxmilmuxw's mother had died young and his father had remarried Wiigyet's sister and moved to her village of Gitsegukla.

46 Some interviewees say that Axtiwigenox was Milton and Hall's father, although that name does not appear on any of the records of names held by a Gitxsan House.

A white trader, Charlie Youmans, regularly hired Gitxsan men to help bring supplies by canoe up the Skeena River from Port Essington on the coast to his store in the village. In the high spring runoff of 1884 a youth, Hisnu'utkshlgana'o[47] (Billy Owen), fell out of one of Youmans's canoes in Kitselas Canyon and drowned. Youmans travelled by land to Gitanmaax ahead of his canoes, but for two or three days failed to mention Owen's death despite being asked by the villagers if all had gone well. When the canoes eventually arrived, news of what happened spread quickly through the village. The people said that Youmans was in the wrong for not telling them beforehand. Owen's father, Haa'atxw,[48] tried to talk to Youmans, but the trader paid no attention to him and did not respond to his questions. Haa'atxw then fatally stabbed Youmans. The following August, the provincial police arrested Haa'atxw.

The highest-ranking chief in Gitanmaax, Gedimgaldo'o, wrote to Provincial Secretary John Robson explaining the Gitxsan law that applied to the case. He laid out the two salient requirements: first, that when an accident or death occurs on a joint venture, the "survivors shall immediately, or as soon as possible, make it known to the friends[49] of the injured or deceased what has taken place"; and second, that "the survivor makes a present corresponding to his ability, to show his sympathy and good will to the friends of the deceased." Robson's response was to concede that although it would have been better if Youmans had followed Gitxsan law, it did not bind him and therefore his killing must be punished. The provincial secretary rhetorically asked Gedimgaldo'o, "Do you not now see that the Queen's law is better than yours?"

At his trial, Haa'atxw was defended by Montague Tyrwhitt-Drake, QC,[50] who argued along the lines already laid out by Gidemgaldo'o, that his client had acted under Gitxsan law and that this justified the jury to exercise its understanding and mercy. In an earlier attempt to integrate indigenous law with the colonial common law, Tyrwhitt-Drake

---

47  A boy's name in the House of Kyeexw, Wolf Clan, Gitanmaax. This House had become extinct by the 1920s: *Totem Poles, supra* note 4 at 126.

48  Haa'atxw, House of Ts'iin, Frog Clan, Gitanmaax.

49  Gedimgaldo'o's letter was put into writing by a D. Jennings (probably Dennis Jennings, an Anglican missionary) who likely translated and transcribed an oral Gitxsan dictation into English. The term "friends" in this case may well have been a somewhat loose approximation in English of more precise Gitxsan kinship terms. Indeed, the conciliatory tone of the letter indicates that it was, in parts, more the missionary scribe's view of what Gitxsan law should be than what, perhaps, Gedimgaldo'o was telling him in Gitxsanmx.

50  Tyrwhitt-Drake was a former mayor of Victoria, a member of the British Columbia Legislative Assembly, and a future Supreme Court of British Columbia judge.

had suggested to Indian Superintendent Powell in 1873, "As the Indians in their tribal condition have established almost universally a system of recompense for almost all offences, why should not that system be carried out and only offences brought before the Supreme Court which couldn't be dealt with in this manner?"[51] The trial judge, Justice Henry Crease, nevertheless instructed the jury that under no system of law was it legal for one man to kill another. Haa'atxw was found guilty of murder and sentenced to hang. Justice Crease did write to the dominion secretary of state laying out the relevant Gitxsan law, but he also carefully stated that such facts could not have been put to the jury. He suggested to the secretary that the governor-general exercise his pardoning power to commute the sentence to ten years' imprisonment. This bit of nineteenth-century judicial activism was a remarkable attempt to reconcile Gitxsan indigenous law and Canadian state law along the lines proposed earlier by Tyrwhitt-Drake. It was successful. Haa'atxw's sentence was commuted to ten years' hard labour, but unfortunately he died in prison two years later.[52]

In the Youmans case, the indigenous law offence was the wilful failure to inform the victim's family and House. In an 1852 case, there were dire consequences for the wilful failure of Hlidax, a Nisga'a Wolf chief, to inform his own House and community that he had killed two chiefs from a neighbouring people, the Tsetsaut. As the missionary R.B. McCullagh later observed, the Nisga'a killer "kept the matter a profound secret from the Nisga'a people, a mean thing to do because according to Indian law, the lives of two Nisga'a chiefs were now forfeit." The Tsetsaut later ambushed and killed a party of Nisga'a, including two of their chiefs. Some Kitwancool people, who were travelling with the Nisga'a, were also killed in the attack, again including two of their chiefs. The Tsetsaut gave the Kitwancool Wolf House of 'Wiilitsxw their Meziadin Lake territory as *xsiisxw* – compensation – for the collateral deaths.[53]

---

51  Hamar Foster, "'The Queen's Law is Better Than Yours': International Homicide in Early British Columbia" in Jim Phillips, Tina Loo & Susan Lewthwaite, eds, *Essays in the History of Criminal Law*, vol. 5: *Crime and Criminal Justice* (Toronto: University of Toronto Press, 1994) 41 at 83–4 ["Queen's Law"].

52  The accounts of the Youmans/Haa'atxw incident are from *Mapping, supra* note 27 at 276–9; Geoff Mynett, *Murders on the Skeena* (Qualicum Beach, BC: Caitlin, 2021) at 32–6; and "Queen's Law," *supra* note 51 at 41–4.

53  *Tribal Boundaries, supra* note 44 at 44–53.

The actions of Gamgaxmilmuxw following Niitsxw's death and those of Charlie Youmans following Billy Owen's death show the distinction between a killing and a murder under Gitxsan law: the one public and legally amendable, the other secret and legally incorrigible. In the latter case, the offender becomes an outlaw in the sense of being outside of the law, not of merely breaking the law. An outlaw is vulnerable to being killed in retaliation without the support of his House and without being provided the opportunity to pay compensation.

When the party bearing Niitsxw reached Gitsegukla, the Fireweed chiefs, Wiigyet, Guuxsan, Haxpegwootxw, and Xsgogmlaxha, each sang a *limx'oy* or dirge to acknowledge Niitsxw's death. They placed his body at the back of Gisax'itutkibu's house. She went to the house of her father, Niisgagwit,[54] who looked after her. Many in the village saw her as the cause of the troubles and wanted to attack her. Others wanted to attack Kitwancool. The resident missionary, William Pierce, advised them "not to take the law into their own hands but to lay their complaint before the government."[55] It is unclear whether Pierce's remonstrations or the inherent restraints of Gitxsan kinship connections and conflict law were responsible, but no attack on Kitwancool took place.

After the shooting, Wiigyet again sent *tets* messengers to invite people from Gitwangak and Kitwancool to the funeral feast of his uncle, Tse'oyimx, in Gitsegukla. But no one wanted to attend for fear of further trouble. Some people in Gitwangak, likely Frog chiefs as neutral go-betweens,[56] sent word to Kitwancool that the Wolves there should make restitution to Niitsxw's family. The Gitwangak chiefs also sent a message to the Gitsegukla Fireweeds that if they wanted to host a big feast, they must ask Gamgaxmilmuxw and his family "to make a compensation." 'Wiixa responded that if Niitsxw's family agreed to accept a payment, "everything would be alright." The Gitsegukla people and, in particular, Niitsxw's kin agreed, after the leading Fireweed chief, Wiigyet, had consulted with the other clan chiefs.

These exchanges exemplify the critical role of the *simgigyet* – the House Chiefs, literally "the real people" – as mediators in the settlement of conflicts. In this case, the dispute was between Houses of different

---

54  House of Haakasxw, Frog, Gitsegukla.

55  Pierce, *supra* note 25 at 58–9.

56  This supposition is given credibility by the fact that a detailed description of these exchanges was given to Barbeau by Jim Laganitz, who in 1923 held the names Laganitsxw and Hlengwax, which then and in 1888 were the House chief names of the leading Frog Clan House in Gitwangak.

clans and from different villages. The mediation was conducted by the chiefs from a third clan in a village not directly involved in the dispute. They employed the classic mediation technique of first putting forward a settlement proposal to each party separately before attempting to bring them together in an agreement.

Two days later, the Gitsegukla Fireweeds armed themselves in case things turned ugly and travelled to Gitwangak and then on to Kitwancool to seek compensation. When they arrived, they stood outside 'Wiixa's house and called for Gamgaxmilmuxw to come out: "Where is 'Wiixa's nephew? Come out, come out and bring everything. Pay for this, pay for this and you will settle for this." In this way, they presented their demand for blood money. Gamgaxmilmuxw came out dressed in grizzly skin regalia,[57] which was his crest, and carrying in his teeth a *hayetsxw* or copper shield, the highest form of wealth in northern Northwest Coast societies. He was on all fours, which meant he was going to pay. One account says that Gamgaxmilmuxw sang a *limx ganx*, a peace song, and placed an eagle feather in the headdress of Niitsxw's nearest relative, his brother. By accepting the feather, the brother promised there would be peace between them.[58] Behind Gamgaxmilmuxw, House of 'Wiixa members and other Wolves were singing as they brought out the most valuable things they had: blankets, coats, guns, beaver pelts, moosehides, and other skins, together worth more than five hundred dollars. They invited the Gitsegukla visitors into their house. There, 'Wiixa had on his dancing regalia, and performed the *gawagani*, a *halayt* peace-making ceremony. The Gitsegukla chiefs retired to the house of Yee'l, the Kitwancool Fireweed House, to consider if the *xsiisxw* compensation offered was sufficient. They decided it was and returned with it to Gitsegukla.

Yee'l, as the single Fireweed House in Kitwancool, was anomalous in a village traditionally comprised of only Wolf and Frog Houses. The two principal names in Yee'l had come relatively recently from the Gitsegukla House of Wiigyet as a consequence of two disputes internal to the Fireweeds. First, two brothers from the House of Wiigyet attempted to succeed a former Haxpegwootxw, chief of another Fireweed House that was close to extinction, by paying for his commemorative feast and thus assuming his and his House's possessions. The coup was

---

57 Most interviewees describe the bear regalia. Niistaw, House of Gwagl'lo, Frog, Gitsegukla (Anna Campbell), however, told Barbeau that Gamgaxmilmuxw wore red-headed woodpecker regalia. The woodpecker is a crest of the House of 'Wiixa.
58 Per Anna Campbell.

unsuccessful and the brothers had to leave, taking the name Yee'l with them to Kitwancool. Second, the holder of the name Yawadzek in the House of Wiigyet killed a House relative around 1870 and fled to Kitwancool to join Yee'l.[59] These incidents show how individuals are deterred from acting against their fellow House members. In each case, the exiled family groups went from being part of the leading House in their village to being outcasts in a place where there were no other clan members for support and where they would have to rely solely on marriage ties to access hunting territories and fishing sites.

Because the dispute arising from the shooting of Niitsxw had been settled, it was now safe for the usual business conducted at the winter feasts to continue. For the third time, Wiigyet sent *tets* messengers to Gitwangak and Kitwancool to attend the feast for his uncle. Everyone came to Gitsegukla except Gamgaxmilmuxw. Wiigyet danced the peace dance and blew white down over the visitors, meaning they could not fight anymore. After the payment was made, "It was all over."

Wiigyet was said to have been a peacemaker "by profession and by nature."[60] This description could define the principal function of every Gitxsan chief. They served as a mediator both within the House and in its dealings with other Houses and clans. Within the House, the chief's function was, first, to maintain its identity by reasserting its histories, names, crests, and territories and, second, to keep the group together and manage it as a functioning economic unit. Before the settlement of Niitsxw's killing in Kitwancool, for example, Wiigyet consulted with the other Gitsegukla Fireweeds as to whether to accept the compensation being offered. We have seen that in interactions with others, the chief embodied his or her House by taking its consensus of what needed to be done and then presenting it to the other Houses. In this way, the Frog chiefs in Gitwangak mediated between the Gitsegukla Fireweeds and the Kitwancool Wolves to bring about the *xsiisxw*.

As has been described, the *xsiisxw* payment is made at a *halayt* ceremony between the two disputing parties. 'Wiixa performed it for the Gitsegukla Fireweeds in Kitwancool and Wiigyet performed it for the Kitwancool Wolves in Gitsegukla. But it could not be considered binding until the Fireweeds hosted a *yukw* feast where they announced their acceptance of the settlement and the invited chiefs validated their

---

59  Wilson Duff, Duff Tsimshian Files, University of British Columbia, Museum of
    Anthropology Archives, Box 41, File 126 [Duff Files]. These files contain Wilson
    Duff's extensive notes compiled between 1960 and 1972 from the Barbeau/Beynon
    notebooks archived at what is now the Canadian Museum of History.
60  Gamayam, Fireweed, Gitsegukla (Charles Mark) to Barbeau in 1923.

decision as lawful. This was done at Wiigyet's funeral feast for his uncle, Tse'oyimx, before everyone dispersed to their territories for spring hunting. Under Gitxsan law, the matter could be neither acted upon nor mentioned again.

But as events unfolded, it was.

*Gamgaxmilmuxw*

In Gitsegukla lived an American store owner, Burzilla Walter Washburn, who for understandable reasons called himself B.W. Washburn. He was considered by his descendants to have been "an opportunist, an adventurer and always trying to make an easy buck."[61] In 1884 he had been one of the Upper Skeena traders and miners who had asked the provincial secretary for a pre-emptive armed attack on the Gitxsan as protection against a perceived uprising after the Youmans killing.[62] Washburn was married to Niitsxw's niece, Gilgallaget (Lucy Washburn). He had seen a copy of an 1872 agreement made on a gunboat sent up to Metlakatla in the Skeena estuary. Provincial government representatives, including Lieutenant-Governor Trutch and the attorney general, had settled a dispute with five Gitxsan chiefs over the burning of Gitsegukla due to white prospectors' negligence. The written document does not appear to have survived, but apparently gave the Gitsegukla chiefs a payment for the losses of the village's poles, buildings, and household effects. In return, the chiefs had promised to "behave themselves" and to stop blocking settler canoe traffic up the river to force their compensation demands.[63] Such an arrangement could easily have been interpreted by each party as being consistent with its own legal regime. Based on his reading of the agreement, however, Washburn began to insist that colonial criminal justice prevail over Gitxsan dispute-resolution processes.

First, Washburn told the Gitsegukla Fireweeds to return all the compensation they had received from the Kitwancool Wolves. This they tried to do, but Gamgaxmilmuxw's family refused to accept the return. The Gitwangak Frog House of Lulak was attempting to mediate the restoration of peace between the families. But Washburn stepped in again, advising the Fireweeds not to accept the compensation but to return

---

61  Ted Johnston, *Ted Johnston Memoirs: Life with Terrace Area Pioneers* (Prince George, BC: Crescentia Harrison, 2005) at 3. Ted Johnston's mother was B.W. and Lucy Washburn's daughter, Martha.

62  Mynett, *supra* note 52 at 28.

63  RM Galois, "The Burning of Kitsegukla, 1872" (1992) 94 BC Studies 59.

the gifts a second time. It is unclear from the evidence whether he was acting out of a passion for British justice, in response to pressure from his in-laws to renege on the *xsiisxw*,[64] or because, as his family suggest, "leading the posse would give Washburn a very soft job."[65] Accounts tell that some Gitsegukla Fireweeds, likely influenced by missionary Pierce, were renouncing Gitxsan law and advocating that people acquiesce to settler law.[66] Mark Wiget, later a leader at the Salvation Army commune of Andimaul,[67] said that after Niitsxw's death he attempted to calm people by reminding them that in 1872 at Metlakatla, "the officials told us that we must not kill each other, but we must bring all our troubles to them and they would judge them." Lucy Laganitz told Barbeau that Niitsxw's relatives had become Christians and refused "the overtures of idolatry" from the Wolves.

As soon as Gamgaxmilmuxw heard that the Fireweeds had returned the *xsiisxw* compensation, he headed for the woods. This was understandable, as he and other members of his House were once again liable to forfeit a life for Niitsxw's death. Gamgaxmilmuxw spent the spring from about mid-March to mid-June on Wudaxhayetsxw's territory, Lummin Gyahlt'in, between the Kiteen and Cranberry rivers, as well as at associated fishing camps on the Nass River. He would have been able to do so through *amnigwootxw*, the privilege of adult children to use their father's territory during the father's lifetime and with the father's House's permission.[68] He later told Jim Laganitz that at the time, he intended to escape and never come back to the village: "I made [up] my mind to live in the mountains as long as I could live." This is consistent with his statement recorded by missionary Pierce when they met in Kitwancool before Gamgaxmilmuxw left for the Nass: "I do not

---

64   Lelt, Frog, Gitwangak (Solomon Harris) says, "The reason why Washburn laid the information was that he had married the sister of Niitsxw and for that reason he laid the information." Here, "laying an information" refers to an informant, usually the police, sending written evidence of a crime to the public prosecutors for their decision whether to lay charges.

65   Johnston, *supra* note 61 at 2.

66   Pierce, *supra* note 25 at 58 to 60.

67   The Methodists arrived in Gitsegukla in 1884. They encouraged people to stop participating in feasts, causing rifts in the village. In 1898, they set up a new settlement at Carnaby east of Gitsegukla, and the Salvation Army set up their new village at Andimaul just west of Gitsegukla: Charlotte Sampare et al, *Adawkhl Gitsegukla* (Gitsegukla: Kitsegukla Band, 1979) at 5, 6, and 24.

68   *Tribal Boundaries, supra* note 44 at 218–19, based on information from Barbeau's 1923–24 interviews.

want either the constables or the magistrate to hunt for me. Tell them what I say and if they do come I will shoot every one." Pierce told the Port Simpson magistrate, Mr. Hall, what Gamgaxmilmuxw had said.[69]

In any event, Washburn undressed Niitsxw's body and, when the ice left the river, set off for Victoria with the steel shot from the body as evidence of the crime.[70] Although the provincial government in Victoria had known since mid-March of Niitsxw's killing, it was not until the end of April that four special police constables together with Washburn in charge left Victoria for the northwest. They picked up Indian Agent Charles Todd at Metlakatla and started up the Skeena, arriving at Gitanmaax (Hazelton) in late May. Before leaving the party at Gitsegukla to return to the coast, Todd wrote a letter to Gamgaxmilmuxw to be delivered to him on his father's territory. It apparently asked the fugitive to surrender to the police party.[71] Charles Mark told Barbeau that the letter promised Gamgaxmilmuxw that he would come to no harm, that the white man's law would respect the Indian law, but that he would have to go through a trial. In Jim Laganitz's account, Gamgaxmilmuxw also described the letter as saying that he would have to go to court but that it would "settle my cause well" and that "government law would not hang me."

Gitxsan accounts of how Todd's message was conveyed to Gamgaxmilmuxw provide a further window into the constraints on people's actions under their laws. Lelt, a Gitwangak Frog chief (Solomon Harris), was at his camp on the Skeena River at Ansgaxs, near Lorne Creek. The police party stopped there on their way to Hazelton and hired him to deliver Todd's letter[72] to Gamgaxmilmuxw. He was to be paid fifty dollars to take the letter and a further fifty dollars if it was delivered. Lelt accompanied the constables to Gitwangak. On the way they passed his fishing camp at Anlaxhon, near present-day Woodcock. Lelt asked the police party to not pass his house as he was to give a *yukw*

---

69  Pierce, *supra* note 25 at 60.

70  This account is from the second interview Gamayam (Charles Mark) gave to Barbeau. In his first interview, Gamayam said that Washburn took the clothes from Niitsxw's body and took them to Victoria as evidence. Pierce, however, said that Niitsxw's bloody clothing was mailed to the magistrate in Port Simpson by his niece (presumably Gilgallaget, Lucy Washburn): Pierce, *supra* note 25 at 60.

71  "Gitxsan Law," *supra* note 7 at 223–4.

72  Two of the Gitxsan interviewees say that a letter to Gamgaxmilmuxw was written by Richard Loring, one of the other constables who, after working as a prison guard in Victoria, in 1889 was appointed the federal Indian agent based in Hazelton.

feast soon,[73] and if he were seen helping the government authorities he would be taunted that he had used their money to fund his feast. (Recall that the host of a feast needed his announced business to be validated by the chiefs of Houses from other clans in order to be legally binding.) At that point, Lelt must have thought through his situation more thoroughly and declined to help the police further. His actions show the role of public shaming in maintaining normative standards in Gitxsan society, particularly among the *simgigyet*, the real people. The necessity to be seen to maintain a high moral standard in a very public society seems to have been the main driver of behaviour rather than coercion, punishment, or even, perhaps, individual conscience.

At this point, it becomes clear that the police were unwilling to travel to the Nass to arrest Gamgaxmilmuxw. Jim Laganitz recalled that "there were two constables [that] had come with the Captain,[74] one of them was Green, and these two men are afraid to get after Gamgaxmilmuxw." They then paid Gamgaxmilmuxw's wife, Gisax'itutkibu, to take the letter to him on his father's Nass River territory. When she found her husband at Wudaxhayetsxw's fishing camp at Gitanxhon, she told him that Richard Loring[75] was one of the police party. Loring and Gamgaxmilmuxw had apparently worked with each other previously in the Stikine country and had become friends there. Gamgaxmilmuxw did not return with his wife, as he remained angry with her for goading him to kill Niitsxw. On her return to the Skeena, Gisax'itutkibu told the police that her husband would return in May.

When Gamgaxmilmuxw returned to Kitwancool in late May or early June, he visited his friend Jim Laganitz in Gitwangak, reiterating Todd's written reassurance that "the government's law will not hang me." Laganitz, however, was not convinced of this. He responded, "You are expecting that in vain because you are a murderer, but they will try to

---

73 This feast was likely the one at which Harris assumed the name Lelt and raised a pole in Gitwangak to the previous Lelt. Barbeau records in 1924 that Harris did this "less than 40 years ago": *Totem Poles, supra* note 4 at 45.

74 The term "Captain" perhaps erroneously referred to Captain Napoleon Fitzstubbs, who had been appointed gold commissioner and stipendiary magistrate for the region but who did not arrive at his Hazelton post until 23 July 1888: "Gitxsan Law," *supra* note 7 at 225.

75 The account in this paragraph is largely based on Jim Laganitz's interview as it has the most detail. Laganitz, however, identifies Loring as "Mr. Beach," as do other informants. Still others call him "Beach Loring." The source of this misnaming may be the interviewees' confusion of Loring with Edward Hicks Beach, a successor to Fitzstubbs as magistrate in Hazelton. Loring went on to be the Indian agent for the Babine Agency based in Hazelton from 1889 to 1921.

arrest you as long as you live." Gamgaxmilmuxw also told Laganitz that he did not want "one of the Indians among the constables" to take him. Perhaps he was concerned that this would enlarge the circle of parties entangled in the feud triggered by Niitsxw's killing and the Gitsegukla Fireweeds' return of the compensation.

According to Lelt, the police sent Niisgam'ala, another Gitwangak Frog in the House of Hlengwax,[76] to Kitwancool to ask Gamgaxmilmuxw to surrender. In mid-June, Gamgaxmilmuxw moved from Kitwancool to Gitwangak with Ukslax'a'mks, a young woman who was his "cousin," as she was from the House of Gamlaxyeltxw, a Kitwancool Frog House closely related to Gamgaxmilmuxw's father's House, Wudaxhayetsxw. (Ukslax'a'mks was the cousin who had been threatened by the group bearing Niitsxw to Gitsegukla.) The couple stayed and slept together at the house of Liginihla,[77] which was right at the river's edge below the poles and the longer, upper row of houses. If Gamgaxmilmuxw and Ukslax'a'mks were, in fact, lovers, it should be noted that they still maintained the rule against relationships within the same clan.[78] Constables Holmans, Parker, and Green were dispatched from Hazelton to make the arrest.[79] They stayed at the mission house run by Charles Ridley at Xsa'andilgan,[80] two miles upriver from Gitwangak. The people in the village told them that they had not seen Gamgaxmilmuxw. Niisgam'ala, however, immediately reported his presence to the police. According to Jim Laganitz, the police paid Niisgam'ala

---

76 Lelt identifies the letter-carrier as Axgoot, a chief name in the House of Hlengwax, while other interviewees identify him as Niisgam'ala of the same House. It is probable that the latter was his name in 1888 and Axgoot the name he succeeded to later in life. Jim Laganitz told Barbeau that Axgoot/Niisgam'ala died around 1916: MacDonald, *supra* note 44 at 29 and 113.

77 House of Skay'an, Eagle Clan, Gitwangak.

78 Recall that Gamgaxmilmuxw was of the Wolf Clan and Ukslax'a'mks was of the Frog Clan.

79 "Gitxsan Law," *supra* note 7 at 224. Loring later maintained that the three were dispatched to Gitwangak to merely locate Gamgaxmilmuxw with strict instructions not to arrest him: "Skeena Expedition Had Origin in Small Trouble" *Victoria Daily Times* (18 July 1923). Given the fear that all the constables had of Gamgaxmilmuxw and the Gitxsan generally, it seems unlikely that the three in Gitwangak would have disobeyed such strict orders.

80 Ridley was Gwa'gayee, House of Haluus, Frog, Gitwangak. Xsa'andilgan is a Skeena River fishing site belonging to the House of Haluus. Some interviewees refer to the mission house as Mr. Woods's house. This probably refers to R.C. Woods, who in 1884 was the lay preacher at the Gitwangak Mission who wrote a letter to the Victoria *Daily Colonist* urging the province to arrest and prosecute Haa'atxw for Youmans's killing.

"big money"[81] to help them. That night, he spotted Gamgaxmilmuxw going into Liginihla's house with another cousin, Gwildeda'o,[82] the same young man who had separately threatened both Ukslax'a'mks and possibly Gamgaxmilmuxw on the trail when he and the others were carrying Niitsxw back to Gitsegukla. Niisgam'ala went to the mission house that night and informed the constables there of what he had seen. That same evening Gamgaxmilmuxw asked Ridley to come and see him. He showed Ridley the Todd letter, although Ridley later said he understood very little of it. Gamgaxmilmuxw then asked Ridley to write a response to the letter to give to the police. Ridley did not respond, perhaps because he was unable to read and write. He was then given two messages to verbally deliver to the constables: that the police should go back to the coast, and that Gamgaxmilmuxw would be returning to Kitwancool. He also told Ridley that he intended to surrender, but Ridley did not pass that information on to the police as he thought that Gamgaxmilmuxw was not sincere.[83] Very early the next morning, likely June 16, the police made ready and came down the trail to the village. Parker went to the forks of the trail to Kitwancool with "an Indian named Johnny"[84] to intercept Gamgaxmilmuxw should he attempt to flee back to his village.

Events then moved quickly.

Constables Holmans and Green along with Niisgam'ala approached Liginihla's house and tried to open the door. Liginihla's wife, Noxsamgyet,[85] asked who was there. Niisgam'ala answered that he wanted to see Gamgaxmilmuxw. The constables remained silent. Gamgaxmilmuxw was in bed with Ukslax'a'mks. He asked that the door be opened as Niisgam'ala was his cousin. Gwildeda'o did so.[86] Niisgam'ala

---

81  Holmans testified later at Green's trial that Niisgam'ala was to be paid one hundred dollars if Gamgaxmilmuxw was caught in Gitwangak village: "Special Assize Court" *Nanaimo Free Press* (7 November 1888) at 3.

82  House of Gwinuu, Frog, Kitwancool.

83  Charles Ridley's evidence at Green's trial: *supra* note 81. At the end of the trial, Justice Crease "animadverted strongly on the fact that Ridley had failed to report to the Constables that Jim was willing to give himself up to the authorities."

84  James Holmans's evidence: *supra* note 81. "Johnny" may have been Jim Laganitz's son, Johnny Laganitz, Guugaakhl, House of Guuxsan, Fireweed, Gitsegukla.

85  Probably Naxnoxamget, House of Luuxhon, Frog, Kitwancool: Beynon, note 5 at 235.

86  Charles Mark told Barbeau that Ridley, Niisgam'ala, and Gwildeda'o went to Victoria as witnesses at Green's trial. The newspaper report of the trial identified the Gitxsan witnesses as Ridley, Niisgam'ala, and "Snow": *supra* note 81. Lelt told Barbeau that Gwildeda'o opened the door. The evidence of Holmans and "Snow"

entered, leaving the door open and identifying Gamgaxmilmuxw to the police. Holmans and Green quickly followed, but then stood around the fire while Gamgaxmilmuxw dressed. He asked them twice what they wanted and then told them, "If you want to do anything with me, do it now."[87] While the constables were looking at each other as if uncertain what to do next, Gamgaxmilmuxw ran past them out the door. Green later told Holmans that he had not guarded the door because "he was afraid of the many Indians there."[88] The police inside the house started after him, but he had disappeared from their sight. He ran towards the upper row of houses and hid behind Hlawt's house, gun drawn, looking down the trail, waiting for the constables to catch up with him. Simediik said that Gamgaxmilmuxw had run off because his pride would not allow him to surrender without a bit of a struggle. Constable Green, meanwhile, had gone around the other side of Skay'an's house on the upper row and was now behind Gamgaxmilmuxw, who was looking away, watching for Holmans and Niisgam'ala. Green shot him in the back, piercing his lung.

Holmans and Niisgam'ala immediately found Gamgaxmilmuxw mortally wounded. Niisgam'ala and Gamgaxmilmuxw spoke in Gitxsan before Gamgaxmilmuxw said in English, "You son of a bitch, you gave me away." Green arrived to tell Holmans that Gamgaxmilmuxw had fired the first shot. Gamgaxmilmuxw was able to deny that[89] before the police began to take him away.[90] At about that time,

---

at Green's trial was that "Snow" had opened the door. Simon Gunanoot (Geel, Fireweed, Kispiox) told Barbeau in 1923 that a relative of Gamgaxmilmuxw from Kitwancool called 'Noo stayed at the same house as Gamgaxmilmuxw that night and had received fifty dollars from the police to signal to them when Gamgaxmilmuxw was inside. From this it can be surmised that Gwildeda'o, Snow, and 'Noo were the same person who, along with Niisgam'ala, was a police informer.

87 According to Simediik, Gamgaxmilmuxw rhetorically asked the police at this point, "This is none of your affair. Are any of you the brothers of the man I killed? It would [then] be alright for you to come and be revenged." This statement may be more Simediik editorializing a correct statement of the relevant Gitxsan law than an accurate retelling of what was actually said.

88 Holmans's evidence at Green's trial, *supra* note 81.

89 Other statements at Green's trial corroborated that Gamgaxmilmuxw had not shot at Green.

90 Ridley told Jim Laganitz that after Gamgaxmilmuxw was shot, the police wanted to behead him and take his head to Victoria for evidence. Ridley said that he alerted Hlengwax, the leading chief in Gitwangak, who marshalled the people left in the village and drove the police out. Ridley did not mention this in his evidence at Green's trial.

Ukslax'a'mks found a cache of police guns in front of Haxpegwootxw's house. She wanted to shoot the police but did not know how to fire a gun. The police were taking Gamgaxmilmuxw to the mission house by canoe, but he died before they got there.[91] The three constables immediately set off on foot to Hazelton. Three days later, Washburn and Loring arrived in Gitwangak by canoe. They were met by a hostile crowd and were only able to get ashore after they agreed to lay down their rifles. They examined Gamgaxmilmuxw's body, making notes of his wounds. They promised the people of Gitwangak that Green would be held responsible for his death and then returned to Hazelton, arriving on June 20.[92] Gamgaxmilmuxw was buried in Gitwangak.

The police party soon found themselves involved in another shooting incident in Gitsegukla. Three days after Gamgaxmilmuxw was killed in Gitwangak, his wife, Gisax'itutkibu, looked out from the house of her father, Niisgagwit,[93] to see two men crossing the Skeena River at Winluunu'u, opposite the village. Thinking that they were from Kitwancool and coming to kill her, she shot at them but did not appear to have hit anyone. But a neighbour, Duubisxw,[94] said to be a crazy man, jumped up, alarmed by the sound of the shots. He took his pistol, put a blanket over it, and walked over to Niisgagwit's house. He asked Niisgagwit why he had fired off the shot. Niisgagwit did not answer. Duubisxw walked away, turned, and fatally shot Niisgagwit in the back. Someone set off to tell Niisgagwit's House chiefs, Mool'xan and Haakasxw, at their fishing site a mile or so away. Mool'xan returned, lay siege to Duubisxw's house, and eventually shot him dead. Guuxsan[95] then distributed swan's down to ensure the chiefs kept their peace. When the police under Washburn arrived from Hazelton on 10 July, they found Duubisxw's body in his house and soon arrested Mool'xan.[96] This incident is remarkable in that Niisgagwit, Duubisxw, Haakasxw, and

91  The account of the attempt to apprehend Gamgaxmilmuxw and of his shooting death by Constable Green is largely based on Barbeau's interview with Jim Laganitz and on the 1888 newspaper account of Green's trial: *supra* note 81.

92  The account of Loring and Washburn's visit to Gitwangak is based on Loring's 1923 recollection in the *Victoria Daily Times*: *supra* note 79.

93  House of Haakasxw, Frog, Gitsegukla.

94  House of Gwagl'lo, Frog, Gitsegukla.

95  Guuxsan was the head chief of the House of Guuxsan, a leading Fireweed Clan House in Gitsegukla.

96  This account of the killings of Niisgagwit and Duubisxw is based on Barbeau's interviews with Charles Mark and Dan Guxsan and on "Gitxsan Law," *supra* note 7 at footnote 31 at 244.

Mool'xan were all of the Frog Clan, so the usual rules of compensation between Houses of different clans could not apply. Instead, it may have been a situation where the Frog Clan chiefs determined that Duubisxw's mental instability was such that it threatened the viability of his House and the safety of the whole community. In the wider view, it highlights the society's focus on the survival and health of the lineages and Houses as legal entities.

Back in Hazelton, Washburn and the handful of other settlers were in a state of high agitation due to the "hostile and threatening attitude" of the Gitxsan. A petition was sent to Victoria seeking protection for settler lives and property. Washburn told the attorney general he had promised the Gitxsan that the government would send a "high chief" to listen to their grievances. Gamgaxmilmuxw's Wolf Clan relatives in Kitwancool were more to the point. They wanted the government to pay a *xsiisxw* of one thousand dollars plus "a man in place of the man killed."[97] The province then did what nineteenth-century colonial authorities usually did when faced with such turmoil in the hinterland: it sent a gunboat. HMS *Caroline* arrived at Port Essington at the mouth of the Skeena with eighty-four soldiers under a Colonel Holmes and twelve police constables under Police Superintendent Roycraft. Victoria branded the exercise the "Skeena Expedition." Only the police journeyed upriver to Hazelton, arriving there on 1 August. A week earlier, Captain Fitzstubbs had also arrived to take up his post as stipendiary magistrate. En route he had stopped at Gitwangak, where the chiefs complained "that the whites had interfered with the operation of their own laws and had taken the life of one of their own race, that life being, by the payment of a stipulated sum, no longer forfeit."[98] Fitzstubbs reported this to the attorney general. Thus, both the local and the provincial authorities were aware that the matter of Niitsxw's killing had been settled by compensation under Gitxsan law and that no further repercussions on Gamgaxmilmuxw had been necessary.

Back in Hazelton, Fitzstubbs and Roycraft put in place "a series of measures to demonstrate both the workings of the judicial process and the coercive powers of settler society."[99] A coroner's inquest was conducted into Duubisxw's death. The jury, made up of Roycraft's twelve constables temporarily discharged from their police duties for the

---

97  "Gitxsan Law," *supra* note 7 at 224–5.

98  Fitzstubbs to Attorney General, 24 July 1888, quoted in "Gitxsan Law," *supra* note 7 at 225.

99  "Gitxsan Law," *supra* note 7 at 226.

purpose,[100] returned a verdict of "justifiable homicide" and Mool'xan's release.[101] This result would seem to be a rare convergence of Gitxsan law and colonial law. In the same week, Roycraft and Fitzstubbs held a preliminary hearing into the shooting of Gamgaxmilmuxw, resulting in Constable Green being remanded to trial in Nanaimo. The police squad then displayed the state's enforcement powers by staging a drill and target practice exercise. The following day, Roycraft and most of his specials departed. On their arrival in Victoria, the chief constable informed the attorney general that the Native population seemed to "now perfectly understand our power" and have "promised to keep the law and their chiefs will bring all offenders to justice."[102]

Fitzstubbs's plan to implement settler law was to enrol the Gitxsan chiefs in each village as "special constables." Roycraft promised police badges for the Indian constables. However, within the year Fitzstubbs was meeting resistance not only because of the people's opposition to state law but because of Fitzstubbs's fundamental misunderstanding of the role of House chiefs within the Gitxsan legal order. Both the opposition and the misunderstanding were on display when the magistrate attempted to recruit the Kispiox chiefs as constables during the winter of 1888. He was refused a canoe to ferry his party across the river to the village and had to steal one. He then faced no acknowledgments from the villagers of his "salutations." After preliminary discussions with some chiefs, a public meeting was set up at which Fitzstubbs had hoped to invest the chiefs and hand out their constabular badges. But a "young Indian" rose to say that "he had no wish that his chief should give countenance and aid to the government, they were a people of themselves, had their laws and would acknowledge none other." Others echoed this view, and in the end all the chiefs declined to accept the badge.[103] The change of the chiefs' position in the face of the community's assertions that Gitxsan law was supreme clearly showed the limited scope of a House chief's authority. The chiefs had no power of command over their House members. The events in Kispiox demonstrated both the people's bottom-up powers and the public conduct of decision-making. To underline these two salient points of Gitxsan legal process, Galois recalls an 1874 statement by Gedimgaldo'o, chief of the highest-ranked Frog House in Gitanmaax at the time, to

---

100  Loring's account in the *Victoria Daily Times, supra* note 81.
101  "Gitxsan Law," *supra* note 7 at footnote 31 at 244.
102  "Gitxsan Law," *supra* note 7 at 226.
103  *Ibid* at 236–7.

a Constable Brown when settlers bumped up against Gitxsan law on another occasion:

> Although I am recognised as a Chief, I have not the power enough even to make the people come here to listen to your message. I expressed a wish to have all that were at home here. It is no use for me to make a good speech to send to the Governor, for as soon as you are gone, the people would do as they like and I will be held responsible.[104]

Fitzstubbs's hope, expressed at his and Roycraft's 1888 meeting with a number of Gitxsan chiefs, that each chief would "be held responsible for the behaviour of his people"[105] was therefore doomed to failure.

Meanwhile in Nanaimo, Constable Daniel Franklyn Green was being tried for the murder of Kitwancool Jim (Gamgaxmilmuxw). The one-day hearing was on 5 November 1888 before Mr. Justice Crease. His lordship crystallized the issue for the jury as whether the shooting was necessary to secure Kitwancool Jim's arrest. The only testimony at the trial was from Constable Holmans and the three Gitxsan collaborators, Niisgam'ala, Gwildeda'o ("Snow"), and Gwa'gayee (Charles Ridley). Green was unrepresented, made no statement, and called no witnesses. There was no testimony that Green attempted to arrest Gamgaxmilmuxw, that there was any resistance to an attempt, or that the shooting was necessary to secure any arrest.[106] Nevertheless, after only a few minutes' deliberation the jury returned a verdict that Constable Green was justified in shooting Gamgaxmilmuxw, and he was released. Given settler fears of further "Indian" attacks as indigenous lands were encroached[107] and the historical characterization of the people as savages to facilitate that process, such a verdict was inevitable and commonplace.[108] The collaboration of some Gitxsan individuals with this settler form of justice, however, deserves further investigation from an indigenous law perspective.

---

104  *Ibid* at 237, quoting Brown to Provincial Secretary, 8 September 1874.

105  *Ibid* at 239.

106  Unlike at the Haa'atxw trial, there was no evidence that the applicable Gitxsan law had been followed so that Gamlaxmilmuxw and his House had made all the required reparations for Niitsxw's death.

107  The so-called Chilcotin War in British Columbia was then less than a quarter century old and Riel's Northwest Rebellion in Manitoba had been but three years previously.

108  "Queen's Law," *supra* note 51 at endnote 11 at 88.

Niisgam'ala and Gwa'gayee (Ridley) were both members of closely related Frog House groups in Gitwangak under Hlengwax. In 1924 Jim Laganitz, the leading Gitwangak Frog chief Hlengwax, explained to Barbeau that some twenty years earlier when he hosted a feast to raise a pole for a previous Hlengwax,

> not many members of my family could assist me, when I gave the feast (*yuku*) for its erection and the assumption of new names. Most of them had become Christians and moved down to Minskinish [Robert Tomlinson's mission village at Cedarvale about twenty kilometres downriver from Gitwangak]. My only helpers were my sister Siuhliya and my mother's household – Kamkal'owl.[109]

Ridley, as previously explained, ran a mission house near Gitwangak in 1888. It would seem that many members of the Gitwangak Frog Houses had fallen under the cult-like missionary recruitment strategy then extensively employed by all denominations across western Canada. This strategy included establishing Christian communes a short distance away from the existing indigenous villages, strict rules of behaviour, top-down authority vested in the missionary himself, and complete rejection of indigenous values, social relations, and economies.[110] The arc of Christianity's cult phase in the middle Skeena began in the 1880s[111], reached its apogee in the first two decades of the twentieth century,[112] and had dissipated as a force rejecting Gitxsan law by the 1940s.[113] It

---

109  *Totem Poles, supra* note 4 at 53.

110  See the facsimiles of the 1908 to 1913 rules for the Salvation Army commune at Andimaul outside Gitsegukla "for the purpose in view of keeping law and order, observe sanitary measures, etc., etc." in Sampare et al, *supra* note 67 at 5–9.

111  Robert Tomlinson established the non-denominational, Duncanite commune of Meanskinisht south of Gitwangak in 1888: *Mapping, supra* note 27 at 150. Thomas Crosby and W.H. Pierce established a Methodist mission in Gitseguecla in 1885: Pierce, *supra* note 25 at 51–3. Later, the Salvation Army established a mission there as well. In 1898 both sects established communes away from the village: the Methodists at Carnaby, twelve kilometres upriver, the Salvation Army at Andimaul, eight kilometres downriver: Sampare et al, *supra* note 67 at 5. Kitwancool people moved to Anglican communes set apart from each lower Nass village: *Tribal Boundaries, supra* note 44 at 72–5.

112  On Tomlinson's death in 1913, his followers began to drift back to Gitwangak. By the mid-1920s, both Gitsegukla denominations began to return to their old village, completing the move by the mid-1930s: Sampare et al, *supra* note 67 at 5, 6, and 24. Similarly, Kitwancool Houses and chiefs moved back to Kitwancool from the Nass over a similar period: Duff, *supra* note 10 at 13.

113  Beynon, *supra* note 5 at 68 and 69, noting that *yukw* feasts were even being held on Sundays.

may be that Niisgam'ala and Gwa'gayee (Ridley) interpreted their Christian conversion and renunciation of Gitxsan legal practices and lineage obligations as an adherence to the colonial justice system.

Gwildeda'o's motives may have been somewhat different. (Recall that he was the young man helping bring Niitsxw back to Gitsegukla who on separate occasions had wanted to shoot both Gamgaxmilmuxw and Ukslax'a'mks but was restrained by his companions.) It is a recurrent theme in northern Northwest Coast oral histories that cooler-headed House members keep a check on young hotheads' urges for immediate, violent revenge and let the compensation process unfold. Colonial law and order as practised in the late nineteenth century was quite different. It was secretive, coercive, and accountable not to the community but to distant authorities. Gwildeda'o may have seen collaboration with the police as an opportunity to avenge Niitsxw's death without indigenous law repercussions for himself and his relatives.

As for B.W. Washburn, in 1892 he abandoned his Gitxsan wife, Lucy, and their two young children to move to Yukon and then to Circle City, Alaska. There in 1896, he was shot to death in a bar-room brawl and was buried in an unmarked grave.[114]

## Subsequent Events

In tracing the consequences of Niitsxw's and Gamgaxmilmuxw's deaths it is necessary to follow not only the subsequent lives of the persons involved but also the subsequent lives of their Gitxsan names, which would have had a succession of individuals occupying them.

### Gisax'itutkibu

Many of Barbeau's interviewees in the mid-1920s put the blame for Niitsxw's and Gamgaxmilmuxw's deaths squarely on Gisax'itutkibu's shoulders. This may be why Fitzstubbs reported to the attorney general later in 1888 that Gamgaxmilmuxw's widow "had been stripped of all she had by the harpies of this tribe and turned out to wander in the woods subsisting as best she could, in constant fear of her life." The magistrate placed her under the protection of the "Chief of her own people"[115] and requested that the provincial government give her a donation of one hundred dollars.[116] It is unclear if any such payment was made.

---

114 Johnston, *supra* note 61 at 3.

115 Probably Wiigyet, the leading Fireweed chief in Gitsegukla.

116 Extract of letter of N Fitzstubbs to Attorney General, the Hon. AEB. Davie (30 September 1888) in B/F/204.17.

Although Fitzstubbs described Gisax'itutkibu as "presenting herself here in tatters," by 1895 she had raised two poles in Gitsegukla. On one of them, the cost of which was shared with Gwa'amaats (Jimmy Good),[117] a carved figure is said to commemorate Gamst'axgu'u, whose death in 1887 precipitated the dispute over the head chieftainship of the House. Gisax'itutkibu said that a figure on the second pole was of Niitsxw, a representation on a pole of the person being commemorated that Barbeau described as exceptional among the Tsimshian.[118] By raising a pole and hosting a feast in Niitsxw's name, she was clearly trying to mend fences within the House and thus re-establish its status and power in the community. It is likely that it was at one of these pole-raising feasts Gisax'itutkibu took the name Hanamuxw as head chief of the House.[119] She had also married Gamgaxmilmuxw's brother, Galaxamx'wan (Peter Johnson), and was by then also known by her Christian name, Fanny Johnson.[120] This marriage follows the common Gitxsan practice of a young widow or widower remarrying their spouse's sibling, thus maintaining the alliance between their Houses. By the early twentieth century Peter and Fanny had joined the Salvation Army commune at Andimaul, Peter's name appearing as a member of the committee keeping missionary and *Indian Act* law and order in that community.[121]

The Skeena River flood of 1936 swept away many of the Gitsegukla poles. Some were recovered, including the older of the two Hanamuxw poles. At a 1945 feast, the then holder of the name Hanamuxw, Jeffrey Johnson, Fanny and Peter Johnson's son and a successful businessman,[122] raised again the reconditioned, washed-out pole in front of his Gitsegukla home.[123] In his speech at the pole-raising feast, Hanamuxw told the *adaawk* or oral history of the Great Snowfall at the storied village of Temlaham many millennia ago, and how his lineage and others escaped this summertime weather catastrophe to settle in Gitsegukla. They brought with them the Person of the Rainbow *ayuk* or crest. Here,

---

117 Gwinuu (Lucy Laganitz) told Barbeau that the original dispute for the head chieftainship of this House was between Niitsxw and Gwa'amaats, indicating perhaps that Gisax'itutkibu was a member of the Gwa'amaats lineage within the House of Gamst'axgu'u/Hanamuxw.

118 *Totem Poles, supra* note 4 at 82 and 83.

119 *Ibid.*

120 *Ibid.*

121 Sampare et al, *supra* note 67 at 6 to 8.

122 Beynon, *supra* note 5 at 45; Sampare et al, *supra* note 67 at 14.

123 Beynon, *supra* note 5 at 165–78.

Hanamuxw identifies a *wil'naat'ahl*, a closely related group of Fireweed Houses from Temlaham that use the Rainbow crest, but also distinguishes his House within that *wil'naat'ahl* by its use of the unique Person of the Rainbow crest. In response to Hanamuxw, the then holder of the name Gamgaxmilmuxw recalled that

> it has always been customary in the past, when Gamlaxyeltxw or 'Wiixa wanted help or advice he always came to Gitsegukla and conferred with chiefs here. And the same with the Gitsegukla chiefs. We are glad that these relations will be maintained. I listened to what you said and was pleased to hear you say that you are going to continue as your uncle did in the past. Many of the chiefs of Gitsegukla are of Kitwancool paternal origin, just as some of the Kitwancool chiefs have Gitsegukla paternal origin.[124]

Recall that Jeffrey Johnson's father, Peter Johnson, was from the Wolf House of 'Wiixa in Kitwancool and that Peter's father was from the Frog House of Wudaxhayetsxw, very closely related to Gamlaxyeltxw. Gamgaxmilmuxw was here reminding Hanamuxw and his audience that iterative marriages among chiefly families not only provided proper education and status for the children but also sealed mutual assistance alliances between unrelated *wil'naat'ahl* from different villages.

In 1991, this same pole was raised for a third time by the then Hanamuxw, Joan Ryan, Fanny Johnson's great-granddaughter. This practice of refurbishing and reraising a crest pole contrasts with the older practice of letting them fall and decay away. In this case, however, it was necessary as the pole raised by Jeffrey Johnson had been taken down by the Gitsegukla *Indian Act* band council without the House's consent.[125] This prompted the House to re-establish its presence and its *daxgyet*, or bundle of powers, in the village. At the same time, Joan Ryan raised her own Rainbow Person pole with a different base carving – the crest of her Frog Clan father.[126] The essence of a pole-raising remains the same. It is the public display and feasting of the *ayuks* or crests accompanied by the public telling and validation of the relevant *adaawk* or history that both reaffirms the lineage's identity and raises its status within the society.

---

124  *Ibid* at 176.

125  Daly, *supra* note 29 at endnote 21 at 308.

126  *Ibid* at 101. Joan Ryan's father was Hak'xw, House of Lelt, Frog, Gitwangax (Phillip Ryan): *Wilps Hanamuxw Genealogical Chart* (1988) [unpublished]. See Figure 1.

*Gamgaxmilmuxw*

The consensus of Barbeau's informants was that Gamgaxmilmuxw (Kitwancool Jim) was a good man who spoke English and was friendly with the white settlers. He had been a *hlguwilksihlw*, a chief's son and 'Wiixa's only nephew[127] who in a few years would have succeeded as the *simoogit* , head chief, of his House and would have made a splendid chief.[128] His killing as a high-status person, therefore, required a formal acknowledgement from those responsible, the government authorities. The clothes in which he was shot were kept by his maternal aunts,[129] the women of the House of 'Wiixa, to be displayed at feasts. The same people were also said to have a letter from the government saying that it would compensate the House of 'Wiixa for Gamgaxmilmuxw's killing. As Gamayam[130] told Barbeau in 1923:

> It is because he was a chief that the bad feeling still exists for him. The whole thing would have blown over and the shame of his death might have been washed away if the government had paid something, no matter how small, if they had recognised him as a chief. It was not the value of the ransom but to take away the shame of the death.

This is a succinct statement of the Gitxsan law of compensation: its purpose is to wipe away the shame the House has to bear; it is not an attempt to replace a person's life with goods or money. Under Gitxsan law it seems that all wrongs perpetrated against a House or a lineage may be reduced to the degree of shame brought upon it by the actions of others. Gamayam's reference to Gamgaxmilmuxw being a chief is a reminder that the shame, and thus the compensation, is linked to the status of the person killed or injured. Conversely, if the shame is brought about by the actions of the House's own chief or member, the obligation is on that House to host a feast and to distribute wealth to others, in order to wash away the shame it brought upon itself.[131] The

---

127  Kitwancool Government, Kitwancool Research Submission to the Minister of Indian and Northern Affairs, Hugh Faulkner (1977) (Chapter 3) at 6 ["Kitwancool Research Submission"].

128  Gamayam said that if he had been a white man, he would have been called a gentleman.

129  Gwinuu (Lucy Laganitz) specifically identifies the wife of Hlami (House of Gamlaxyeltxw, Frog, Kitwancool) as still having the clothes in the 1920s.

130  House of Guuxsan, Fireweed, Gitsegukla (Charles Mark).

131  Recall that Lelt's fear of the shame brought on by anticipated taunting prompted his decision to not help the police find Gamlaxmilmuxw.

Tsimshian ethnographer William Beynon had to do this when his boat was caught between the piles of a bridge on an ebbing tide. He was taunted as being "a wolf hanging up under the bridge." The remark was less about Beynon's poor seamanship and more about the fact that he had yet to hold a feast to validate his position as Wolf Clan chief of the Tsimshian Gitlan tribe. He and his House were then obliged to give a feast to wipe away the shame of the insult and for Beynon to properly assume his *simoogit* name.[132] Shame operates by significantly reducing the ranking of a House and its chief within the society. This, in turn, reduces the House's say in the community's decisions by placing it further down the list of speakers at feasts and other events. It also reduces the potential for marriage alliances with high-ranking Houses for mutual economic and other benefits.

Dominion officials felt the full force of their obligations under Gitxsan compensation law ten years later at an 1898 meeting in Kitwancool, ostensibly called to explain their policies on the creation of reserves under the *Indian Act*.[133] Constance Cox[134] was their interpreter and later gave this account of the proceedings:

[The Kitwancool people] got a house ready, a big potlatch house, and they had in the four corners of their house ... grizzlie... like smaller totem poles.[135] They had a chair for Mr. Vowell to sit on covered with a grizzly bear [skin] and they had a head of a grizzly with the face on the right side of the chair. They meant this for honour and not for discomfort. But Vowell always took it the other way and he refused to sit on that ... [T]hey had a great seat for me with a great big shawl on it, Loring had Indian blankets spread over [his chair], and the surveyor, Ashton [*sic*] Green, had likewise ...

The shirt that [Jim] had on, they kept it, blanket and all, with a hole (bullet) through the shirt. And they spread it in front of Mr. Vowell and laid the bullet on it and said: "Do you see that there? When we are made satisfied and this blanket is wiped away by gifts from the government, then you can talk reserve to us."

---

132  Beynon, *supra* note 5 at 9.

133  The government party was made up of Arthur W. Vowell, Indian reserve commissioner, Richard Loring, Indian agent, Babine Agency, and Ashdown Green, surveyor, Indian Reserve Commission.

134  Constance Cox was born in Hazelton of Gitxsan and settler parentage and spoke fluent Gitxsan. She translated for Marius Barbeau and Wilson Duff, as well as for government officials as she was doing in 1898: *Mapping, supra* note 27 at 125–7.

135  This would have been the feast-house of 'Wiixa, who was Gamgaxmilmuxw's House chief. Barbeau described its four carved grizzly posts, although the house was gone by the time he visited Kitwancool in the 1920s: *Totem Poles, supra* note 4 at 117.

And Vowell went around and picked [*sic* poked?] the grizzly bear with his stick and said, "What do you mean by setting this thing up?" And there was a woman who said, "What a bad-tempered man he is. I suppose he does not know anything. Does he not know that we are [representing?] ourselves?" That did not worry Vowell that they were reprimanding [him] ...

When Vowell got back, I was talking to him and I said to him, "Oh, I thought you were afraid of those wooden bears." And he said, "Well, I should not have listened to them. I should have laid out the reserve. I cannot stand Indians dictating to me."[136]

Indian Agent Loring gives a corroborating account of the event with more particulars in a 1924 letter to Barbeau, part of which states:

We betook ourselves to the largest of the community houses, which was elaborately prepared for us. The three of us were conducted to a sort of dais at the back or rear of the hall.[137] The first procedure was that a light grey undershirt, very much stained with blood, was spread in front of Mr. Vowell's feet, at which the latter gentleman became somewhat incensed. Then heatedly demanded to know what that meant and attempted to push forward the said shirt.

Thereafter followed the demand of the Indians that an expensive tombstone be delivered at Gitwancool in the memory of the late Gitwancool Jim, ere any talk would by them be listened to concerning reserves or anything else. Thereat Mr. Vowell could not very well conceal his temper and it brought about rather a sudden termination of the meeting. At the latter Headchief We-hah ['Wiixa] was present and had very little to say on behalf of the Indians;[138] and here may add that the most defiant at the said meeting were three women named Noss-wye, Noss-glee-alch and Gun-ah.[139]

---

136 Constance Cox interview with Marius Barbeau, 1920: B/F/89.6.

137 Recall that the raised dais at the rear was the place of honour in the feast hall matrix, usually occupied by the House hosting the feast.

138 It is the usual practice for a wing chief, the *galdim'algax,* to speak on behalf of the House. "The chief himself never talks. He just looks at his speaker, who knows what to say, having been given his instructions before the meeting": Duff, *supra* note 10 at 38.

139 Letter of RE Loring to Chs M Barbeau (5 January 1924): B/F/204.2. It is not possible to identify the three defiant women from Loring's rendition of their names. His Gun-ah may be Gwinuu (later held by Lucy Laganitz), and the other two are likely named as the mothers (*Noxs*) of chiefly sons. The Cox and Loring accounts were corroborated in summary form by Luuxhon (George Derrick), Gamayam (Charles Mark), and Simediik.

The Kitwancool Frog chief Luuxhon said in 1924 that the protests to Vowell had been led by the Wolves, Gamgaxmilmuxw's clan. "Until this day," he said, "they are against the establishment of a reserve and it is because the government has not compensated for the death of Gamgaxmilmuxw."

For the Kitwancool, then, this was a negotiation hosted by 'Wiixa in his feast-house to get the government to fulfil its obligations under Gitxsan law. It shows the high priority the Wolf Houses placed on washing away the shame of Gamgaxmilmuxw's death. The matter of the surveys and laying out of reserves appears to have been a bargaining tactic to nudge the officials towards a settlement. The staged seating of the guests in the feast house[140] was to elevate them to the level of chiefs and thus signal the Wolves' intent to use the occasion as an opportunity for negotiations between equals. Vowell misread all these signals. He remained committed to enforcing the *Indian Act* and reserves on the indigenous communities.

Over the next quarter century surveyors, settlers, missionaries, and police were rebuffed from the Kitwancool Valley.[141] In August 1910 the Indian Affairs surveyor, Ashdown Green, was instructed to visit Kitwancool again in response to Alfred Douse[142] telling Prime Minister Laurier by telegram that the Kitwancool valley was being surveyed for white men and "no land left for us." As the government party approached the village, a messenger told them, "Kitwancool Jim's family is very strong … and they may seek revenge."[143] When Green arrived, he was told by the leading Kitwancool Wolf and Frog chiefs, 'Wiixa and Gamlaxyeltxw, that the whole country belonged to the Kitwancool. As Green reported to Ottawa afterwards, " I believe that the majority, both in Kitwancool and Andimaul, would gladly have their reserves defined were it not for an agreement made by all the tribes on the Nass and Skeena to accept of no reservations until a decision had been arrived at as to their claim to the whole country, they are afraid that the acceptance of a reserve would invalidate their claim."[144] This would appear to

---

140  See the description of the seating matrix at the Gitwangak *halayt* performances at page 73.

141  "Two White Perspectives," *supra* note 1 at 24 and 28; *Tribal Boundaries, supra* note 46 at 60–2 and 84–7.

142  Albert Douse held the name Biiyoosxw in the House of 'Wiixa. He was the first president of Kitwancool, a position established by all the chiefs to protect the laws and territories of Kitwancool against settler and Crown encroachment: "Kitwancool Research Submission," *supra* note 127 at 5; Duff, *supra* note 10 at 36.

143  "Kitwancool Research Submission," *supra* note 127 at 6.

144  *Ibid* at 7.

be the moment that the Kitwancool decided to emphasize the aboriginal title claim against reserve surveys along with the indigenous law claim for compensation for the killing of Gamgaxmilmuxw.

In the summer of 1927, the Indian agent in Hazelton asked the RCMP to protect a party of dominion reserve surveyors who were scheduled to once again venture into the Kitwancool Houses' territories. The anticipated confrontation ensued, resulting in five Kitwancool men being convicted by the Smithers magistrate for the Criminal Code offence of preventing someone from doing what they had a lawful right to do. The essence of the alleged criminal acts was a failed attempt to take a surveyor's transit and the throwing of an axe in a creek. Four of the men were given terms of up to four months in Oakalla prison; the fifth received a suspended sentence because of his age. Two of the convicted were Albert Williams and his son, Peter Williams, the then president and secretary respectively of the organization set up by the Kitwancool House chiefs to advance their land rights with the imperial, dominion, and provincial governments. The identities of the other three are more relevant to this chapter. They were Richard Douse (Gwashlaa'm), his brother Samuel Douse (Biiyoosxw), and Walter Derrick (later to hold the name Gamgaxmilmuxw and eventually 'Wiixa), all of the House of 'Wiixa.[145]

In their reports, the police attempted to portray a division of the community into two factions: the five arrested land rights advocates, together with Mrs. Richard Douse and an unnamed man;[146] versus the majority of the village and its *Indian Act* band chief, Alexander Smith, who, the police reported to their superiors, "took no part in the disturbance ... and ... seems to be relieved that most of them have been removed."[147] Smith, however, also held the name 'Wiixa, then the highest-ranked Kitwancool House chief,[148] who certainly would have known about and approved the actions of his wing-chiefs in their confrontation with the surveyors and, later, with the police escort. 'Wiixa in 1927 was thus performing the same role as 'Wiixa in 1898 at the meeting with Commissioner Vowell. He had sent a carefully worded, non-threatening note to the surveyors before they arrived suggesting that they not come to Kitwancool "until the trouble had been settled."[149] When his message

---

145  "Two White Perspectives," *supra* note 1 at 32–40.
146  *Ibid* at 37, 38, and 41.
147  *Ibid* at 38 and 41.
148  Duff Files, *supra* note 59, Box 41, File 125.
149  "Two White Perspectives," *supra* note 1 at 31.

was ignored, he let his speakers-cum-warriors take up the face-to-face defence of his House's and his community's territories. As s*imoogit*, a chief embodied his or her House. He or she must ensure their name is not shamed by military defeat, by capture or arrest, by misstep at a feast, or any other public embarrassment. Physical and verbal encounters were left to warriors or a speaker, a *galdim'algax*, so that any stumbles did not seriously reflect the House's rank in the society.

There had been no mention of compensation for Gamgaxmilmuxw's death in the Kitwancool chiefs' communications with the dominion government in the 1920s. The focus was on land rights and the common law legal efforts to secure them in the English courts. In this, the Kitwancool were probably following the advice they had been hearing, perhaps second hand, from the lawyers pursuing claims in the imperial court.[150] Nonetheless, it is telling that the chiefs involved in the 1898, 1910, and 1927 confrontations were predominantly from Gamgaxmilmuxw's House and *wil'naat'ahl*.

There is a sparse record of the later lives of those who collaborated with the police in their attempted arrest of Gamgaxmilmuxw. By 1920 or earlier Mark Holland had taken on Charles Ridley's name of Gwa'gayee.[151] Hlengwax raised a pole to Niisgam'ala in 1919, who probably died some years earlier, having by then assumed the name Axgoot.[152] Jim Laganitz told Barbeau in 1923, "The Kitwancool did not want to let me know anything they said because they were aggrieved against us because Niisgam'ala had warned [the police]. He was one of our uncles." Once again, then, the consequences of an individual's actions were visited upon his House group.

Meanwhile in Kitwancool, the Wolves and Frogs continued to maintain the essential legal structure of their society by feasting each individual successor to a *simoogit* name. Around 1895, the House of 'Wiixa raised a pole to Gamgaxmilmuxw. He had originally chosen and cut the tree himself when it had been intended to commemorate a former Gwashlaa'm of the House. Gwinuu (Lucy Laganitz) remarked that "It was erected by Gamgaxmilmuxw's relatives. Even the children helped

---

150 The main thrust of the Kitwancool presentations was its support for the 1909 Cowichan Petition, which asked the Imperial Privy Council in England to refer the question of aboriginal title to the Judicial Committee of the Privy Council, the highest court dealing with colonial decisions: *Tribal Boundaries, supra* note 44 at 61; "Two White Perspectives," *supra* note 1 at 8–9.

151 *Mapping, supra* note 27 at 150–2.

152 See note 76.

pay for it."[153] This was one of the poles that so entranced Emily Carr when she visited Kitwancool in 1928. Her artist's eye especially noticed that "the big wooden hands holding the child were so full of tenderness they had to be distorted enormously in order to contain it all."[154] As indicated above, the name Gamgaxmilmuxw was held by various individuals until at least the late 1950s.[155]

*Ukslax'a'mks*

Recall that Ukslax'a'mks probably also had the name Lisee'iw, and by 1910 had succeeded to the name and House chieftainship of Gamlaxyeltxw.[156] As Gamlaxyeltxw, she spoke to surveyor Ashdown Green along with other Kitwancool chiefs in August 1910. According to Green's notes, she asked him if he had heard of the Kitwancool petition and then said, "We cannot get a living on the reserves[,] they are too small. We do not want reserves[,] we are not so foolish. We know the land belongs to us and we will hold it till we die. Our hunting grounds are our bank."[157]

A 1910 photograph identifies Miriam Douse as Gamlaxyeltxw standing with her daughter, Margaret Good, then holding her mother's previous name, Lisee'iw.[158] By 1927 Arthur Derrick, living in the Lower Nass village of Gitlaxdamix, was said to have held the name Gamlaxyeltxw.[159] At that time, however, when many Kitwancool people

---

153 *Totem Poles, supra* note 4 at 119–20.

154 "Two White Perspectives," *supra* note 1 at 49, quoting Emily Carr, *Klee Wyck* (Vancouver: Douglas & McIntyre, 2003) at 145. Carr's painting of the base of Gamgaxmilmuxw's pole, entitled "Totem Mother," is shown in the left-hand panel of Foster, "Two White Perspectives," Figure 9. Barbeau notes that by the 1920s when Carr would have seen it, the figure was missing its attached nose. He records that it was an ancient Wolf Clan crest portraying a supernatural being that used its long, sharp nose to kill children before it and its similarly endowed sister were slain by Wolf Clan members: *Totem Poles, supra* note 4 at 119 and 128.

155 By 1924, the name was held by Michael Inspring Bright in Gitlaxdamks on the Nass: Duff Files, *supra* note 59, Box 41, Files 122 and 123. A later Gamgaxmilmuxw attended the Gitsegukla feasts in 1945, and spoke in response to Hanamuux's speech at his pole-raising feast, although the individual holding the name was not identified: Beynon, *supra* note 5 at 85, 92, 93, 100, 118, 171, and 176. In 1958, the name was held by Walter Derrick: Duff, *supra* note 10 at 5. By 1978, Walter Derrick held the House Chief name of 'Wiixa: *Tribal Boundaries, supra* note 44 at 77.

156 See note 46.

157 *Tribal Boundaries, supra* note 44 at 61, citing Green to McLean, 6 Sept. 1910, NAC, RG 10, vol. 7780, file 27150-3-1.

158 *Tribal Boundaries, supra* note 44 at front and back covers.

159 *Totem Poles, supra* note 4 at 62.

had moved to the Nass River communes established by the Anglican church, some House groups had both a Nass River head chief and a Kitwancool head chief.[160] As the 'Wiixa on the Nass made clear, "When we moved to Gitlaxdamks, we did not go into the House of K'eexkw [a closely related Wolf House]. We took our own power with us."[161] This exodus began in the 1880s and 1890s, reached its zenith in the early twentieth century, and the chiefs' powers were fully restored in Kitwancool by the 1940s.[162]

So it was with the House of Gamlaxyeltxw. Hamar Foster quotes a statement from a Mrs. Richard Douse to RCMP Sergeant Taylor during the 1927 Kitwancool swoop to arrest the Oakalla five for resisting the dominion reserve survey team. After instructing Taylor to look after his prisoners and feed them well, she said:

> The Kitwancool Valley had been given to them by Almighty God, and was the property of their grandfathers, and that the whole valley belonged to them. She said she was wearing poor clothes because all her money had been given to the cause of keeping the Kitwancool Valley for the public wealth in the hands of the Indians.[163]

Emily Carr tells of staying with Mr. and Mrs. Douse in Kitwancool when she journeyed there in the summer of 1928 to paint the poles.[164] Carr thought that "Mrs. Douse was more important than Mr. Douse; she was a chieftainess in her own right, and had great dignity … The two best poles in the village belonged to Mrs. Douse." The Mrs. Douse that Carr met and sketched was Miriam Douse, who then held the name Gamlaxyeltxw.[165] It was a remarkable household that Carr had dropped into. She describes Miriam and Richard living in an earth-floored

---

160  For example, by the mid-1920s the House of Gwinuu had moved to two locations – Dan Kweenu holding the chief name in Gitlaxdamix on the Nass and Lucy Laganitz holding the chief name in Kitwancool: *Totem Poles*, *supra* note 4 at 32. Similarly, while Alexander Smith held the name 'Wiixa in Kitwancool, Robert Pearl was 'Wiixa in Gitlaxdamks: Duff Files, *supra* note 59, Box 41, File 125.

161  Duff Files, *supra* note 59, Box 41, File 125.

162  Duff, *supra* note 10 at 13. In 1881, the population of Kitwancool was 212, but by 1901 it had fallen to 69 with another 115 village members living in Nass River villages: *Mapping*, *supra* note 27 at 145 and 158, citing Canadian 1881 census reports and Department of Indian Affairs Annual Report, Babine Agency, 1905.

163  "Two White Perspectives," *supra* note 1 at 35.

164  *Ibid* at 6, 42–58, citing Carr, *Klee Wyck* (Vancouver: Douglas & McIntyre, 2003).

165  India Rael Young, "By Any Other Name" (Winter 2020) What's Insight (Royal BC Museum) 4 at 5.

dwelling with a central fire that vented through the roof, with salmon smoke-drying on racks. The rest of the family – two married daughters, a son, and an adopted orphan girl – lived in a new house in front. One of the daughters would likely have been Margaret Good who, while not succeeding to her mother's chief name, was nevertheless a guiding force in the House of Gamlaxyeltxw into the 1950s.[166] The other daughter, as Hamar Foster surmises, was married to Peter Williams, who interpreted for his mother-in-law at various times to Carr, the police, and government officials.[167] Williams was "the hero" who shared Carr's wagon ride into Kitwancool , having just returned from Oakalla Prison as one of the Kitwancool chiefs convicted of confronting the reserve surveyors. Later, as the president of Kitwancool, Williams was to guide the chiefs for over a half century in their legal entanglements with settler governments.[168] The young son, whom Carr calls Aleck,[169] was probably Albert Douse who, in 1945, held his mother's name of Gamlaxyeltxw.[170] By that time, each House once again had just one *simoogit* who lived in Kitwancool.

### Agency

Yet as firmly bound by kin and marriage ties as Gitxsan individuals were, there was surprising leeway for personal agency. Consider the remarkable lives of the two strong women central to this account, Fanny Johnson and Miriam Douse. Gisax'itutkibu's fierce, entrepreneurial drive was directed at advancing her close family within the Gitxsan order. She pushed the law's boundaries by placing her son Gamaxon in the *simoogit* seat when he was barely a teenager, by claiming against

---

166 As Lisee'iw, Margaret Good signed the 1958 agreement with the Royal British Columbia Museum on behalf of all the Kitwancool Frog Clan Houses to preserve three Kitwancool poles and to publish the House chiefs' account of their society and laws: Duff, *supra* note 10 at 4. Her husband was Fred Good, later Niishlaganuus, House of Malii, Wolf, Kitwancool.

167 "Two White Perspectives," *supra* note 1 at 57.

168 *Ibid*.

169 It was Carr's common practice to invent names for the indigenous individuals in her writing: "Two White Perspectives," *supra* note 1 at 43. A caption on the 1910 George Emmons photograph of Miriam Douse and Margaret Good states that Mrs. Richard Douse (Miriam) was the mother of Albert Douse: University of Washington Libraries, Digital Collections, accessed on 12 December 2021 at https://digitalcollections.lib.washington.edu/digital/collection/loc/id/1416/rec/449.

170 Beynon, *supra* note 5 at 234. Note that this was a different Albert Douse from the one who held the name Biiyoosxw and was the president of Kitwancool in 1910.

all evidence that her rival Niitsxw had used his *swansk* powers to cause Gamaxon's death, and then by goading her husband Gamgaxmilmuxw to shoot Niitsxw, a member of her own House. All this she did on her own by sheer force of personality but not without legal consequences. Many of the 1920s interviewees blamed her for the subsequent cascade of events. Fitzstubbs's report of Gisax'itutkibu being "stripped of all she had by the harpies of this tribe" after Gamgaxminmuxw was killed indicates widespread shaming. Yet within a few years, she managed to marry Gamgaxmilmuxw's brother, assume the name of Hanamuxw for herself, and organize two poles to be erected, one of them in memory of Niitsxw. She did this, however, from the relative sanctuary of the mission village of Andimaul. While her son, Jeffrey Johnson, himself a noted entrepreneur, succeeded her as Hanamuxw, it wasn't until her granddaughter, Gwaans (Olive Ryan), returned to Gitsegukla from Andimaul in the early 1990s to complete the funeral feasts for her uncle and to oversee the re-raising of the House's poles in the village that the House's *daxgyet* began to be restored.

Ukslax'a'mks is first encountered being threatened by the party bearing Niitsxw because she was related to Gamgaxmilmuxw on his father's side. Later that year, she becomes his lover, staying with him the night before he was shot and attempting to revenge his death, only to be thwarted by not knowing how to fire a gun. This fiery young woman then married the Gitwangak Eagle chief, Simediik, perhaps as his second wife, and by 1910 had succeeded to the Kitwancool Frog House chief name of Gamlaxyeltxw. In that role, she became increasingly bound up in Kitwancool's resistance to the reserve surveyors and police as the spokesperson for the Frog Houses. She remarried into the Kitwancool Wolf House of 'Wiixa, becoming the matriarch of an extended family of kin and in-laws that was on the front line of the legal and physical operations of that resistance. Her leadership there was apparent even to the apolitical Emily Carr in 1928. Miriam Doust saw her role as one that required her to engage in the larger political and legal arena of Kitwancool's struggle against settler incursions into their territories and suppression of their legal order.

Gamgaxmilmuxw's conversations with William Pierce, his friend Jim Laganitz and with Charles Ridley record his anguished uncertainty as to how to extract himself from the trap formed by the pressing and conflicting demands of two disparate legal orders. He died largely because he dithered between following the consequences of his actions under Gitxsan law by living on his or his father's House territories beyond the reach of colonial authorities, as Simon Gunanoot was to do some time later, versus following state law by surrendering to the police posse.

This conundrum continues to haunt the Gitxsan and their neighbours to the present day.

## Conclusions

So, what can be said about Gitxsan law at the turn of the nineteenth and twentieth centuries based on the legal processes engaged and legal decisions made in the events surrounding the deaths of Gamaxon, Niitsxw, and Gamgaxmilmukw? And what can be said about the semiotic role of stories, performances, and images in those legal processes?

Every Gitxsan person encountered in these notes was born with an identity that enabled them to place themselves at a nexus within an ever-widening web of legal connections. The connections through their mother established their kinship identity and thus the groups to which they would belong and share privileges and responsibilities. The connections through their father identified the groups from whom they would receive status and education and, through their later lives, who would be the primary monitors of their actions. Recall that Gamgaxmilmukw was admonished by both his House chief and his father after he killed Niitsxw. The connections widened by including each individual within a group, each such group within a larger group, and so on until the whole society and, with a bit more effort, neighbouring societies formed a resilient, non-hierarchical, nested network that guided each person's responsibilities for others. "Non-hierarchical" means that everyone had a part in governance and legal decisions, everyone had to inform themselves on the relevant law and legal process. Stories, performances, and images were the signposts that helped everyone navigate their way safely and usefully through that network.

Kinship connections were invoked in the narrowest sense to identify a person's membership in a particular lineage and in the broadest sense to identify their membership in one of four clans. Oral histories (*adaawk*), crests (*ayuks*), spirit powers (*naxnox*), and sung laments (*limx'oy*) were used both to create a unique lineage identity and to identify relationships with related lineages that together made up a *wil'naat'ahl*. A lineage possessed a unique set of histories and associated crest images, while a *wil'naat'ahl* was made up of lineages with some common histories and crests. Hanamuxw explained this in 1945 when he identified his closely related Fireweed *wil'naat'ahl* that had the Temlaham dispersal history, and whose member lineages displayed the Rainbow crest while his particular lineage that made up the House of Hanamuxw also had the unique Person of Rainbow crest. Kinship connections were stable, subject only to a lineage becoming extinct when there were no women members to carry on the matriline and when it was unable to adopt members from related lineages. Lineages that shrank too small to be economically viable would have joined with closely related lineages to form a self-sufficient House group, which held the amalgamated lineages' treasury of names, histories, and crests. A House, then, was an economic unit made up of one or more closely related lineages and managed by a *simoogit* or House chief.

Marriage connections sealed alliances between unrelated Houses. Clan exogamy ensured that marriages were alliances between Houses from different clans. As Houses of each clan would require at least half of the intermarrying population to be from other clans, no one clan could dominate a village or the larger society. In a marriage alliance, the father's role in educating his children and enhancing their rank encouraged each House to maintain good relations with Houses of other clans so that their future members were properly educated and had high standing in the society. The father's House's role in arranging his children's end-of-life ceremonies cemented these ties. It was young men from Niitsxw's father's House of Gwinuu who searched for him and bore his body home. The connection, then, might more properly be called a parenting alliance rather than a marriage alliance. This interaction of many inherited, fixed connections and many negotiated connections across the society as a whole gave it the structural stability to cohere as a fully functional social entity yet be adaptable to changing conditions. Within such a network, an individual and a group could exercise considerable agency, as did Gisax'itutkibu and Ukslax'amks, albeit subject to close monitoring by the people, particularly the *nidinsxwit*, those most firmly allied with the person and his or her House group. It is the *nidinsxwit* to whom a House looked at its *yukw* feast to review its decisions and validate them as being lawful. Thus, when Gaxsbgabaxs included the contested Ganuget crest on the pole he was raising in 1945, at his pole-raising feast he told the *adaawk* that the image encoded. Wiiseeks, his Fireweed *nidinsxwit*, validated Gaxsbgabaxs's privilege to display the crest: "And you have done the proper thing in showing this to your fellow chiefs, who know that what you say is true."

Within the fabric woven from kinship and marriage threads, dynamic adjustments were possible through the ranking either of individuals within a House or of Houses within a village community. The nature of a person's role within their group would have been signalled by a series of feast-names bestowed on them by the House at their various life stages. Each House had its own unique set of names. Individuals could elevate their standing within their House either by competing for high names, as when Gisax'itutkibu propelled her young son into the House chief's seat at the 1888 Kitwanga feast, or by raising the status of the name they had, as when Gisax'itutkibu later took the name Hanamuxw and raised it to that of the *simoogit* of the House of Hanamuxw. Usually, however, such competition took place at a House feast or *li'liget*, away from the gaze of the wider public and ethnologists. Ranking was a continuous adjustment to the standing of individuals within groups and of groups amongst each other based on their *daxgyet*. As the word's literal translation signifies, this was the power that firmly bound each individual to their House and bound each House to other Houses and to the spirits of its territories. A House without territory was the lowest ranked, as was the Fireweed House of Yee'l when it had to leave its Gitsegukla territories and move to Kitwancool. At the inter-village *yukw* feasts, ranking was less about striving to get ahead of other Houses and more about maintaining at least a nominal equality among them. It therefore had more of a cooperative aspect, as Gamgaxmilmukw showed in 1945 when he described how iterative marriage ties between the Houses of Hanamukw, 'Wiixa, and Gamlaxyeltxw had led to their mutual support. But for all the lineages' striving through the personage of their House chiefs, ranking depended on iterative, bottom-up assessments, the results of which were reflected in *halayt* and feast seating and speaking order. Authority came from the trust publicly given by others.

The role of a House chief, then, becomes clearer. The *simoogit* not only embodied his or her House but had a critical role in maintaining its ranking by managing it as a well-functioning social and economic unit. Legal management included mediating internal House disputes but sometimes also removing incorrigible members, such as Wiigyet's banishment of the Yee'l individuals or, in extreme cases, killing them, as appeared to happen when Mool'xan shot his deranged House member, Duubisxw. A chief was also called upon to mediate disputes between other Houses, as the Gitwangak Frog chief Lulak did in the compensation negotiations between the Kitwancool Wolves and the Gitsegukla Fireweeds over Niitsxw's killing. It is apparent that the legal order did not depend on any overarching sovereign authority. There is no record of anyone or any entity being able to command, legislate, or enforce positive laws. We hear of no village chiefs, of clan chiefs, or of a high chief or council of the Gitxsan. Even the House chiefs, as Gedimgaldo'o told Constable Brown, "have not the power enough even to make the people come here to listen to your message." Magistrate Fitzstubbs fell victim to this limitation on chiefs' power when he thought he had a deal with the Kispiox chiefs only to have it overturned by their House members at a public meeting.

Nineteenth-century Gitxsan society was a complex, highly connected network of individuals and groups capable of adaptive evolution through very slow-changing lineages, moderately slow-changing marriage alliances, and relatively fast-changing individual and House ranking. In Gamlaxyeltxw's words, its inherent balance of stability and adaptability resulted in "public wealth in the hands of the Indians." Parts of the law focused on maintaining the network – the rules of matrilineal inheritance of lineage membership, forbidding marriage within a person's clan, and the duties of a father's lineage to his children. Other parts focused on keeping information and transparent decision-making flowing through the network – the *halayt* ceremonies and the seating matrix, the requirement for a House to hold a *li'liget* feast of its members to reach its decision on critical matters, and for it to host a *yukw* feast to have that decision legally reviewed and validated by Houses of other clans. Critical parts of the law focused on the resolution of disputes, not just to deter them but to ensure they did not disrupt or paralyse society.

The field notes in this chapter have largely been observations of those conflict-resolution processes. Gitxsan case law is clear that the legal actor was not the individual disputant but her or his lineage. The righting of wrongs, including injuries and deaths, was not a matter between the wrongdoer and the wronged but between their respective kin groups – Gamgaxmilmuxw's House of 'Wiixa and Niitsxw's House of Gamst'axgu'u/Hanamuxw, for example. The key mechanism to resolve such disputes was shame. It operated on groups as legal actors the same way that conscience operates on individuals as legal actors. It served to remind each disputant how their subsequent actions would affect their and their House's ranking. Shame is manifested through the talk of others. Taunting or the anticipation of it was one way others' assessment of behaviour was communicated to the legal actor and to the wider society. Lelt stepped away from helping the police posse hunting Gamgaxmilmuxw when it appeared his participation would become public knowledge and subject to taunts affecting his upcoming succession *yukw*. William Beynon held the feast to announce his succession to the chieftainship of the Tsimshian Gitsis tribe after he was taunted about it. Later, at the 1945 Gitsegukla *halayt* performances and feasts, he recorded the role that taunting songs played in the resolution of the crest dispute that wove its way through those ceremonies. It is worth repeating at this point Gamayam's assessment of the government's failure to acknowledge Gamgaxmilmuxw's killing: "The whole thing would have blown over and the shame of his death might have been washed away if the government had paid something, no matter how small, if they had recognised him as a chief. It was not the value of the ransom but to take away the shame of the death." Shame, therefore, did not just hang over those responsible for a death; it also hung over the kin of the deceased.

The law also disregarded intent when someone was harmed. Harm from accidents was to be settled in the same way as harm from wrongs. There was responsibility for an accident if it occurred on your territory or if it occurred on a joint venture with you. Charlie Youmans failed to act on this, as he also failed to publicly acknowledge the harm done. Gamgaxmilmuxw acknowledged his culpability within a day of Niitsxw's death. This resulted in repercussions for him within his House but it also enabled his House and Nittsxw's House to quickly agree on suitable compensation. The shaming of both lineages involved, the disregard of intent, and the expeditious acknowledgement of the harm all served to encourage the parties to focus on dealing with the effect of an incident on their society as a whole. The law thus dealt with the repercussions on everyone, not just on the person who initiated a conflict. It follows that while the required compensation was negotiated at the *gawagani* ceremony between the groups directly involved, each party then had to host a *yukw* feast so the wider community could validate the deal.

*Halayt* theatre encapsulated, perhaps, the deepest sense of how Gitxsan society functioned. The restoring to life of the comatose *simoogit* or "real person" dramatized the immortality of names and lineages. This was a vision that together the people were engaged in something larger than their individual lives, something that had an eternal life of its own. So, when the *halayts* enacted the human traits that harmed others only to see them banished from the feast hall, participants were reminded of the moral behaviour required to nurture the social organism.

Gitxsan art was thus imbued with legal meanings. Legal identity was informed by narrative art – feast names and oral histories; by visual art – crest images on poles and worn regalia; and by sung art – the laments that grieved the past loss of territories and connections with other lineages. A group's identity told the world to whom it was related and from whom it should be distinguished. Legal process was informed by performed art signalling intent: the floating of eagle down to show no harm, Gamgaxmilmuxw appearing before the Kitsegukla Fireweeds in his regalia and on all fours to show his House would compensate them for Niitsxw's death, and the ubiquitous taunting songs at feasts that showed a group it was courting trouble if certain matters were not righted. Art not so much for art's sake but for law's sake.

APPENDIX: PRINCIPAL ETHNOGRAPHIC SOURCES

| Chief Name* | House | Clan | Village | Christian Name | Archival Reference** |
|---|---|---|---|---|---|
| 'Niistaw | Gwagl'lo | Frog | Gitsegukla | Anna Campbell | B/F/68.2 |
| Wiigyet | Wiigyet | Fireweed | Andimaul | Mark Wiget | B/F/68.7 |
| Lelt | Lelt | Frog | Gitwangak | Solomon Harris | B/F/89.2 |
| Luuxhon | Luuxhon | Frog | Kitwancool | George Derrick | B/F/89.3 |
| Simediik (I) | Simediik | Eagle | Gitwangak | none given | B/F/89.4 |
| Guuxsan | Guuxsan | Fireweed | Gitsegukla | Dan Guxsan | B/F/89.7 |
| Tsi'igwii | Wiigyet | Fireweed | Gitsegukla | Isaac Tens | B/F/89.8 |
| Gamayam (I) | Guuxsan | Fireweed | Gitsegukla | Charles Mark | B/F/89.9 |
| Geel | Geel | Fireweed | Kispiox | Simon Gunanoot | B/F/90.1 |
| Simediik (II) | Simediik | Eagle | Gitwangak | none given | B/F/201.3 |
| Gamayam (II) | Guuxsan | Fireweed | Gitsegukla | Charles Mark | B/F/201.5 |
| Gwinuu | Gwinuu | Frog | Kitwancool | Lucy Laganitz | B/F/201.6 |
| Hlengwax | Hlengwax | Frog | Gitwangak | Jim Laganitz | B/F/201.7 |

* Feast name held at the time of Barbeau's interviews. The chiefs Simediik and Gamayam each gave two interviews.
** Canadian Museum of History, Barbeau/Beynon Northwest Coast Files.

## BIBLIOGRAPHY


Barbeau, C. Marius. *The Downfall of Temlaham* (Edmonton: Hurtig, 1973 [1928]).

Barbeau, C. Marius. *Totem Poles of the Gitksan, Upper Skeena River, British Columbia* (Ottawa: Department of Mines, National Museum of Canada, 1929).

Beynon, William. *Potlatch at Gitsegukla: William Beynon's 1945 Field Notebooks*, ed Margaret Anderson and Marjorie Halpin (Vancouver: UBC Press, 2000).

Carr, Emily. *Klee Wyck* (Vancouver: Douglas & McIntyre, 2003).

Daly, Richard. *Our Box Was Full: An Ethnography for the Delgamuukw Plaintiffs* (Vancouver: UBC Press, 2005).

Duff, Wilson. Duff Tsimshian Files, University of British Columbia, Museum of Anthropology Archives, Box 41, File 126.

Duff, Wilson, ed. *Histories, Territories and Laws of the Kitwancool* (Victoria: Royal British Columbia Museum, 1989).

Foster, Hamar. "'The Queen's Law Is Better than Yours': International Homicide in Early British Columbia" in Jim Phillips, Tina Loo & Susan Lewthwaite, eds, *Essays in the History of Criminal Law*, vol. 5: *Crime and Criminal Justice* (Toronto: University of Toronto Press, 1994) 41.

Foster, Hamar. "Two 'White' Perspectives on Indigenous Resistance: Emily Carr's *Klee Wyck*, the RCMP, and Title to the Kitwancool Valley in 1927" (2021) 43:1 Manitoba L J 1.

Galois, RM. "The Burning of Kitsegukla, 1872" (1992) 94 BC Studies 59.

Galois, RM. "Gitxsan Law and Settler Disorder: The Skeena 'Uprising' of 1888" in Theodore Binnema & Susan Neylan, eds, *New Histories for Old: Changing Perspectives on Canada's Native Pasts* (Vancouver: UBC Press, 1992).

Johnston, Ted. *Ted Johnston Memoirs: Life with Terrace Area Pioneers* (Prince George, BC: Crescentia Harrison, 2005).

Kitwancool Government. Kitwancool Research Submission to the Minister of Indian and Northern Affairs, Hugh Faulkner (1977).

MacDonald, George F, ed. *The Totem Poles and Monuments of Gitwangak Village* (Ottawa: Environment Canada, Parks Canada, 1984).

MacDonald, George F & John J Cove, eds. *Tsimshian Narratives*, vol. 2: *Trade and Warfare* (Ottawa: Canadian Museum of Civilisation, 1987) at x–xvii.

MacDonald, Joanne. *Gitwangak Village Life: A Museum Collection* (Ottawa: Minister of Environment, Parks Canada, 1984).

Mynett, Geoff. *Murders on the Skeena* (Qualicum Beach, BC: Caitlin, 2021).

Pierce, William Henry. *From Potlatch to Pulpit* (Vancouver: Vancouver Bindery, 1933).

Sampare, Charlotte et al. *Adawkhl Gitsegukla* (Gitsegukla: Kitsegukla Band, 1979).

"Skeena Expedition Had Origin in Small Trouble." *Victoria Daily Times* (18 July 1923).

"Special Assize Court." *Nanaimo Free Press* (7 November 1888).

Sterritt, Neil J. *Mapping My Way Home: A Gitxsan History* (Smithers: Creekstone, 2016).

Sterritt, Neil et al. *Tribal Boundaries in the Nass Watershed* (Vancouver: UBC Press, 1998).

Young, India Rael. "By Any Other Name" (Winter 2020) What's Insight (Royal BC Museum) 4.

# 4 Indigenous Intellectual Property in the Public Domain: The Case of Hawaiian *hula*

DEBRA McKENZIE

Like all legal concepts, Western intellectual property rights have particular cultural and economic groundings. The modern Western legal concept of intellectual property law has its roots in the seventeenth century.[1] The earlier Lockean theory viewed copyright law as "vindication of the author's natural right to the products of her labour."[2] If one applied their labour to creation, design, or invention, then they should have a right to control, and exclude others from, the product of that labour. The creator held legal property in the knowledge that led to the development of the product. Later, Bentham posited a theory of utilitarianism whereby the goal was to encourage and maximize invention and progress by creating property rights in knowledge because "creators would not invest the time or capital necessary to produce such products, if others could copy or reverse engineer them freely."[3] This theory aligns with the modern capitalist state's rationale for a legislative framework[4] whereby an inventor, artist, or author is encouraged to produce innovative products by statutory authority that guarantees exclusive control of, and thus all the profits arising from, the product for a number of years.

In effect, the development of a Western state legal regime of intellectual property rights created the "propertization of creative activity."[5]

---

1 Rajshree Chandra, *Knowledge as Property: Issues in the Moral Grounding of Intellectual Property Rights* (New Delhi: Oxford University Press, 2010) at 6.

2 Abraham Drassinower, "A Rights-Based View of the Idea/Expression Dichotomy in Copyright Law" (2003) 16 Can J L & Jurisprudence 3 at 6.

3 Chandra, *supra* note 1 at 92.

4 In Canada the administration of IPRs is undertaken through the *Patent Act*, RSC 1985, c P-4; *Trademarks Act*, RSC 1985, c T-13; *Copyright Act*, RSC 1985, c C-42; and *Industrial Design Act*, RSC 1985.

5 Hanoch Dagan, "Property and the Public Domain" (2013) 18 Yale J L & Human 84 at 84.

One could hold legal property rights in knowledge, inventions, or creative works. If no one held legal rights, then the creative activity was relegated to the so-called public domain where access to the creative idea was freely available. Generally, intellectual property was deemed part of the public domain on the expiration of the term of protection granted by state law. However, some notions of creativity were never amenable to legal protection. A dichotomy of ideas and expressions is a fundamental doctrine in Western intellectual property law[6] whereby only "expressions" of "ideas" are protectable property. Ideas themselves are relegated to the public domain. For example, no one can hold a protectable right to mathematical theories, but the inventor who develops a machine that utilizes that theory has a protectable right in the application. A musical note is not protectable, but string as few as four together and you have a protectable musical work.[7] In dance, steps such as the waltz or the moonwalk are not protectable,[8] but choreographed works are.

The dichotomy of unprotectable ideas and protectable expressions is a constructed legal concept that was developed in order to resolve the quandary inherent in awarding intellectual property rights to an individual creator, author, or inventor when the creation of an expression very rarely represented an individual effort. Chandra explained:

> Knowledge and the capabilities arising thereof are constituted both socially and culturally … the creation of an idea has an unmistakable social and historical component, … invention, writing and thought do not happen in a vacuum. Ideas, knowledge and thoughts of a person are crucially dependent on ideas and thoughts of the preceding generation.[9]

The idea/expression dichotomy served to limit the natural rights of creators, and left a pool of ideas for others to access.[10] The ultimate

---

6 For discussions of this topic, see Edward Samuels, "The Idea-Expression Dichotomy in Copyright Law" (1988–1989) 56 Tenn L R 321; Drassinower, *supra* note 2; Marisa C Schutz, "Is *Gray v Perry* the One That Got Away? The Idea-Expression Dichotomy and Music Copyright Infringement" (2020–2021) 20 UIC Rev Intell Prop L 290.

7 In *Lawson v Dundas* [1985] The Times 13 (Eng Ch Div) the Court held that the four-note theme used as part of the Channel 4 signature tune was protected as a musical work.

8 Diane Busuttil, "Choreographic Authorship Using Two Case Studies: Anne Teresa De Keersmaeker v Beyonce and Ann Van den Broed and Figgis" (2015) Macquarie University, Sydney, online: <https://shorturl.at/zJN13>.

9 Chandra, *supra* note 1 at 68.

10 *Ibid* at 70.

inventor was prevented from reaping the totality of the benefit from all the labour that had been put into the project before their involvement. From a utilitarian viewpoint, the tension was resolved through statutory instruments by which the state "control[led] the utilization of an idea."[11]

Indigenous knowledge, or the societal/cultural expressions particular to an Indigenous society, are often relegated to the public domain.[12] A basic building block of Indigenous knowledge may resemble an "idea" in that it has no specific and named creator, and it is a standardized feature of evolving iterations of a tradition, fitting nicely into Chandra's definition of an idea cited above. On some levels it may be possible to view Indigenous knowledge as analogous to a mathematical theory, a dance step, or a musical note, as a *part* of an expression. However, in the case of many Indigenous societal/cultural expressions, the standardized elements are precisely that which imbue the knowledge with societal relevance. Even as the manifestation of an expression may evolve over generations and become part of something different, the ideas are the integral building blocks that have flowed through the minds of generations in that society. Expressions cannot easily be separated from ideas, and why should they be artificially bifurcated by a constructed Western legal concept in any case?

Indigenous communities have always had their own laws that permitted or limited access to local knowledge. This volume considers the ownership of intangible knowledge by the Secwepemc peoples and the Gitxsan peoples. Although the two societies are organized very differently, it is clear that in them certain societal/cultural expressions were held proprietarily. The knowledge was not shared freely with outsiders, and in the case of the Gitxsan, rules and protocols also governed the use of the knowledge internally. However, because the underpinning of the proprietorship of Indigenous intangible property is different, both across Indigenous societies and in contrast to Western states, it faces a dilemma when considered in a Western legal context.

If Indigenous law is not considered as a valid source of legal control over the use of intellectual property, and Indigenous knowledge, relegated to the public domain, is not protectable under Western copyright law, it follows that Indigenous intellectual property is very vulnerable to unauthorized appropriation. This is a colonial notion that allows non-Indigenous parties to attain proprietary interests in

---

11 *Ibid* at 89.

12 See James [Sa'ke'j] Youngblood Henderson, "The Indigenous Domain and Intellectual Property Rights" (2021) 4:2 Lakehead L J 93.

Indigenous-held intellectual property because those proprietary rights are unprotected under an imposed Western legal system.

In the following case study, a non-Hawaiian photographer was able to utilize movements from Hawaiian *hula* as the subject matter of a lucrative photography business. The *hula* movements were characterized as "ideas" by the court. Thus, those movements were relegated to the public domain where they could be freely appropriated and utilized as the foundation of a so-called expression that could be protected by state copyright law. Three important issues regarding the vulnerability of Indigenous knowledge to appropriation and misuse arise from this case. First, the court relegated the *hula* movement to the public domain, a Western legal construct, without considering the movement as an integral part of existing Indigenous intellectual property. Second, the court did not recognize the Hawaiian rules and protocols that directed the practice and performance of *hula* as the governing law. Last, the court addressed the type of legal harm that may flow from the appropriation of Indigenous knowledge. Although this was not a case in which the court considered legal harm, discourse surrounding the case illustrated how the Hawaiian and non-Hawaiian parties differently valued *hula*. The economic model of Western intellectual property law does not consider the societal harm that may flow from the appropriation of Indigenous art and societal/cultural expressions.

## Considering the *Hula* Case

In 2006 a non-Hawaiian photographer in Hawaii filed a complaint for copyright infringement against a Hawaiian artist and art gallery.[13] The complainant alleged that a stained-glass artwork of a woman performing a traditional *hula* movement was an unauthorized copy of his photograph of the same *hula* movement.

The complainant, Reece, had enjoyed a very lucrative living through his photography of images of Hawaiian *hula* dancing since 1979. He incorporated his images within a wide range of products, including prints, coasters, lamps, and scarves.[14] His current product website (https://kimtaylorreece.com/about) describes him as "Hawaii's

---

13  *Reece v Island Treasures Art Gallery*, Inc (2006), 468 F Supp 2d 1197 (D Hawai'i) [*Reece*].

14  See Kim Taylor Reece's website at <https://kimtaylorreece.com/shop/ols /products> for a full range of products.

foremost fine art photographer" whose "art helps to preserve the *hula* and enrich lives." Reece reports on his website that he has studied the history, motions, ceremony, and costumes of *hula kahiko*[15] for nearly twenty-five years.

Reece sought a preliminary injunction to prevent the Hawaiian art gallery from displaying or selling the stained-glass artwork that he alleged was an unauthorized copy of his photograph entitled *Makanani*. Reece published this photograph as a poster in 1988, and in the ensuing eighteen years leading up to this action had licensed the image for use on greeting cards, T-shirts, and picture frame inserts. The court noted that the photograph had been widely disseminated. It was used as an insert in koa picture frames sold at all Hawaii Longs, Walmart, and Kmart stores from 1995 to 2003, and an estimated ten thousand posters and twenty-thousand greeting cards bearing the image had been sold.[16]

The stained-glass artwork at issue was created by Hawaiian artist and *hula* dancer Leialoha Colucci. She stated that her inspiration came from years of doing *hula*, and that the *'ike* motion portrayed in the artwork was one of her favourites. At the hearing Colucci testified that she drew from memories and photographs of her niece dancing *hula* and from other *hula* performances.[17]

Both works portrayed an image of a woman kneeling on the beach performing in the *hula kahiko* tradition, and performing an *'ike* motion (which means "knowledge") whereby the "dancer raises one hand out and one arm is bent at the elbow and the hand is open and placed behind the eye with the thumb facing downwards and the finger to show the seeing motion."[18]

The stained-glass artwork was on display in Island Treasures Art Gallery when the complainant, Reece, demanded that the gallery remove the "unauthorized copy"[19] of his photograph. The gallery temporarily removed the artwork but later put it back on display, albeit not for sale. At that time Reece filed a complaint for copyright infringement, and sought an order for a preliminary injunction to prohibit the artist or gallery from displaying or selling the artwork until the copyright issue was resolved.

---

15 *Kahiko* is the ancient form of hula. It is a solemn hula with strong purpose and is not performed with a grass skirt or accompanied by a ukulele.

16 *Reece, supra* note 13 at 1204.

17 *Ibid* at 1201.

18 *Ibid*. The Court quotes *kumu hula* M Puana de Silva.

19 *Ibid* at 1200.

The court denied the complainant a preliminary injunction pending trial. However, the defendants agreed to a settlement before going to trial. The defendants paid US $60,000 to Reece for legal expenses and were permanently enjoined from displaying or selling the stained-glass artwork.[20] One can safely assume that the defendants settled because there was a real concern that Reece would be successful in his copyright infringement claim at trial. In fact, Gail Allen, owner of the Island Treasures gallery where the stained-glass artwork was displayed, revealed that "[after the lawsuit was filed] all of the artists who had *hula* artwork on display in Island Treasures removed them out of fear they too could be sued."[21]

It seems incongruous that a non-Hawaiian photographer could be in a position to legally prevent Hawaiian artisans from interpreting their own cultural expressions, or from freely using their own knowledge. However, under the existing US state copyright law Reece was in a position to accomplish just that. Reece argued that *hula* was in the public domain, and that his own artistic renditions of *hula* were protected by copyright law. He explained to a reporter that he owned rights to the image and that the defendant artist "was not copying the *hula*" but "copying the image [from his photograph]."[22]

A master *hula* teacher (*kumu hula*) and expert witness at the hearing, Vicky Holt Takamine, responded to Reece's assertions: "He wants exclusive rights to our *hula* and to our *hula* motions. He's taken pictures and photographs of *hula* dancers for the last 20 years; we have never infringed on his right to go and sell those photographs."[23] Takamine's comment reflected the quandary that surrounds Indigenous intellectual property. There is the possessive "our" *hula*, which rightly connotes some sort of ownership of a dance created and danced by countless generations of Indigenous Hawaiians. However, Takamine also recognized the Western legal right that allowed Reece to benefit from

---

20  The settlement agreement is available at <https://storage.courtlistener.com/recap/gov.uscourts.hid.71109.96.2.pdf>.

21  Kazuya Hayakawa & Yasunobu Ito, "Diversity of Reactions among Local People upon Commercialization of Traditional Knowledge under Intellectual Property Rights Systems" (2016) Proceedings of PECMET'16: Technology Management for Social Innovation 1495 at 1500, online: <http://www.picmet.org/db/member/proceedings/2016/data/polopoly_fs/1.3251286.1472157486!/fileserver/file/680779/filename/16A0025.pdf>.

22  Joann Shin, "Art or Copyright Infringement?" Hawaii News Now (3 November 2006), online: <http://www.hawaiinewsnow.com/story/5628631/art-or-copyright-infringement>.

23  *Ibid.*

his photographs of *hula*. Any type of ownership or stewardship that Hawaiians held over *hula* failed to bring with it any enforceable legal control recognized in a Western court.

It was an unusual situation whereby a non-Indigenous artist sued an Indigenous artist for infringement of copyright where it was clear that the complainant based his artwork on an Indigenous knowledge. The court was presented with a scenario whereby a non-Hawaiian artist sought to enforce greater legal rights to Indigenous knowledge than the Hawaiians held themselves. In an interview Reece stated that he sued to enforce his copyright because "if not protected, there's no incentive for [an] artist or a musician to produce this stuff and there's no creativity."[24] Reece was not off the mark when he publicly alluded to a Benthamic utilitarian philosophy[25] in order to rationalize his bold move to sue a Hawaiian artist. After all, this was the theoretical basis for his lawsuit under American copyright legislation. The statement ignored the fact that it was Hawaiian creativity that had developed the *hula* movements over many generations, albeit with a collective authorship rather than a single creator. Further, although Reece professed a great knowledge of *hula*, he failed to note the rules and protocols that had always surrounded the Hawaiian dance.

Reece was making his case according to the legislation that was in place, and likewise, the Hawaiian court could only consider the application within the confines of Western law. Thus, in rendering the decision, the court narrowly focused on the issue of whether an image of *hula kahiko* could be a protectable element under copyright law. In other words, could the plaintiff have any intellectual property rights in the image beyond the elements of photographic expertise that he applied to the image? The district court in Hawaii began with what could be described as an homage to *hula*, and the place of *hula* in Hawaiian culture:

> Hula is a vital expression of Hawaiian culture … For many, it is an articulation of nature and beauty, of respect for the ancient gods and goddesses, of historical memory and legends and of daily life. Hula plays a role in preserving Hawaiian culture and history.[26] Although Hawaiian was not

---

24  *Ibid.*

25  Chandra, *supra* note 1 at 26.

26  *Reece, supra* note 13 at 1200. In support of this statement, the Court cited the Declaration of *kumu hula* Victoria Takamine: "For years hula was the incubator of all our cultural practices. At a time when many such practices were being destroyed, hula traditions provided a place where those cultural practices could be preserved and incubated."

originally a written language, Native Hawaiians have "an extensive literature accumulated in memory, added to from generation to generation, and handed down by word of mouth." Historically, "it consisted of *meles* (songs) of various kinds, genealogies and honorific chants, stories and traditional lore in which were imbedded fragments of history and biography," and which were "used as an accompaniment to the *hula*, a large part of it being composed especially for that purpose."[27]

The movement portrayed in the artworks was one of *hula kahiko* described by *kumu hula* Victoria Takamine as "the ancient style of *hula* where the movements and materials use are "historically standard ... Traditional *hula* draws from a body of motions and has a definite framework in which it works.[28] Further, the court was informed that proper dress was required for a traditional performance, and the choice of material chosen for the *lei* worn on the head held significant meaning.[29]

The movement portrayed in both artworks was that of a female dancer in traditional dress wearing a maile *lei*.[30] The court noted that the *lei* was a *piko lei*, "a *lei* that ties us to our ancestors".[31] Both works depicted a woman kneeling on the beach performing an *'ike* motion. Takamine explained that "the *'ike* motion is used in many *hula* to mean to see, to view, to behold."[32] The two images before the court had many similarities because they both depicted the same traditional *hula* movement. Elements of tradition were obvious in the movement itself, in the dancer's choice of dress, and in the selected lei. Nothing depicted in the artworks was a random choice because each of these elements held meaning in the *hula*, and was integral to the movement portrayed.

After the description of the traditional *hula* movement, the court went on to consider which elements of the complainant's photograph were protectable by the copyright he held. The traditionality of the elements and their cultural and societal significance to Hawaiian culture and history were not considered. Rather, the court applied the law of Western copyright, and set out to distinguish protectable elements from

---

27  *Ibid.* The court is quoting from Ralph S Kuykendall, *The Hawaiian Kingdom* (Honolulu: University of Hawaii, 1938) at 10.

28  *Ibid.*

29  *Ibid.*

30  *Ibid.* Maile is a fragrant vine endemic to Hawaii. The leaves of the vine are twisted together to fashion a lei.

31  *Ibid.*

32  *Ibid* at 1201.

unprotectable elements in the idea-expression dichotomy.[33] As we saw above, in copyright law only the expression or manifestation of an idea is protectable. Ideas themselves are not. The court decided that the expression of the idea portrayed in the photograph included the photographic elements of angle, timing, lighting, and the expression itself of the *hula kahiko* performance and dress.[34] However, the image of a *hula* dancer performing an *'ike* movement, as well as her dress and lei, constituted ideas and were unprotectable elements in copyright law. All of these elements particular and standard to the tradition of *hula kahiko* were characterized by the court as *scènes à faire*.[35]

The term *scènes à faire* translates to "scene to be made" or "scene that must be done." It is a copyright law doctrine whereby certain elements are considered standard in the depiction of a given topic.[36] Thus, the *hula* movement and the dress and adornment of the dancer represented standardized ideas that were expressed in different media by both artists. As such, only the technical elements of the photograph could be copyrighted, and it is on those elements that the works were compared for similarities.

Because standardized elements or *scènes à faire* are unprotectable in copyright law, they are legally situated in the public domain. No one could point to the individual creator of *hula*; it was an Indigenous societal/cultural expression that had been known and shared by Hawaiian society for countless generations. The movement depicted in the artworks was a standard gesture used in *hula kahiko*. In intellectual property law, this kind of standard knowledge, unclaimed by an individual creator, is relegated to the public domain where a third party such as Reece is able to access it freely and then put it to commercial use.

## Indigenous Knowledge in the Public Domain

As mentioned above, Chandra justified the notion of the public domain on the basis that the fundamental ideas developed over time should always be freely available because no one person should reap all the benefit from an idea developed over generations. The state entered the picture to "control the utilization of the idea."[37]

---

33  Carl Mazurek, "Through the Looking Glass: Photography and the Idea/Expression Dichotomy" (2017) J of Intell Prop and Entertainment L 278 at 281.

34  *Reece, supra* note 13 at 1206.

35  *Ibid* at 1207.

36  Defined by *Black's Law Dictionary* (11th ed. 2019) as "standard or general themes that are common to a wide variety of works and therefore are not copyrightable."

37  Chandra, note 1 at 89.

With Indigenous knowledge, it can be argued that ideas and expressions are not so easily separated. If rules and protocols control its use, then it is likely that the same peoples that developed the ideas over time are the ones that will utilize the idea. Marilyn Strathern noted the difficulty of separating idea and expression in Indigenous art: "A painting executed in reference to ancestral images contains its own conditions of reproduction: the design itself indexes who has the right to paint it. In this manner, artist belongs to painting rather than painting to artist."[38]

This is the argument that is missing in a consideration of the public domain and Indigenous intellectual property. This is not to suggest that an Indigenous artisan or author may not have rights of ownership over their own creative work. However, if the artisan or author is part of an Indigenous community, and their creative work draws upon the generations of Indigenous knowledge of the community, *and* they are enabled or allowed to do so by that community, then every artistic *expression* under these conditions carries with it the *ideas* of local Indigenous knowledge. Indigenous artists and authors may be policed by laws that are found in the protocols and rules that control production and dissemination of local intellectual property. It might be said that Indigenous artists enjoy a communal ownership of the underlying knowledge utilized in their artworks, but even that ownership does not carry with it an unfettered right to use the ideas.

The movements of *hula* are more than steps to a dance. *Hula* has a long history in Hawaii. The first *hulas* are linked to myth wherein *hula* schools were established and conducted by the gods, and these became the model for the *hālau* (*hula* schools) "set up by mortals."[39] The *hula* was danced by the original settlers of the Hawaiian Islands in the fifth century. It was never considered to be only dance, but "a form of narration accompanied by movement"[40] that "cannot be danced in the absence of a prayer, poem, or story," because the movements of the *hula* interpret the words.[41] Nor was it ever simply enjoyed for entertainment, as it served religious, political, and social purposes as well.[42] It is

---

38  Marilyn Strathern, "Intellectual Property and Rights: An Anthropological Perspective" in Christopher Tilley, Webb Keane & Susanne Kuechler-Fogden, eds, *Handbook of Material Culture* (London: Sage, 2006) 447 at 451.

39  George Hu'eu Sanford Kanahele, *Kū Kanaka Stand Tall: A Search for Hawaiian Values* (Honolulu: University of Hawaii Press, 1986) 106.

40  Māhelaani Uchiyama, *The Haumāna Hula Handbook for Students of Hawaiian Dance* (Berkeley: North Atlantic Books, 2016) 1.

41  *Ibid.*

42  Sharon Mahealani Rowe, "We Dance for Knowledge" (2008) Dance Research J 31 at 36.

representative of a Hawaiian way of knowing, a knowing "grounded in the natural environment and in the ancestral line of family."[43] Hawaiian knowledge is infused with spirituality, utility, relationship, and reciprocity, and *hula* represents those values.[44] Sharon Mahealani Rowe situates these values in elements of the dance, holding that these elements do not merely accompany the dance, but are constitutive of it:

> They are exemplified in the basic *aiha'a* stance with knees bent and feet flat, in full contact with the earth. One feels its rhythms and responds to its contours. Rather than seeking to leave the earth, this stance indicates a responsive connection to earth. Here the values of humility and reciprocity inform the movement, not just of hands but of face and eyes, and the rhythmic sway of hips ... synchronizes the body with the constant movement of the wind and waves. Values and meaning are found in the adornments of *lei* and costume where meaning is communicated in the choice of color and style and in the types of plants, shells, or other objects from which *lei* are woven. They are acknowledged in the protocols of respect that once accompanied every facet of hula, and they reverberate most powerfully in the sound and rhythm of the *ipu* and other implements and through the words and tones of the *mele*.[45]

The *'ike* movement portrayed by Reece is of ancient origins. It was part of the *hula* that was strictly governed by rules and protocols. Even today it is an exacting activity. The annual Merrie Monarch festival is a *hula* competition that has been held in Hawaii since 1963. The judges are often descendants of generations of *hula* teachers. It is structured as a "friendly exchange that replicates the competition of the nineteenth century."[46] The rules for *kahiko* (traditional) chants specify that the chant had to be composed before 1893. Small innovations are allowed in the movements, but the changes must be within the traditional framework in order to be acceptable.[47] The gestures and chants are viewed as a whole that tell a story and connect Hawaiians to their past as it informs their present.

---

43  Manulani Aluli Meyer, *Ho'oulu: Our Time of Becoming* (Honolulu: 'Ai Pohaku, 2003) at 93.

44  Rowe, *supra* note 42 at 39.

45  *Ibid.*

46  Teri Leigh Skillman, *The Merrie Monarch Festival in Hilo Hawai'i: Sovereign Spaces Reclaimed and Created through Hula Competition 1963–2010* (dissertation, University of Hawai'i, 2012) at 112, online: <https://scholarspace.manoa.hawaii.edu/server/api/core/bitstreams/33b8f74e-ec39-45b4-ab29-8a5bc06f967a/content>.

47  *Ibid* at 122.

The steps and gestures of *hula* are not simply parts of a choreographed performance as ballet positions, movements, and steps might be. *Hula* has a social and political context that Western dance forms such as ballet do not have.[48] Rowe pointed out that "the West has had a long tradition of appreciating both art and knowledge for their own sakes without regard to any pragmatic purpose."[49] The movements of *hula*, which always interpret a chant, are imbued with meaning and purpose. Today modern *hula* provides a political voice for Hawaiians. Jane C. Desmond observed that "even the [*hula*] shows at the Sheraton sometimes include a reference to sovereignty."[50]

Prior to the so-called Age of Enlightenment, European dance also held meaning in itself.[51] However, Cartesian rationalism "introduce[d] a methodical approach that was applied to all branches of knowledge, including artistic production and the training of artists."[52] Dance movement was separated into steps and movements that could be combined and mixed by a choreographer.[53] This illustrates an example of the genesis of the dichotomy of ideas and expression. Dance itself was no longer imbued with meaning: modern Western dance may carry a political message, but the story is conveyed by the characters. By contrast, there are no characters in *hula*. The story is told by the song and dance, and the entire performance makes up the holistic expression. Here is the key to the problem of the public domain in the *hula* case: the movements of traditional *hula* are not divisible into ideas and expression.

## Indigenous Rules and Protocol: The Law

In their reasons, the court appeared to understand the cultural significance of *hula* to Hawaiian society; but this was not enough to keep *hula* out of the public domain of Western copyright law. The problem was that the court did not consider the legal position of *hula* in Hawaiian law. All too often Indigenous legal principles are regarded as community or cultural principles, with the result that they cannot be treated

---

48  Rowe, *supra* note 42 at 36.

49  *Ibid.*

50  Jane C. Desmond, "Invoking 'the Native': Body Politics in Contemporary Hawaiian Tourist Shows" (1997) 41:4 TDR/The Drama Rev 83 at 103.

51  Rowe, *supra* note 42 at 34.

52  *Ibid.*

53  *Ibid* at 35.

seriously as "law" by Western courts.[54] In effect, these so-called cultural and community principles become invisible in a Western court of law.

In a similar scenario, Marie Hadley discussed the invisibility of Māori cultural appropriation in an American case about a Māori tattoo that pitted a non-Māori tattoo artist against Warner Bros. Entertainment.[55] The issue in the case centred on a facial tattoo designed by and tattooed on boxer Mike Tyson by tattoo artist S. Victor Whitmill. The tattoo was, according to Whitmill, an "American tribal tattoo inspired by some of the movement that you would see in a Māori piece."[56] Tyson signed a "Tattoo Release" document confirming Whitmill's copyright of the image. In 2003 Tyson's tattoo was unveiled to the public, and within a week the tattoo design was reported to be a misappropriation of Māori cultural tattoos.[57] Hadley reported that "Tyson's identity as a controversial public figure was initially objected to as much as the tattoo's composition as an unauthorised and illegitimate use of Māori culture."[58]

In 2011 Whitmill commenced a copyright infringement action against Warner Bros. Studios, alleging unauthorized use of his facial tattoo design by the studio in their *Hangover II* movie. The reaction from the Māori community in New Zealand was one of incredulity. Ngahuia Te Awekotuku, author of *Mau Moko: The World of Māori Tattoo*,[59] stated: "It is astounding that a *Pakeha* (non-Māori) tattooist who inscribes an African-American's flesh with what he considers to be a Māori design has the gall to claim … that design as his intellectual property."[60]

Even though Whitmill stated in 2003 that he was inspired by Māori design, and Tyson, in a 2008 documentary, spoke of the tattoo as representative of a "New Zealand warrior tribe called the Māori's,"[61] the

---

54  For example, see Val Napoleon & Hadley Friedland, "Indigenous Legal Traditions: Roots to Renaissance" in Markus D Dubber & Tatjana Hornle, eds, *The Oxford Handbook of Criminal Law* (Oxford: Oxford University Press, 2014) 225.

55  Marie Hadley, "Whitmill v Warner Bros. and the Visibility of Cultural Appropriation Claims in Copyright Law" (2020) 42:4 European Intellectual Property Rev 223.

56  Quoted in *ibid* at 224.

57  *Ibid* at 225.

58  *Ibid* at 224.

59  Ngahuia Te Awekotuku, *Mau Moko: The World of Māori Tattoo* (Auckland: Viking, 2007).

60  Leon Tan, "Intellectual Property Law and the Globalization of Indigenous Cultural Expressions: *Māori* Tattoo and the Whitmill versus Warner Bros. Case" (2013) 30:3 Theory, Culture & Society 61 at 66.

61  *Ibid* at 64.

court made no mention of the cultural origins of the tattoo. The court confirmed that Whitmill held a valid copyright to the design. There was no discussion of the fact that he had dipped into the public domain for inspiration, and then rendered a typical Māori facial tattoo on Mike Tyson's face. The defence did not raise the issue of the Māori design, and neither did the court. The Māori law that directed the appropriate usage of facial tattoos did not come up in the American courtroom. The economic basis of Western intellectual property law kept consideration of an intellectual property legal regime based in cultural and societal values outside the realm of legal argument.

As Indigenous intellectual property, the facial tattoos held meaning outside of the marketplace. Leon Tan explained: "The *moko* is not a surviving trace of an ancestral lineage at some other place and time, but belongs to an ancestral body *in the here and now*. The *moko* artist (*tohunga ta moko*) and those wearing the tattoos are but fragments of a real ancestral body, a historically individuated collective system of action, connected by blood, flesh, ink and memory."[62]

*Moko* artist Mark Kopua was consulted by New Zealand's Waitangi Tribunal, a commission of inquiry, on *ta moko*. He said:

> There is a need for regulation to prevent non-Māori who want to wear the moko as a fashion statement or to help sell records or magazines or branded apparel. This is because their motivation differs radically from those descendants of moko wearers in the past. I want a law that would prevent a Mike Tyson or a Robbie Williams or large non-Māori companies from wearing and exploiting the moko.[63]

These statements indicate that the historical, cultural, and societal knowledge in tattoo designs, like the *hula* movements, represent more than simply ideas that should be available in the public domain for commercial exploitation by anyone. They possess meaning and importance beyond their marketability. It is not always the case that this knowledge is sacred, or that its use is somehow forbidden. Rather, the unauthorized and uncontrolled commodification of this knowledge by those outside of the community is unacceptable to the Indigenous community, and, importantly, is contrary to existing Indigenous law.

In her critique of the *Reece* decision Danielle M. Conway noted the failure of the court to recognize Indigenous law. She suggested that

---

62  *Ibid* at 67.
63  *Ibid* at 66.

in this case the court "was presented with a case ripe for, at the very least, recognition of Indigenous rights and law" and "overlook[ed] an opportunity to acknowledge jurisprudence recognizing Native Hawaiian rights that are vital to protecting Native Hawaiian resources and intangible assets."[64] Conway pointed out that the decision did not allude to Hawaiian legal precedent that recognized "Hawai'i's constitutional mandate to protect traditional and customary Native Hawaiian rights."[65] She recognized that the earlier cases dealt with rights associated with land, but argued that those cases, along with the then recent adoption of UNDRIP, represented "strong, persuasive authority critically relevant to recognizing and protecting rights in Indigenous resources and intangible assets."[66]

Aside from the opening description of the place of *hula* in Hawaiian society (quoted above), the court did not allude to the fact that there may be some different legal considerations where Indigenous intellectual property is concerned. In contrast, Conway pointed to the language of the Supreme Court of Hawaii in a land case: "In order for [N]ative Hawaiian rights to be enforceable, an appropriate analytic framework for enforcement is needed. Such an analytic framework must endeavour to accommodate the competing interests of protecting [N]ative Hawaiian culture and rights, on the one hand, and economic development and security, on the other."[67]

Conway noted that this reasoning was not touched upon at all in the *hula* case. I suggest that the problem is that Western intellectual property law gives the court no legal basis upon which to consider the control or protection of Indigenous intellectual property where the rationale for control is not economic considerations. The balance of interests in the land cases mentioned by Conway comes easier. Interests in land are similar across different societies or peoples. They relate to occupation and use of resources. Recently, several jurisdictions[68] have upheld a different notion of a legal personality in rivers and mountains that recognizes legal difference in relationship to land, but at the end

---

64  Danielle M Conway, "Indigenizing Intellectual Property Law: Customary Law, Legal Pluralism, and the Protection of Indigenous Peoples' Rights, Identity, and Resources" (2009) 15 Tex Wesleyan L Rev 207 at 241.

65  *Ibid* at 242.

66  *Ibid* at 245.

67  *Ibid* at 242 citing *Ka Pu'akai o Ka'aina*, 7 P.3d at 1082.

68  For example, in 2014 the Te Urewera National Park in New Zealand was declared a legal entity; in 2017 Mount Taranaki in New Zealand was granted legal personality; in 2021 the Magpie River in Quebec, Canada, was legally recognized as a person.

of the day, these legal personalities can be rationalized by the courts as related to land and resource use. Conversely, when the courts consider Indigenous intellectual property within the confines of Western law, the balance or comparison with non-Indigenous interests is difficult. There may be no economic or legal overlap available in order to find a balancing of interests to lead to a solution. The starting point is different where there are important societal and cultural interests rather than market interests that underlie legal control of the proprietorial interests in intangible property.[69]

It should not be necessary to find analogies with Western law or to resort to a Western legal mandate in order to protect Indigenous knowledge when there are prevailing Indigenous legal rules and protocols already in place to govern access to and use of that knowledge, as is the case with both Hawaiian *hula* and Māori facial tattoos. This is the governing intellectual property law, which is applicable to all those who access the knowledge. It follows that Indigenous knowledge that is subject to rules and protocols of use must hold an important place in society. It must play a role other than mere decoration, activity, or sport. *Hula* exemplifies this notion, as its teaching and performance has always been controlled by protocols.

*Hula* is performed with *mele*, which is defined as Hawaiian poetry.[70] *Mele* comprise records containing social, political, and legal information, and can be in the form of prayers, name chants, love songs, and songs about the land.[71] There was a *mele* for every occasion: "prayers and prophecies for planting, fishing, building, etc.; name chants that lauded the chief and the heroic deeds of ancestors; genealogies; dirges; love songs; war poems; poems in derogation of an individual; and other topical poems for contest, clothing, etc."[72]

Specific *hula* training was given at the *hālau* (*hula* school). The Hawaiian king ordered the construction of the *hālau*, and during their training students were not allowed to go out of the school or have contact with anyone else.[73] The students' conduct was strictly regulated: they were

---

69 For an example of a different approach, see Fiona MacMillan, *Intellectual and Cultural Property: Between Market and Community* (Abingdon, UK: Routledge, Taylor & Francis, 2021).

70 Violet Lovelena Witt, *Aloha in the Desert: Ideologies of Ka'ōlelo hawaii'I a mēheuheu* (master's thesis, University of New Mexico, 2016) at 22, online: <https://digitalrepository.unm.edu/ling_etds/44>.

71 *Ibid.*

72 ES Craighill Handy et al, *Ancient Hawaiian Civilization* (Vermont: Charles E Tutte, 1965) at 204.

73 *Ibid* at 56.

required to maintain proper demeanour, practice sexual abstinence, and avoid specific foods and contacts.[74] There were songs and protocol for every step leading up to a performance, including gathering woodland decorations for the altar, celebrating graduation, and visiting the altar of the *halau*. Special songs accompanied the donning of each required article of the *hula* costume.[75]

Every facet of *hula* was part of an "organized, premeditated affair."[76] One could not just dance *hula* on a whim, for every step of the instruction was governed by strict rules and protocols. No mistakes were allowed, as errors were considered to be an ill omen: "Make a mistake in the *hula* during a solemn ritual performance, public shame – and the god's displeasure – followed.[77]

The practice of *hula* was interrupted in 1842 when Calvinist missionaries outlawed *hula* as a heathen practice. Plantation owners were happy to have *hula* regulated, as they recognized the centrality of *hula* to Hawaiian political structure and chiefly power.[78] Banning *hula* was seen as part of an effort to Europeanize Hawaiians.[79] The practice of *hula* moved underground at this time, but resurfaced with the reign of King David Kalakaua (1874–91), who invited *hula* practitioners to practise at the palace. After the overthrow of the Hawaiian monarchy in 1893 *hula* again declined. During the 1930s and 1940s the practice of *hula* shifted from a serious repository of Hawaiian history and culture to a commodified and sexualized dance form catering to Western audiences.[80] The "phony" Hawaiian music became a "symbol of Hawaiian culture in the minds of many and was incorporated into Waikiki stage shows."[81]

In the 1970s Hawaii underwent a cultural renaissance of sorts.[82] Hawaiian people sought to reclaim their societal/cultural expressions that had been re-invented in order to provide entertainment to tourists and movie goers. "The flowering of cultural practice occurred after

---

74  Nathaniel B Emerson, *Unwritten Literature of Hawaii: The Sacred Songs of the Hula* (Washington: Government Printing Office, 1909) at 12.

75  *Ibid* at 58.

76  *Ibid* at 10.

77  Kanahele, *supra* note 39 at 297.

78  Skillman, *supra* note 46 at 29.

79  *Ibid* at 30.

80  Witt, *supra* note 70 at 23.

81  George H Lewis, "Style in Revolt: Music, Social Protest, and the Hawaiian Cultural Renaissance" (Autumn 1987) 62:4 International Social Science Rev 168 at 172.

82  Widely referred to as the Hawaiian Renaissance.

decades of assimilation and Americanization."[83] There was a resurgence of interest in learning the Hawaiian language and in rediscovering Hawaiian music. The study and performance of *hula* became prominent once again. Students avoided Westernized *hula* in favour of the traditional *hula kahiko,* and senior masters who had been trained earlier in the century disseminated the repertoires they had maintained.[84] Skillman eloquently summed up the importance to the Hawaiians of returning to *hula*: "Who a people are as a corporately social entity is shaped by what they remember of the past, how they explain themselves into being, and how they generate historical narratives in order to memorialize who they are and their forbears are. For Hawaiians, the *hula* encodes and transmits key knowledge about the historical past through which they define themselves."[85]

## The Public Domain and Societal Harm

As discussed above, there are important reasons why *hula* should not be included in the public domain, and why the local law that governs access to *hula* should not be ignored by Western courts. These are not only theoretical concerns. There is real harm suffered by Indigenous societies when their Indigenous knowledge is appropriated and used without regard to local rules and protocols. It is worth repeating that the rationale behind Western intellectual property law is economic. One obtains a copyright so that they can produce and market a unique product. In Western law, copyright infringement can be adequately compensated financially.

The harms suffered by a society as a result of the misappropriation and/or misuse of Indigenous knowledge may be beyond the economic. In three well-known Australian cases, Indigenous Australians explained the harm suffered when Indigenous knowledge was shared without the proper rules and protocols in place. In each case, the harms go to the very heart of the local society.

The early case of *Foster and Others v Mountford and Rigby Ltd*[86] considered the publication and distribution of a book that contained details and pictures of secret ceremonies of Central Australian Aborigines.

---

83  Amy Ku'uleialoha Stillman, "Re-Membering the History of the Hawaiian Hula" in Jeannette Marie Mageo, ed, *Cultural Memory: Reconfiguring History and Identity in the Postcolonial Pacific* (Honolulu: University of Hawaii Press, 2001) 187 at 197.

84  *Ibid.*

85  *Ibid* at 187.

86  *Foster and Others v Mountford and Rigby Ltd* (1976) 14 ALR 71 (OL)

Anthropologist Mountford had obtained this information thirty-five years prior to the publication of his work, *Nomads of the Australian Desert*.[87] The Pitjantjatjara Council brought an action to prevent the distribution of the book in the Northern Territories. The court granted an injunction accepting the council's argument "that revelation of the secrets to their women, children and uninitiated men could undermine the social and religious stability of the community, a serious loss which would not be reparable by an award of damages."[88]

In *Yumbulul v Reserve Bank of Australia*,[89] the issue was the reproduction of the image of a Morning Star Pole on ten-dollar Australian bank notes. The Morning Star Pole in question was made by Australian Aboriginal artist Terry Yumbulul. He inherited the legal right to make the pole from his mother's clan group.[90] The poles played an important role in ceremonies commemorating the deaths of important persons, and in inter-clan relationships.[91] Yumbulul held an Australian copyright to this particular pole, and the reproduction of the pole was made pursuant to a sub-licence of the copyright to the bank granted by the Aboriginal Artists Agency Limited. Yumbulul had previously signed an exclusive licence agreement with this agency.

In an unsuccessful bid to have the licensing agreement declared invalid, the court heard from the senior members of the clan. A senior member of the Rirratjigu clan and a leader among Aboriginal people testified that some traditional objects such as the Morning Star Pole can be made for sale to a museum or craft shop because "it is important that white people learn to respect the Aboriginal people and their land."[92] However, he added that "the subject of mass reproduction of paintings and important objects is very sensitive because it takes the ability and right to produce and supervise the production of these objects out of the hands of the Aboriginal people."[93] Further, he specified that "objects such as the Morning Star Pole are only meant to be made in a sacred camp by men who have been properly taught the rules relating to their production. It is not right for such objects to be made by children,

---

87 Charles P Mountford, *Nomads of the Australian Desert* (Adelaide: Rigby, 1976).

88 Sue Bunting, "Limitations of Australian Copyright Law in the Protection of Indigenous Music and Culture" (Autumn 2000) 18 Context 15 at 19.

89 *Yumbulul v Reserve Bank of Australia, Aboriginal Artists Agency Ltd* [1991] FCA 448; 21 IPR 481.

90 *Ibid*, para 3.

91 *Ibid*, para 3.

92 *Ibid*, para 4.

93 *Ibid*.

women or men who do not understand their meaning and power and who have not been given the right to make such things."[94]

In *John Bulun Bulun &Anor v Nejlam Investments*[95] the case concerned the unauthorized reproduction of a painting by Ganalbingu artist Bulun Bulun. The painting depicted the place of creation of the Ganalbingu people. Bulun Bulun painted the dreaming stories of his clan, as his father had done. His father had taught him the traditional techniques of bark painting as well as the dreaming traditions and images of the clan.[96] In affidavit evidence, Bulun Bulun explained:

> My work is very closely associated with an affinity for the land. This affinity is at the essence of my religious beliefs. The unauthorized reproduction of artworks is a very sensitive issue in all Aboriginal communities. The impetus for the creation of works remains their importance in ceremony, and the creation of artworks is an important step in the preservation of important traditional customs. It is an activity which occupies the normal part of the day-to-day activities of the members of my tribe and represents an important part of the cultural continuity of the tribe.[97]

In this case, the Indigenous artist had earlier been successful in an Australian copyright infringement action. Here, the community sought declaratory relief from the court as "equitable owners" of the copyright. The court held that the artist had a fiduciary duty to his community to ensure that the artwork was not exploited in a way that was contrary to the laws and customs of his people, but that fell short of equitable ownership.

These three cases illustrate the existence of Indigenous law that controlled the making and/or use of knowledge or artwork that held knowledge. In each case there was evidence of existing protocols of creation as well as rules controlling the means of dissemination and the use of societal/cultural expressions. When the Indigenous law was not followed, the harms went beyond the economic.

As discussed above, *hula* also holds an important legal, social, and political position in Hawaiian society. Mass production of Indigenous knowledge for commercial gain ignores local laws, devalues and denigrates whole societies, and serves to disrupt the continuity of a peoples.

---

94  *Ibid.*

95  *Bulun Bulun v R&T Textiles Pty Ltd* (1998) 41 IPR 513.

96  *Bulun Bulun v Nejlam Investments*: Affidavit of Johny Bulun Bulun, undated [1989] Indig L Res 3.

97  *Ibid* at 7–8.

Hawaiians are familiar with the misappropriation of their Indigenous knowledge. Their songs and dance were famously appropriated and then adapted into new formats in order to attract tourism to the islands. Recently Walt Disney studios copyrighted the soundtrack of the animated movie *Lilo & Stitch*, and two of the songs were name chants, or *mele inoa*. These particular chants, sung by a cartoon character in the movie, were sacred chants that were once sung to honour King Kalakaua and Queen Lili'uokalani.[98] Here, there is disdain and a lack of respect shown for Hawaiian history and law.

The misappropriation of *hula* also has a more dangerous edge, as it perpetuates a colonial trope of Hawaiian women. Although Reece styled himself as someone who worked and studied to preserve *hula*, his posed photographs of young women and muscled men did a disservice to *hula* and Hawaiians. Andrea Marata Tamaira noted that Reece's models "promote a lusty sensuality to excite and titillate."[99] Further, "Reece draws unabashedly on the familiar trope of the 'Lovely Hula Girl': bare breasted, curvaceous hips swaying, adorned with head and neck garlands, dark tresses blowing in the wind, and gesturing hands aflutter or open wide in welcome."[100] In regard to Reece's photographic style, Tamaira pointed out a book called *How to Photograph Hawaii*[101] wherein Reece advised that creating an image of Hawaii "necessarily requires exotic glimpses of grass hula skirts, white sand, palm-fringed beaches and sultry little brown gals."[102] It appears that Reece was not using his art to promote and preserve the Hawaiian culture as he claimed, but rather to continue to profit from a colonial trope that objectified Hawaiian women. His stated simplistic view of Hawaiian culture and his one-dimensional *hula* of pretty pictures belies the important social, legal, and political role of *hula*. However, Reece was able to perpetuate his interpretation through his prolific artwork. Herein lies the problem with open access to Hawaiian intellectual property facilitated by its inclusion in the public domain. Hawaiians cannot control the narrative of their own society and social history.

---

98　Hayakawa & Ito, *supra* note 21 at 1495.

99　Andrea Marata Tamaira, *Envisioning Contemporary Kanaka Maoli Art in Hawai'i* (dissertation, Australian National University, 2015) at 57, online: <https://open-research-repository.anu.edu.au/bitstream/1885/13866/1/Tamaira%20Thesis%20 2015.pdf>.

100　*Ibid* at 57–8.

101　Robert Wenkam, *How to Photograph Hawaii* (Chicago: Rand McNally, 1973).

102　*Ibid* at 25.

Indeed, *hula* dancers and Hawaiian women have been stereotyped since the first Europeans to view *hula* objectified the female body in pictures and text.[103] Europeans viewed the performance of *hula* as entertainment, rather than as the value-laden ceremony it was. In the Euro-American culture, only so-called women of ill repute danced for entertainment, and the result of that erroneous assumption was devastating for *hula* dancers.[104] In the words of Amy Skillman, "The depiction of eroticism from the Western male's gaze has stereotyped female *hula* dancers and Hawaiian women for two centuries. It is precisely this gaze that has made contemporary photographers in Hawai'i such as Kim Taylor Reece successful in the global marketing of *hula* dancers' images in the guise of 'nostalgia' since 1983."[105] Lisa Kahaleole Hall explained that the *hula* trope has made Hawaiian women "hypervisible, while still unseen … through the sexualized marketing of the "hula girl" … turning a cultural form with sacred, political, and sexual dimensions into a kitsch spectacle."[106] The women in the images are never named, and become objectified in art and in life as the "ideal native."[107] The Indigenous law of *hula is* ignored, much to the detriment of Hawaiian women.

## Conclusion

The marketing of the "exotic" through the misappropriation and misrepresentation of Indigenous societal and cultural expressions is a problem faced by Indigenous societies the world over. Nicole MacDonald stated that "Māori are prepared to fight to protect their traditions, to hide them, if necessary, from the bored, fascinated eyes of a world hungry for the 'exotic.'"[108] As long as Indigenous art that contains societal/cultural expressions is relegated to the public domain, there is no Western legal mechanism available to Indigenous societies to control the external use and misuse of their intellectual property. Further, the rationale underlying the Western intellectual property model is

---

103  Skillman, *supra* note 46 at 3.

104  *Ibid* at 24.

105  *Ibid* at 26–7.

106  Lisa Kahaleole Hall, "Navigating Our Own 'Sea of Islands': Remapping a Theoretical Space for Hawaiian Women and Indigenous Feminism" (2009) 24:2 Wicazo Sa Rev 15 at 17.

107  Jane C. Desmond, *Staging Tourism: Bodies on Display from Waikiki to Sea World* (Chicago: University of Chicago Press, 1999) at 6.

108  In Hans Neleman, *Moko: Maori Tattoos* (Zurich: Edition Stemmle, 1999) at 11.

not necessarily relevant to intellectual property that is also valued for non-economic reasons. In the cases of Hawaiian *hula* and Māori tattoos, it was not only the appropriation of the Indigenous artforms that was troubling. It was also the sense of entitlement that the non-Indigenous parties exhibited towards their use of Indigenous intellectual property. Granted, the Western law of the public domain was on their side.

Western law courts are ill suited to the task of controlling access to and use of Indigenous societal and cultural expressions. And why should they be asked to do so? There are existing Indigenous legal orders that control access to Indigenous intellectual property. That is not to say that the rules and protocols that once controlled access to *hula* could be perfectly reinstated. That is impossible given the societal and governance changes that have altered Hawaiian societies. However, legal systems are responsive to change. The Western regime of intellectual property law did not arise organically, but was devised in order to economically reward creativity, invention, and innovation. Indigenous legal systems can also respond to the threat of unauthorized use of their intellectual property through Indigenous legal means. Importantly, there must be universal recognition of the proprietary interest that Indigenous societies hold in their cultural and societal expressions, which is well evidenced by the long-standing rules and protocols that governed (and still may govern) their use. Here is the starting point for the development of an Indigenous legal means to control intellectual property.

Noenoe K. Silva[109] bemoans the fact that first missionaries and then colonialism changed foreigners' perception of *hula* in Hawaii. A "solemn, religious, yet entertaining *hula*" became viewed as a "*hula* danced by women for money as entertainment for men."[110] Silva describes *hula* as it was once performed before it was disrupted by missionaries as "protocol and entertainment."[111] Importantly, it was never performed for the exchange of goods or the titillation of men.[112] In the world of the stories told by *hula*, women have agency and power.[113] The misinterpretation of *hula* has disempowered and misrepresented women not only in the *hula* stories, but also in modern Hawaiian life.

---

109 Noenoe K Silva, "Talking Back to Law and Empire: Hula in Hawaiian-Language Literature in 1861" in Sally Engle Merry & Donald Brennies, eds., *Law and Empire in the Pacific: Fiji and Hawaii* (Santa Fe: SAR, 2004) 101 at 110.
110 *Ibid*
111 *Ibid* at 119.
112 *Ibid*.
113 *Ibid* at 120.

The basis of intellectual property law concerns the control of proprietary knowledge. Given the rules and protocol that surrounded the performance of *hula*, there is a clear indication of existing property rights in that knowledge. Hawaiian peoples lost control of the use and interpretation of *hula* when they were overtaken by European powers who did not respect the existence of Hawaiian laws. The results have been devastating, particularly for women. The Reece case discussed above illustrates the difficulty of rectifying the situation through the application of Western legal principles. The constructed public domain acts as a repository for Indigenous societal/cultural expressions because they fit within the Western legal notion of "ideas." The way to the development of a viable Indigenous intellectual property legal regime is to look to the existing Indigenous legal system as a starting point. In this way, control of the use of Indigenous intellectual property can remain in the hands of those who know its true history, meaning, and significance, and control may be exercised in the context of that knowledge.

## BIBLIOGRAPHY


Bunting, Sue. "Limitations of Australian Copyright Law in the Protection of Indigenous Music and Culture" (Autumn 2000) 18 Context 15.

Busuttil, Diane. "Choreographic Authorship Using Two Case Studies: Anne Teresa De Keersmaeker v Beyonce and Ann Van den Broed and Figgis" (2015) Macquarie University, Sydney, online: <https://shorturl.at/zJN13>.

Chandra, Rajshree. *Knowledge as Property: Issues in the Moral Grounding of Intellectual Property Rights* (New Delhi: Oxford University Press, 2010).

Conway, Danielle M. "Indigenizing Intellectual Property Law: Customary Law, Legal Pluralism, and the Protection of Indigenous Peoples' Rights, Identity, and Resources" (2009) 15 Tex Wesleyan L Rev 207.

Dagan, Hanoch. "Property and the Public Domain" (2013) 18 Yale J L & Human 84.

Desmond, Jane C. "Invoking 'the Native': Body Politics in Contemporary Hawaiian Tourist Shows" (1997) 41(4) TDR/The Drama Rev 83.

Desmond, Jane C. *Staging Tourism: Bodies on Display from Waikiki to Sea World* (Chicago: University of Chicago Press, 1999).

Drassinower, Abraham. "A Rights-Based View of the Idea/Expression Dichotomy in Copyright Law" (2003) 16 Can J L & Jurisprudence 3.

Emerson, Nathaniel B. *Unwritten Literature of Hawaii: The Sacred Songs of the Hula* (Washington: Government Printing Office, 1909).

Hadley, Marie. "Whitmill v Warner Bros. and the Visibility of Cultural Appropriation Claims in Copyright Law" (2020) 42:4 European Intellectual Property Rev 223.

Hall, Lisa Kahaleole. "Navigating Our Own 'Sea of Islands': Remapping a Theoretical Space for Hawaiian Women and Indigenous Feminism" (2009) 24:2 Wicazo Sa Review 15.

Handy, ES. Craighill et al. *Ancient Hawaiian Civilization* (Clarendon, VT: Charles E Tuttle, 1965).

Hayakawa, Kazuya & Yasunobu Ito. "Diversity of Reactions among Local People upon Commercialization of Traditional Knowledge under Intellectual Property Rights Systems" (2016) Proceedings of PECMET'16: Technology Management for Social Innovation 1495, online: <http:// www.picmet.org/db/member/proceedings/2016/data/polopoly_fs /1.3251286.1472157486!/fileserver/file/680779/filename/16A0025.pdf>.

Henderson, James [Sa'ke'j] Youngblood. "The Indigenous Domain and Intellectual Property Rights" (2021) 4:2 Lakehead L J 93.

Kanahele, George Hu'eu Sanford. *Kū Kanaka Stand Tall: A Search for Hawaiian Values* (Honolulu: University of Hawaii Press, 1986).

Lewis, George H. "Style in Revolt: Music, Social Protest, and the Hawaiian Cultural Renaissance" (Autumn 1987) 62:4 International Social Science Rev 168.

MacMillan, Fiona. *Intellectual and Cultural Property: Between Market and Community* (Abingdon, UK: Routledge, Taylor & Francis, 2021).

Mazurek, Carl. "Through the Looking Glass: Photography and the Idea /Expression Dichotomy" (2017) J of Intellectual Property and Entertainment L 278.

Meyer, Manulani Aluli. *Ho'oulu: Our Time of Becoming* (Honolulu: 'Ai Pohaku, 2003).

Mountford, Charles P. *Nomads of the Australian Desert* (Adelaide: Rigby, 1976).

Napoleon, Val & Hadley Friedland. "Indigenous Legal Traditions: Roots to Renaissance" in Markus D Dubber & Tatjana Hornle, eds, *The Oxford Handbook of Criminal Law* (Oxford: Oxford University Press, 2014) 225.

Neleman, Hans. *Moko: Maori Tattoos* (Zurich: Edition Stemmle, 1999).

Rowe, Sharon Mahealani. "We Dance for Knowledge" (2008) Dance Research J 31.

Samuels, Edward. "The Idea-Expression Dichotomy in Copyright Law" (1988–89) 56 Tenn L R 321.

Schutz, Marisa C. "Is *Gray v Perry* the One That Got Away? The Idea-expression Dichotomy and Music Copyright Infringement" (2020–2021) 20 UIC Rev Intell Prop L 290.

Shin, Joann. "Art or Copyright Infringement?" Hawaii News Now (3 November 2006), online: <http://www.hawaiinewsnow.com/story/5628631/art -or-copyright-infringement>.

Silva, Noenoe K. "Talking Back to Law and Empire: Hula in Hawaiian-Language Literature in 1861" in Sally Engle Merry & Donald Brennies, eds, *Law and Empire in the Pacific: Fiji and Hawaii* (Santa Fe: SAR, 2004) 101.

Skillman, Teri Leigh. *The Merrie Monarch Festival in Hilo Hawai'i: Sovereign Spaces Reclaimed and Created through Hula Competition 1963–2010* (dissertation., University of Hawai'i, 2012) [unpublished].

Stillman, Amy Ku'uleialoha. "Re-Membering the History of the Hawaiian Hula" in Jeannette Marie Mageo, ed, *Cultural Memory: Reconfiguring History and Identity in the Postcolonial Pacific* (Honolulu: University of Hawaii Press, 2001) 187.

Strathern, Marilyn. "Intellectual Property and Rights: An Anthropological Perspective" in Christopher Tilley, Webb Keane & Susanne Kuechler-Fogden, eds, *Handbook of Material Culture* (London: Sage, 2006) 447.

Tamaira, Andrea Marata. *Envisioning Contemporary Kanaka Maoli Art in Hawai'i* (dissertation, Australian National University, 2015).

Tan, Leon. "Intellectual Property Law and the Globalization of Indigenous Cultural Expressions: *Māori* Tattoo and the Whitmill versus Warner Bros. Case" (2013) 30:3 Theory, Culture & Society 61.

Te Awekotuku, Ngahuia. *Mau Moko: The World of Māori Tattoo* (Auckland: Viking, 2007).

Uchiyama, Māhelaani. *The Haumāna Hula Handbook for Students of Hawaiian Dance* (Berkeley: North Atlantic Books, 2016).

Wenkam, Robert. *How to Photograph Hawaii* (Chicago: Rand McNally, 1973).

Witt, Violet Lovelena. *Aloha in the Desert: Ideologies of Ka'ōlelo hawaii'I a mēheuheu* (master's thesis, University of New Mexico, 2016).

## LEGISLATION CITED

*Copyright Act*, RSC 1985, c C-42.

*Industrial Design Act*, RSC 1985.

*Patent Act*, RSC 1985, c P-4.

*Trademarks Act*, RSC 1985, c T-13.

**Jurisprudence Cited**

*Bulun Bulun* v *R&T Textiles Pty Ltd* (1998) 41 IPR 513.

*Foster and Others v Mountford and Rigby Ltd* (1976) 14 ALR 71 (OL).

*Lawson v Dundas* [1985] The Times 13 (Eng Ch Div).

*Reece v Island Treasures Art Gallery, Inc* (2006), 468 F Supp 2d 1197 (D Hawai'i).

*Whitmill v Warner Bros Entertainment* (ED Mo, no. 4:11-CV-752m complaint dismissed 22 June 2011).

*Yumbulul v Reserve Bank of Australia, Aboriginal Artists Agency Ltd* [1991] FCA 448; 21 IPR 481.

# 5 Conversational Flows: Indigenous Intellectual Property in the Law School Lounge

REBECCA JOHNSON

This chapter explores the interface of a number of complicated questions that have emerged in conversations with colleagues and friends about the concepts of intellectual property and cultural property, in the context of both Western and various Indigenous legal orders. These questions take us into the realm of tangibles and intangibles, as well as different structures of valuing intellectual property (IP). They also invite conversations about identifying IP-related harms in the world around us, and about the kinds of remedies that might be appropriate in a world where ideas have value and we encounter disputes around how those ideas are used, shared, and controlled. In what follows, I draw on an IP conflict that emerged in British Columbia in 2013, involving a pair of Hupacasath masks. I imagine a set of conversations occurring in the law school lounge as first- and upper-year students grapple with the questions raised by the case.[1]

***

[Setting: the student lounge on the main floor of the law school.[2] A glass wall opens out to a courtyard, hedged by towering trees. It is a late fall day, and leaves lie on the ground, occasionally scooped up by a lazy

---

1 I take influence here from Val Napoleon, "Indigenous Women Talking: The Work of Indigenous Feminisms in the World" in *Critical Indigenous Feminisms*, ed Emily Snyder et al (Toronto: University of Toronto Press, forthcoming), online: https://ilru.ca/wp-content/uploads/2020/08/Napoleon-Indigenous-Women-Talking-0072.pdf. That work is influenced in turn by Miriam Toews's novel *Women Talking* (Toronto: Alfred A. Knopf, 2018).

2 Gillian Calder notes that the student lounge is often a site of both rich conversation and ongoing harm. See Calder, "Embodied Law: Theatre of the Oppressed in the Law School Classroom" (2009) 1 Masks: Online J of Law and Theatre 1.

breeze. Students sit in groups, and a low buzz of conversation hums as students move in and out of the space.]

Evie and Dawn, two first-year students, enter the lounge, still in conversation about their criminal law class. They join the queue at the snack bar and grab cups of coffee. They see Ami and Shiloh, their upper-year "law buddies," sitting at a table near the window. Shiloh also notices the pair of first-year students and beckons them over.

Evie rolls her shoulders as she sits down. "Wow. Crim law. My head is feeling fuzzy from class today. I'm just not sure what to make of that masks case."

Ami raises an eyebrow, curious. "Masks? I don't remember a masks case from first year crim. What kind of masks are we talking about here?"

Evie pulls out her laptop, brings up a newspaper article, and reads out the headline: "BC families search for sacred cedar masks sold at auction."[3]

She turns the screen to face Ami, who pulls the laptop closer and looks at the screen. The article opens with a black and white photo of a young Indigenous dancer with a large headdress in the shape of a sea serpent attached to their head. The young person, face painted and staring directly at the camera, is standing against the backdrop of a painted screen portraying a coiled sea serpent, posed so that the head-dress almost appears to emerge from the screen itself.

"Cool photo," says Ami. "I like seeing the mask actually on a person's head. You usually get photos of masks that look like they are in a museum or gallery. Interesting to see the mask in action! It says here this photo was taken in 2006 at a memorial feast in Port Alberni, where the mask was last danced."

He slides the laptop back to Evie. "So," he continues, "you are talking Indigenous masks and dances in crim law?! I'm intrigued. What happened in class? How did this mask question come up?"

"Well," she said, "we were looking at two different crimes: theft, and possession of stolen goods. We were talking about the differences between actually "stealing" something and "having" something in your possession that is stolen. The focus was on what it is that makes either of these things a crime. Basically, the point was related to knowledge and intent: having both *mens rea* and doing the *actus reus*. You know the routine."

---

3   Keven Drews, "B.C. Families Search for Sacred Cedar Masks Sold at Auction," *Globe and Mail* (29 November 2012), online: <https://www.theglobeandmail.com/news /british-columbia/bc-families-search-for-sacred-cedar-masks-sold-at-auction /article5789775/> [Drews, "BC Families"].

Dawn grins while slowly walking her fingers across the table to Ami's phone, and starts sliding it towards herself. "Like if I *accidentally* pick up your phone and walk away with it, thinking it is mine, then that is not theft …"

Ami raises an eyebrow, places his hand on top of his phone, and slides it back to his side of the table.

Dawn shrugs, and continues: "If I buy something from the pawn shop at the corner, and it turns out to have been stolen, but I didn't 'know' that it was stolen, then I'm not guilty of being in possession of stolen goods. You know, stuff like that. People were raising all sorts of hypothetical examples. What if, for example, you intend to steal your neighbour's umbrella, but accidentally end up taking your own? Is it still theft?"

Craig, an upper-year student sitting at the next table, rolls his eyes and gives an exasperated huff. "Why do our profs waste time talking hypotheticals instead of taking on the elephant in the room? Why are we talking about stolen umbrellas instead of stolen land? If she's gonna talk about possession of stolen property, why not talk about what it means for people today to argue that they 'own' land in this province?"[4]

Shiloh turns to the side with a smile, acknowledging her friend, "Hi Craig!" She turns back to the table, saying, "Introductions are in order. Evie and Dawn, I'm not sure if you know Craig yet? Craig and I were in legal process class together in first year. He's Wet'suwet'en, and has family who were deeply involved with the Unist'oten land defence camp. It was pretty tough. We've had lots of conversations about which laws get enforced and which ones don't."[5]

Craig nods at the first-years. Shiloh shifts her chair to the side and draws him into the conversation. "While I can see that your hearing superpowers seem intact, why don't you join us? We're talking about what the first-years did in class today." Craig shrugs and pulls his chair over to their table.

Evie returns to the story. "Actually, Craig's question about stolen land has been bumping around in my head since we had that talk on

---

<ol start="4">
<li>Shiri Pasternak & Nadine Scott Dayna, "Introduction: Getting Back the Land" (2020) 119:2 South Atlantic Quarterly 205. See also Nicholas Xemtoltw Claxton & John Price, "Whose Land Is It? Rethinking Sovereignty in British Columbia" (2019–20) 204 BC Studies 125.</li>
<li>Irina Ceric, "Beyond Contempt: Injunctions, Land Defense, and the Criminalization of Indigenous Resistance" (2020) 119:2 South Atlantic Quarterly 353. See also Val Napoleon, "Behind the Blockade" (2010) 9:1 Indigenous L J 1.</li>
</ol>

the Douglas Treaties in our property law class.[6] And then today, while we were trying to figure out the differences between theft and possession, the prof invited us to think about something more concrete. Basically, she told us about these carved masks belonging to an Indigenous family here on Vancouver Island. One of the younger family members took the masks and sold them to an auction house. Some community member had been scanning the web, and recognized the masks listed for sale on the auction company's website. They told the family, who then tried to get the auction house to stop the sale. But the auction house wouldn't, and so the masks were sold to an anonymous buyer for something like $25,000."

"Actually," says Dawn, scrolling down on her phone, "The report said it was $22,500 for the male mask, and $4,000 for the female mask."[7]

"What?!" says Shiloh.

"I know, eh?" Dawn grimaces, "A piece of me wants to talk about the differential valuing of the male and female masks, and maybe also about what makes a mask 'male' or 'female' in the first place, but maybe that can wait for another day. Let me just read you a bit from the news article on the case itself:

> For the Hamilton and Sayers families, the two cedar masks depicting male and female serpents and known as hinkeets to the Hupacasath culture of Vancouver Island were among the most sacred of possessions. Accompanied by shawls and even a specific dance, the masks were born of royal roots and for more than 100 years had been passed down the generations for their safe keeping – until they were sold unbeknownst to family members at an auction at the beginning of November. The families say one of their own, a relation entrusted with their safe keeping, was behind the sale, and now they're pleading for whomever may have bought them for a chance to negotiate their return. The family member responsible for the masks was out of the country and could not be reached for comment."

Dawn pauses, and Evie picks the story back up. "The prof then asked us to think about all the wrongdoing in the story. What can be said about the woman who took the mask to the auction company? Is it theft? Or

---

6  Peter Cook et al, eds, *To Share, Not Surrender: Indigenous and Settler Visions of Treaty Making in the Colonies of Vancouver Island and British Columbia* (Vancouver: UBC Press, 2021).

7  Drews, "BC families," *supra* note 3.

some fraud in her telling them that she had the right to sell the mask when she didn't? What about the auction company and the person who eventually bought the mask? Were they in possession of stolen goods?"

"So, was anyone charged with a crime in this case?" Craig asks.

"No," Evie replies. "The auction company claimed that the person who gave them the mask also showed them a will saying that this person had been left all of her grandmother's 'household possessions.' I guess that included the masks. That is why the auction company refused to call off the sale. The mask was sold to an anonymous buyer, and that was that."

Ami tilts his head. "So, just stop there. The auction firm saw a copy of the will? If there was a will, then the sale was lawful, and it can't really be crime, so why are you talking about this case in criminal law? If anything, its sounds like a family fight that belongs in a wills and estates class, or maybe in a property class?"

Evie furrows her brow, and rolls her shoulders again. "I am told that this is how generations of students have learned law, but I've gotta say that it's confusing trying to figure what kind of legal problem you are dealing with. What *is* the difference between a crim law and a property law question and a wills and estates question anyways?!"

Dawn picks up the thread. "You are not alone in asking the question, Ami. Do you know our classmate Karen, or 'IKEA' for short?"

Evie added, "IKEA is shorthand for 'I Know Everything Already.' Maybe you've got someone like that in your year? Anyway, our increasingly vocal classmate piped up in class to tell the prof that the story already got mentioned in her section of property law, and so she didn't know why the prof was talking about it in crim law."

Dawn interjects, adopting a somewhat cranky voice: "And this isn't going to be on the exam, right?"

Evie gives a bit of a sigh, and continues, "It's not that I think questions can't be asked, but I am irritated by how often she challenges the prof about what we are supposed to be learning. Like, she thinks the rest of us don't notice that she doesn't act like that with our male professors?"

Shiloh laughs. "Gender dynamics, my friend. Power dynamics are part of the field and something that needs taking up in so many contexts. But tell me more. What did the prof say?"

"Well," says Dawn, flipping out her notebook and reading off a list, "the prof said that categories of thought were exactly what we should be thinking about. This is in fact a case that you could study in property, tort law, contracts, criminal law, evidence, remedies, conflicts, and more. Part of the difficulty, she said, is that the design of legal education can sometimes leave us believing that law exists in silos. She cautioned us to avoid getting constrained by our own habits of thought about law."[8]

Dawn stops and looks up. "I like her phrase, habits of thought." She drops her eyes back to her notebook. "The professor also said that, and I quote [she continues reading, but adopting a lofty and sonorous tone of voice], "In learning law in these times, we have to continually stop to ask about the scaffolding that supports our understanding of law. And we must remember that the scaffold is often internalized." She pauses and laughs. "Whatever that means!"

She returns to her notes and continues. "The prof told us that this case tells quite a bit about the auction house, and about its ideas about property ownership, and about criminal law. Those ideas, she said, are based on their beliefs about Canadian property law and Canadian criminal law. She told us that, particularly when asking about a Hupacasath mask, we should be asking what Hupacasath law might say about this problem. We needed to ask questions about our own assumptions about what it is 'to own' something, or to take something that doesn't belong to you, and about what kinds of remedies are possible when something has been taken."

Evie picks up the thread, "Basically, she reminded us that we live in a multi-juridical Canada, so we need to spend a bit longer thinking about how the questions and answers might shift depending on the legal regimes, traditions, and orders that we draw upon. She told us that this case is a good one for thinking about complications and entanglements between Indigenous legal orders and the Canadian common law system. So, she told us to think about this mask using both Canadian law and Hupacasath law. And then she gave us a list of questions to look at over the weekend."

Dawn lets out a huff of air and rolls her eyes. "As usual, she gives us more questions and no answers.[9] I ask you, would it be so hard to just give us a *few* answers?!"

Ami sniggers. "Yep, she does that all the time! OK. So out with it. What were the questions?"

Evie looks back at her notebook. "Well. She said that we should be at least thinking about how this case makes sense from the perspective

---

8   There are many ongoing conversations about the challenges of teaching in ways that don't reinforce those silos.

9   Rebecca Johnson, "Questions about Questions: Law and Film Reflections on the Duty to Learn" (2020) 50 Northern Review 83.

of Hupacasath law. She said we should be asking at least five different questions:[10]

1  What kind of property is this?
2  Who is the owner?
3  What is the underlying purpose of the property?
4  What is the legal harm or injury?
5  What are the range of historic and present-day remedies?

In class, the prof told us that if we think only through the common law, it is easy to presume that one person has the authority over what happens to the mask. But this needn't be the same in Hupacasath law."

"Yikes," says Ami. "I have to say that the questions make me nervous, since I don't know very much about Hupacasath law."

Dawn cracks a smile. "Karen raised that in class, and the prof reminded her that we are only a few months into law school, and that we don't know much about Canadian law either!"

Shiloh grins back. "I gotta say that certainly feels right!" Shifting in her seat, she adds, "I take comfort in those reminders that the goal isn't to know things, but to begin learning how to learn."

Craig, nodding slowly says, "Well, that means getting comfortable with discomfort. It means taking seriously that we live in a country that has multiple legal traditions at play when dealing with almost any legal issue."

Shiloh, who had pulled up the news account on her phone and was scrolling through it, says in surprise, "Get out! This story has a local connection. I think the Sayers family here includes Dr. Judith Sayers! She gave a guest lecture in our business associations class on some run-of-river project up near Port Alberni, and we did get a bit of background on the Hupacasath. The Hupacasath are part of the Nu-chah-nulth legal order, right?" She looks over to the coffee line-up and says, "Hey, there's Lauren! She is in my IP class and friends with Dr. Sayers. I'm pretty sure she will know more about this case. You guys shift over and make space!" She jumps up, strolls over to the line-up, and starts chatting animatedly with an older woman.

Dawn raises an eyebrow. Ami plows in, "Lauren's in third year. She started law school after her kids were all grown and having their own

___________

10  See the introductory chapter in this volume. See also Val Napoleon et al, *An Interrupted Intergenerational Conversation: Indigenous Art and Society/Cultural Expression* (Victoria: Indigenous Law Research Unit, 2021) at 8.

kids. She was a serious activist in her younger days, and is bit of a radical grandmother to lots of people. I think she's Kwakwaka'wakw."

Lauren comes over to the table, setting her books and coffee down and reaching into her knapsack for a lunch bag. She pulls out a couple of apples and a well-used Swiss Army knife, and starts coring the fruit. "So, Shiloh says you guys are looking at the stolen hinkeets case in criminal law? I would love to hear what you are thinking about the problem."

Evie glances down at her notes again. "Well, the first and second questions seem a bit tangled to me: what kind of property is it, and who is the owner? The conflict here is over ownership. According to the woman who sold it, she was the owner because her grandmother left the masks to her in her will. At least, that is, if you think that masks like these belong to the category of 'household possessions.'"

Lauren smiles, placing sections of cut apple on a napkin in the middle of the table. "'Household possessions' is such an interesting term, isn't it? Have a slice of apple." She thoughtfully folds the knife back on itself, and returns it to her knapsack. "It makes you think of something you would use in your kitchen, or something you might use to decorate your living room."

"Exactly!" Evie says. "And the newspaper article emphasized that. The family said that the masks were cultural property, and not household possessions. They said the masks were sacred. The prof told us that some masks aren't just like 'art pieces,' but also have intangibles attached to them."

Dawn pipes up, "As you might imagine, at this point, I was thinkin' my brain was gonna liquefy and pour out my ear. Cultural property? Intangibles? I don't even know what she means. Anyways, she tells us that these masks also have songs and dances that go with them. And of course, at the same time she is talking, I can hear Karen still muttering away behind me that this is obviously just a family fight, or an intellectual property problem and not a crim law problem."

Lauren smiles. "It sounds like different people are thinking about different aspects of the problem. The distinction between private law and public law can be helpful, but also make it tricky. In the Canadian legal system, criminal law is used for harms to the public. So, one might ask what kind of harm there was in the selling of this mask. And to know what kind of harm it was, you still need to have a sense of what kind of property it was. A mask like this needs to be understood as part of a legal order in which the potlach was an important piece of public ceremony."

Lauren pauses, looking out the window at some leaves caught in a small gust of wind, and then continues. "I'm not sure how much background you two have on the potlach. Have you taken it up in criminal law class yet?"

Evie nods. "Well, just a bit. Basically, that the potlach was a crime from 1885 to 1951."

Ami adds, "I did my undergrad in anthropology, and there is so much stuff written from an anthropological perspective about potlach.[11] We did learn that there were many different kinds of potlach ceremonies, and they could mark different kinds of legally important events: naming ceremonies, passing of chieftainships, marriages, memorials. They took significant preparation, could continue for days, and would involve dances and songs from both the hosting nation or family and others who were invited. They would conclude with the giving of gifts to all who were in attendance. Sir John A. referred to them as Indian festivals of debauchery.[12] People who held potlach ceremonies were given mandatory jail sentences, and masks and regalia were confiscated by the state."

Craig jumps in: "Debauchery?! And this from the man who introduced both the Chinese head tax and the Indian residential schools as a program for nation-wide assimilation?! Man, if that isn't the pot calling the kettle black! Basically, it is one state criminalizing the legal institutions of another state!"

Lauren picks up another slice of apple and says, "You could think of potlach as a kind of institutional structure within the legal cultures of the West Coast, many of which are structured through a nuanced and sophisticated gift economy. The masks and dances are part of the process of publicly validating the legal events occurring at those ceremonies. A mask like this would have songs and dances associated with it. Different songs or dances would be associated with events like marriages, naming ceremonies, memorial potlaches, and more. They would have been part of the processes through which legally important activities were publicly affirmed."

Shiloh says, "So, if I hear you right, the important point is that masks like these are not just beautiful objects, but are associated with legal proceedings? So, you are saying that when we see them, the word 'law' should actually come to mind."

Lauren continues. "Sometimes. Not all masks function as law. But sometimes they do. It has been easy for the general Canadian

---

11   Christopher Bracken, *The Potlatch Papers: A Colonial Case History* (Chicago: University of Chicago Press, 1997).

12   Sir John A MacDonald (1894). For a fact sheet of quotes, see <https://educ.queensu.ca/sites/educwww/files/uploaded_files/JAM%20Fact%20Sheet.pdf>. For background, history, and a showcase of Potlatch culture, see <https://potlatch6767.com/>.

population to think about the masks primarily as art because so many of these masks, regalia, and other objects ended up in museums and private collections when they were confiscated, or forfeited, or sold in the years when everything associated with potlach was made a crime. You sometimes hear people talk about these masks as if they are remnants of a vanished past, but that is not a helpful view. Potlaches definitely moved underground during the years of criminalization, but the practices continued.[13] People in community continue to organize potlach ceremonies for important legal events. During the pandemic, we even saw people adapting by moving some ceremonies online."[14]

Dawn nods. "And I guess that explains the present, since museums and private collections around the world are full of objects forfeited during the years of the ban."

Evie adds, "So maybe it's unsurprising that there's been the development of a market for West Coast art. And I wonder if this idea of the masks as former legal objects contributes to their current value in the art world? Do you think that makes them more valuable objects to trade?'

Ami picks up another slice of apple and says, "But that photo in the paper was from a potlach in 2006, right? People were still dancing this specific mask at contemporary potlach ceremonies? So then the masks, the songs, and the dances were still doing the work of law?"

He pauses, looking out the window, then continues: "What a story. To be honest, I can't believe the sister sold the masks. It does feel like theft."

The group sits quietly for a moment, listening to the swirl of conversation in the room around them. Evie says, "I think I feel that way too, Craig. It makes me think about the question of the injury. The selling of the mask seems obviously wrong."

She looks back to her open laptop, scrolling down through the article. "So, they quote her brother about the masks. He says:

> They are not chattel to be bought and sold; they are our family histories over thousands of years, and our place within Hupacasath and Nuu-chah-nulth

---

13   For a visual introduction to Potlatch, see <https://umistapotlatch.ca/potlatch-eng.php>. See also resources from the Bill Reid museum at Simon Fraser University: <https://www.sfu.ca/brc/our-work/multimedia.html#potlatch>.

14   Ren "Wikinanish" Louie, "Persistent to Potlatch: The Continuity of Nuu-Chah-Nulth Potlatches through Covid-19," *Martlet* (1 February 2021), online: <https://www.martlet.ca/potlach-nuu-chah-nulth-covid-19/>.

culture … If you were to even hint at the idea of selling those masks, my mother would have slapped the taste right out of your mouth."[15]

Dawn leans back and sighs. "OK. I am all opposed to violence yada yada yada, but I like how he put that. It sounds like the family members understood pretty clearly the significance of the masks. It says in the paper that their sister sold the masks without telling anyone, took the money, and then left the country with her boyfriend. Obviously she knew that what she did was wrong."

Again, Craig shakes his head. "And so we just circle back to the beginning. Wrong according to whose law? It is like Canadian law still can't *see* Hupacasath law. Or is it *pretending* not to see it? I don't get how the auction company, or the police, or the government can just rely on a narrow interpretation of 'household possessions' in order to dispossess a group of people of their cultural heritage. It is like they are totally ignoring the cultural value of the masks."

"Can we stop for a minute?" Dawn asked. "I still don't really get why we are using the word 'cultural.' I mean, if we are saying the mask does the work of law, then why aren't we talking about its legal value? Or is talking about cultural value just a way of saying that the mask has non-market value?"

Lauren says, "This brings us back to those 'habits of thought' you mentioned, Dawn. One habit here is the treatment of the mask as only a thing of beauty, without seeing the intellectual property in it, the 'IP.' The mask *means* something, and it *does* something. There will certainly be stewards for masks like these, and maybe the word 'steward' is richer than the word 'owner,' but it is certainly the case that the use of the mask is *controlled* by those who have authority to make decisions about its use. IP, even in the West, is not just about the protection of ideas. It is also about who 'controls' the use of that intellectual property. This is perhaps an even bigger problem where the value of the IP leans in the direction of something that we might call the sacred. The Western habit of separating reason and emotion sometimes stumbles with intangible cultural and societal expressions that operate on a spiritual level."

Craig jumps in again. "Even raising language about the sacred or spiritual gets you in trouble. The Western legal system prioritizes 'the rational' and mocks what it doesn't understand, treating it as

---

15   David Wiwchar, "Sacred First Nation Masks Sold to Highest Bidder," *Indian Country Today* (10 December 2012), online: <https://ictnews.org/archive/sacred-first -nation-masks-sold-to-highest-bidder>.

unsophisticated or primitive. Many of these masks and dances are part of a sophisticated intellectual tradition that links the past, present, and future together in different ways. Focusing on the mask as just a piece of art to be bought and sold means Indigenous peoples are denied the right to control the ways we gather and organize our own knowledge. Or, for it to make sense, we are required to talk about the spiritual values in our knowledge using Western terms like 'epistemology' and 'ontology.' The system treats us like a vanishing vulnerable population, at best, offering to protect a limited number of our artefacts like some collection of dinosaur bones from the past!"

Dawn points to her laptop again. "OK. What about the question of remedies? The prof asked us if the way we describe the harm shapes the kinds of remedies we can imagine. So, can we talk more about terminology here? I heard you say both 'cultural heritage' and 'intellectual property.' I'm not sure that I exactly get what you mean. Are these two different things?

"We were talking about the terminology in our IP class today," says Lauren, "and about the overlaps between cultural heritage and intellectual property." She opens her notebook. "One of the articles we looked at defined cultural heritage as 'the legacy of physical artifacts and intangible attributes of a group or society that are inherited from past generations, maintained in the present and bestowed for the benefit of future generations.'[16] You can see in that definition the idea of an inheritance that is shared, not something passed on to just one person."

Evie nods, saying, "So that fits here. If the masks are cultural heritage, then they have a shared inheritance. They didn't belong just to the sister, even if she was left them in her grandmother's will. What she was given was something more like stewardship than ownership."

Lauren continues. "Another challenge is that cultural heritage can take tangible and intangible forms. The tangible stuff seems obvious: things you can see and touch – monuments, works of art, objects, even places and landscapes. Intangible cultural heritage is a bit more slippery. It's all that which is non-physical and only visible through tangible expression. Things like language, ritual, songs, music, and social practices. The intangibles here are things of great value to the Hupacasath, though they seem to be invisible to the auction house."

---

16  Folarin Shylloin, "Cultural Heritage and Intellectual Property: Convergence, Divergence, and Interface" in William Logan, Máiréad Nic Craith & Ullrich Kockel, eds, *A Companion to Heritage Studies* (Hoboken: John Wiley & Sons, 2016) 55 at 55.

Ami, who had continued to wander through news reports on the web, says, "Well, that does seem to link us back to the intellectual property questions, since the family reported that the masks came with rights, responsibilities, and privileges. That's quite strong language. And it seems to bridge both the tangible and the intangible."

"Yes," Lauren says, "it *is* strong language. The IP with the masks would be of significant value to the family. There would likely be important protocols for engaging with the masks. There would be a number of family members with the right to access the masks on certain occasions. Someone would have been charged with the care of the masks. And there might have been others responsible for teaching family members the songs and dances that went with the masks. There is significant additional intangible value because of the IP. We bump into a conflict when we start to commodify that value – how can you put a price on the value to the Hupacasath of the IP associated with those specific masks?"

Evie grimaces, saying, "I can't help it! Now I have those irritating Mastercard commercials running through my mind. You know, the ones telling you to use your credit card to generate priceless moments"?

Dawn rocks back in her chair. "You know, the article said that the mask does have royal roots. So, does royalty make a difference to our story? I mean, does the story still work if we imagine telling it using British royalty? Can you imagine this scenario: an elderly woman comes into the auction house; her name is Liz. She wants to sell a bunch of jewels she has, say, a diamond tiara. Or the Crown jewels. Who owns or controls the family jewels? Who decides when and where they are displayed publicly? Can they be sold? Can a royal family also have household objects that could be passed down?"

Craig says, "Well, the analogy is interesting, but I wonder if it overshoots the mark. One difference might be that the queen may well own some family jewels, but the state owns the Crown jewels. In the Hupacasath context, there isn't a nation-state structure.[17] Another difference is that even if the Crown jewels get trotted out for special occasions, they don't really perform a legal or governance function. For example, they are not associated with legal ceremonies that legitimize a marriage or adoption as these masks might do. They are important cultural objects, but I don't see the intangibles, or the IP."

---

17   Val Napoleon, "Thinking about Indigenous Legal Orders" in René Provost & Colleen Sheppard, eds, *Dialogues on Human Rights and Legal Pluralism* (Dordrecht: Springer, 2013) 229.

"I don't know," Shiloh said, taking a long slow breath. "What you say seems right, and still … with how much talk there is about 'the honour of the Crown' in constitutional law class, it seems too quick to say that the actual Crown has *no* governance function. I mean, what about that magical moment what when a new king or queen gets crowned, and suddenly has two bodies?[18] Don't you think that during a coronation, the physical crown itself is maybe doing some legal work? Maybe there is a difference between family jewels and '*the* Crown'?"

Ami gives Dawn a sympathetic glance and says, "Nice try at constructing a hypothetical exam fact pattern, Dawn." Slipping into a passable imitation of Yoda's voice, he continues, "Patience, young Padawan. Much you still have to learn!"

Dawn shrugs. "No doubt we all do! I will confess I am still uncertain about the differences between cultural property and intellectual property. Maybe I just have to wait until next year to figure this out?"

Lauren smiles and says, "No point in waiting! Might as well start grappling with the challenge now! The bottom line is that intellectual property does have some overlap with cultural property. Intellectual property law deals with creations of the mind, with things produced by human intellect. In Canadian IP law, some forms of protection acknowledge the economic interest in property.[19] One branch of IP deals with things like patents, trademarks, registered designs. In class, we discussed how some people call these industrial property rights since they emerge out of questions about industry and commerce in our society. The other common branch of IP law is linked to the artistic world, in the form of copyright. You know, artistic creations of the mind like poems, novels, films, paintings. Some of the protection here is also rooted in economic questions, but some of it takes us to questions about identity. But these distinctions might get us back to the masks and that question your professor asked you about the *purpose* of the property."[20]

Ami jumps in. "I know Craig said no hypotheticals, but this sort of gets me curious. I know we are only asking about the sale of the mask itself, but now I find myself wondering about other IP questions. Like, who owns the IP on the mask itself? Is it the new owner of the mask,

---

18   Ernst H Kantorowicz, *The King's Two Bodies: A Study in Medieval Political Theology* (Princeton: Princeton University Press, 1957).

19   Robert Uerpmann-Wittzack, "Introduction: Cultural Heritage Law and the Quest for Human Identities" in Evelyne Lagrange, Stefam Oeter & Robert Uerpmann-Wittzack, eds, *Cultural Heritage and International Law: Objects, Means and Ends of International Protection* (Cham, Switzerland: Springer, 2018) 1 at 22.

20   Shylloin, *supra* note 16 at 59.

or the person who carved it in the first place? I know this mask is one hundred years old, so the carver is probably long dead, but what if the Hupacasath family wanted to make a new copy of the mask? A replica to use? Do they have to ask the original carver or the new owner for permission to make a copy? What if someone did want to make a replica? Who would they go to to get permission?"

Shiloh adds, "This is not totally hypothetical, of course. These problems come up in IP law all the time. This is the point. If someone wants to make a copy of an Indigenous cultural or intellectual product, or wants to use Indigenous cultural property for economic purposes, then you end up heading to IP law to ask who actually gets to make that decision. But you can see how tricky it starts to be. For sure, in order to know who you would ask, you can see there are some law questions. I am guessing you have probably seen cases about this in the news: fashion designers copying Inuit shaman's coats,[21] or Neiman Markus making cloaks using a Tlinkit design.[22] In those US cases, people have been making use of the *Indian Arts and Crafts Act* to deal with anyone wrongly making use of Indigenous intellectual property. In Canada, we don't have that kind of legislation yet. But there are parts of Canadian IP or copyright or heritage legislation can deal with some of the questions that come up."

"In the case you guys are looking at," adds Lauren, "the Sayers and Hamilton families tried to make an argument that the masks were protected from sale under the BC *Heritage Conservation Act*. But that legislation treats the ownership of such cultural pieces as individual rather than collective. Because this interacts with BC provincial laws that treat inherited objects as individually owned, there is a kind of erasure of the Nu-chah-nulth understanding of collective ownership."

Dawn says, "I know I am just in first year. I know I am just a baby learner, but ..." She trails off, and then takes a slow breath. "Well, that seems a bit wrong. So BC inheritance law trumps Nuu-chah-nulth cultural heritage law? Surely it is time that such a law be changed?!"

---

21  Teresa Scassa, "Copying of Inuit Robe Highlights Gaps in Canadian Legal Framework" (26 November 2015), online (blog): Teressa Scassa <http://www .teresascassa.ca/index.php?option=com_k2&view=item&id=200:copying-of -inuit-robe-highlights-gaps-in-canadian-legal-framework>; Sima Sahar Zerehi, "Inuit Shaman Parka 'Copied' by KTZ Design Well-Studied by Anthropologists," CBC News (2 December 2015), online: <https://www.cbc.ca/news/canada/north /inuit-shaman-parka-design-history-1.3345968>.

22  Yereth Rosen, "Neiman Marcus Agrees to Settle in Landmark Indigenous Property Rights Case," Arctic Today (24 March 2021), online: <https://www.arctictoday .com/neiman-marcus-agrees-to-settle-in-landmark-indigenous-property-rights -case/?wallit_nosession=1>.

Shiloh pops up: "It says here that there is a working group of First Nations leaders and provincial government representatives who are looking at the question.[23] But as you can imagine, there are lots of political questions there, since there are many different First Nations. Do they have to come to an agreement with the province first about their own legal orders? And if you want to see Craig blow his top again, you just remind him that the provincial body that is working with First Nations to address possible changes to the Heritage Conservation Act is the Ministry of Forests, Lands and Natural Resources."

Evie adds, "I guess that is what the family members were saying too. Wawmeesh Hamilton says these masks were among the most sacred of possessions. So that brings us back to the prof's question three about underlying purposes, right. It sounds like you are saying that it doesn't make sense to talk about the mask as if it were just a piece of art, or just a piece of intellectual property. In this context, the mask seems to be a piece of a governance structuring, or related to establishing the family's place in society. So, there is something artistic, something about governance, something about intangible intellectual property. That is a lot bundled into one object."

Craig breaks in again: "Exactly! And yet Western law continues to flatten things. The *Indian Act* still forces many Indigenous folks to adopt Western-style wills and concepts to deal with the legal transmission of title to such objects. It changes how we think about what's possible. And why do we keep talking this way?" He pauses and shakes his head, adding, "In fact, why am *I* talking this way? I mean, I am irritated listening to myself. Saying 'title' and 'transmission' in the same sentence makes me think of trying to sell my old car."

"Well, there you go, Craig," smiles Lauren. "Driving us towards a conclusion. Pun intended."

Dawn groans at the pun, and then adds, "You know, we have been focusing on the seller and the auction house. But now I'm wondering about the buyer. Do you think the auction company told the buyer about the conflict? I mean, if I try to imagine myself as a buyer, I don't

---

23   Keven Drews, "Woman Asks B.C. To Alter Heritage Law; Family to Punish Member over Masks' Sale," *Global News* (20 January 2013), online: <https://globalnews.ca /news/380655/woman-asks-b-c-to-alter-heritage-law-family-to-punish-member-over-masks-sale-3/>; Judith Lavoie, "Sale of First Nations Masks Sparks Call for Better Legal Protection," *Times Colonist* (21 January 2013), online: https://www .timescolonist.com/local-news/sale-of-first-nations-masks-sparks-call-for-better -legal-protection-4575575.

know that I would feel really great about buying the mask if I knew the story behind it."

Evie turns back to the open computer screen. "I don't know. For sure the auction company knew. The newspaper article says that the family went to the auction company and asked them to stop the sale. Waw-meesh Hamilton, the older brother, said, 'We tried to explain to them that there is a difference between private property and family cultural property, but their heads were full of dollar signs instead of sense. The art auction is a game played by rich people who don't care about cultures or correctness.'[24] He clearly doesn't have a high opinion of the auction house."

Ami adds, "Do you think he's right? Do you think this is a case of people who don't care, or people who actually don't know? I mean, I remember a friend of mine telling a story about his elderly mother taking her first visit to China, and sitting on what looked like a stool but was actually an ancestor shrine of some sort. She had no idea why people were yelling at her. She obviously didn't 'mean' to do harm, but I can see why the local peoples would feel disrespected. I can also see why it would have been better for her to know a bit more about Chinese law/society/culture."

Craig shakes his head. "No way! There is no way the auction company gets to make a claim of innocence here. Let's be honest. They knew there was a conflict. If they specialize in West Coast art, then they know about this history of the potlach and unjust legal dispossession. So, we're going to take seriously their claim that a mask is simply a household possession?! I think that conclusion is contestable even in Canadian law. They are not legislators, and they are not judges, but they get to decide that Hupacasath law is irrelevant, and strip this family of its intellectual property and turn its cultural heritage into a tradable art commodity?!" His voice continues to rise, gathering a few looks from people at the tables close to them. "So what that the potlach is no longer illegal! This is just a continuation of cultural genocide through new means!"

"Strong words, Craig," Ami says. "I am not quite sure what I think about calling it cultural genocide, but … you do leave me wondering. Why is the burden of proof here on the Hupacasath rather than on the auction house? Do you think that a court may be able to take judicial notice of a history of legal dispossession? Maybe the principle of *buyer beware* should be supplemented by the notion of buyer *be aware*.

---

24  Wiwchar, *supra* note 15.

Shiloh adds, "OK. That's a good bumper sticker line." She continues, "I guess if we are going to start talking evidence law, maybe we should also start talking about equity? Why do we assume it is equitable to let the buyer keep the mask?"

There is silence for a few minutes at the table. Lauren pushes another slice of apple over to Craig and says, "The loss of the mask is significant. The family has lost control of it in circumstances they should have been able to control. The mask and its songs and dances were a symbol of their continued cultural existence. They should have been able to maintain control of possession and use of the masks. It speaks to their very continued cultural existence. Having an understanding of the injury can shape how you think about possible remedies."

Evie says, "I guess this is why my head starts aching, trying to figure out how to describe the injury. There's the loss of the mask itself. There is the fact of having your own family member be the one to sell it. There is the injury of being told that criminal law can't help you because this isn't really theft, but only the sale of a household possession. There is a refusal to acknowledge the existence of Hupacasath law, let alone its relevance."

Dawn looks out to the woods behind the school, watching another swirl of leaves caught in a gust of wind. "Part of me is stuck on thinking how sad I would be if something like this were to happen in my own family. In some ways, it would be way easier to have the mask stolen by a stranger than to be sold by your own family member. That must have been so hard on the rest of her family. Well, that is a story that many of us know in our personal lives, eh? Many a family has seen their own members break the law, and has been left trying to figure out how to respond: Change the locks? Call the police to report it? Let it go?"

Lauren says, "Well, the Hupacasath certainly understood the magnitude of the injury that was done here. I assume your professor told you that the sister was stripped of her name?"

Ami tilts his head, "Say what?!"

Evie nods, scrolling down through the article and pushing it over to Ami to read. "Yes, she said that the family held a public ceremony, at which they stripped the family member of her name, title, and responsibilities. Serious business. It sounded a bit like being banished, or excommunicated, or exiled. Or like losing your citizenship."

Ami looks up from the article. "Listen to this: one family member said, 'These things are considered to be some of our very highest property, and they would be covered by our very highest laws, and those laws have consequences to them. It's an egregious offence.'" He pauses for a moment, then says "Now that is weird ..."

"Why do you say that?" Craig snaps at him. "It is not weird at all. In fact, it speaks to all the intellectual property implications in this case. It tells us that the intangible property, you know, the songs and dances that went with the mask, that those make the mask even more valuable to the Hupacasath. You know there has been a big harm where the remedy is so big!"

"Whoa, whoa, whoa!" says Ami, holding up his hands in a defensive posture. "I didn't mean the *ceremony* was weird. I was looking at the way the newspaper reported it. The paper says, "They plan to strip the family member who sold the 'hinkeets' of her royal title and cultural responsibilities at an upcoming ceremony, shedding light on the internal disciplinary proceedings practised by First Nations for generations."[25]

"So, what is the weird part of that?" Craig says, still looking at Ami suspiciously.

"Well," he says, "I just thought it weird that they would describe a ceremony as *"internal disciplinary proceedings."* That's not the language you see in the papers when they are referring to Canadian law. We usually call that stuff 'law.' Calling it 'internal' implies that non-Hupacasath people have no responsibilities when dealing with Indigenous property. And the phrase 'disciplinary proceedings' is something you hear when the hockey league is trying to deal with fights on the ice between its players. It makes it sound like an administrative or bureaucratic process rather than a legal process related to the very highest form of property."

"Ah," says Shiloh, "I see your point. The newspaper describes the problem as a private one for the family to sort out. Not one that implicates Indigenous intellectual property. In effect, the auction house, the buyer, the police, the legislature, and the media all *implicitly* deny the existence of Hupacasath law. Or, put otherwise, they deny that Hupacasath law has any jurisdictional traction in contemporary life. If there is a remedy, it is only of the Hupacasath against one of their own. Hupacasath law has no extra-territorial reach."

Ami says, "So then, are we saying that there is no Indigenous IP problem with this case?"

"Well," Shiloh comments, "I guess I am saying that under the current statutory regime, it is hard to find a harm recognizable for Western IP with the sale of the mask. This reminds me of Professors Morales and

---

25   Keven Drews, "Sale of Island Masks Sparks First Nations Concern over Preservation Of Culture," *Times Colonist* (20 January 2013), online: <https://www.timescolonist .com/national-news/sale-of-island-masks-sparks-first-nations-concern-over -preservation-of-culture-4575445>.

Thom saying that Canadian property laws cast a shadow and make it difficult for Indigenous property laws and principles to be seen and exercised.[26] For the Hupacasath here, there is little in the Canadian legal system that could provide a remedy for the harm done. It does not seem to get them the mask back."

Shiloh turns to Evie. "That was one of the questions the prof asked you, right? About remedies for this kind of legal harm?" Evie nods, and Shiloh continues. "In terms of present-day remedies, it sometimes feels like the Canadian legal order suffers from a lack of imagination."

Lauren interjects, "Before everyone falls into the pit of despair, I think it bears saying that Hupacasath law is not without resources for addressing complex problems like these. In this case, the mask is gone. That is an injury. But you can imagine the mask being lost in other ways. What if, for example, it was lost in a house fire? You would still have questions about the relationship between the mask and the songs. There are protocols in place for making a new mask, and for reconnecting the mask to those songs and dances: there would be a ceremony at which that would happen. And in fact, something like that happened in this case. I am not diminishing the injury in this case. I am only noting that the question of 'what next' is addressed in Hupacasath law. There are legal principles in place to address how one responds to the relationship between the physical object of the mask and the other intangible intellectual and cultural properties that are carried with it. What you see here in the ceremony, however it was reported, was that two big things happened. First, there was a public acknowledgment of the magnitude of the harm. In stripping the sister of her name, they were not just punishing her. They were affirming and enacting the significance of Hupacasath intellectual property law. Second, in carving a new mask and attaching the songs and dances to it, they were enacting a lawful response to and repair of that injury."

Craig adds, "You are reminding me that the issue here is control and not just protection. Because the point is not that a mask like this could never be sold. The question is how the decision gets made and by whom. Sometimes families made decisions to sell masks like these when they were no longer being danced, or when their needs were dire. It would be pretty paternalistic to say that a group could *never* make the decision to sell a mask or another object."

---

26   Sarah Morales & Brian Thom, "The Principle of Sharing and the Shadow of Canadian Property Law" in Angela Cameron, Sari Graben & Val Napoleon, eds, *Creating Indigenous Property: Power, Rights and Relationships* (Toronto: University of Toronto Press, 2022) 120 at 122.

Evie asks, "But this gets us back to the question of how a buyer would know if they could or couldn't buy something. How would you know if someone was selling you someone's family property, or something made for the market?"

Lauren smiles, "There are questions in all markets. In the context of masks, it has always been the case that some are ceremonial, some are for trade. You could probably tell from seeing how well the back of the mask was set up for being worn, with pieces to connect or hold it in place."

"That reminds me of this pair of Inuit sunglasses I have." says Dawn. "My sister brought them back from a trip up North. They look like the glasses in the film *Atanarjuat*. They are carved from some kind of bone or antler, I think. They are beautiful to look at, but not really designed for being worn. I imagine that there would be tons of artistry and time involved to have a pair fitted to wear. Such things, whether worn or hung on the wall, don't seem to raise quite the same questions. They're fabulous functional objects, definitely associated with the North, but not quite raising IP questions. My pair have the artist's name carved on the back and came with a certificate of authenticity. So, I guess they are at least covered by IP law in some way?"

"This gets back to the point," Craig says. "*Whose* intellectual property law? You just can't have a conversation about a Hupacasath mask without having a conversation about Hupacasath law." Both BC and Canada have ratified UNDRIP. Article 31 asserts the right of Indigenous peoples to maintain, control, protect, and develop their cultural heritage. So, the point is, the conversation can't end with Canadian IP law. The rebuilding of right relations with Canada has to involve Indigenous legal orders too."

The group sits quietly for a minute, as the flow of students moves in and out of the space around them. Evie smiles and says, "Well, I guess that is the answer I will be giving in the next crim class: 'The conversation can't end with Canadian IP law! Nor can it end with Canadian criminal law!'"

Evie re-opens her notebook, and taps the list written there, saying, "So let's recap. The prof told us to ask five different questions: (1) What kind of property is this? (2) Who is the owner? (3) What is the underlying purpose of the property? (4) What is the legal harm or injury? and (5) What are the range of historic and present-day remedies?" She raises her eyes and says, "I don't know that I could answer these yet, but I do feel like I understand the questions a little bit better. I really wonder about that last question, about what some of the historic and present-day remedies might be."

Dawn holds out an arm, and says, "Evie! Stop!" She wrinkles up her face and says, "My brain is tired! Lauren, Ami, Shiloh, Craig ... You guys are amazing, and this has been a very tasty intellectual meal, but I am full to the brim. I feel like Mr. Creosote in Monty Python's *The Meaning of Life*. Please, no more! No last 'wafer-thin mint' for me, John Cleese! I think I need some time to digest."

Shiloh laughs, and then looks at her watch. "Time flies! OK, my next class starts in an hour, but I have got to get a bit of fresh air before we head back in there. Are any of you up for a bit of a 'post-meal' walk to speed up the mental digestive juices?"

"Well," Dawn said, "if you are planning to stroll by the parking lot, I would be happy to join you."

"The parking lot?" Shiloh said with a raised eyebrow. "Not exactly the most scenic walk around here. So, I guess that means you're still working on that plan to quit smoking?"

Dawn shrugs and grins, "It's the last designated smoking spot left on campus. Life's a work in progress, you know. But hey! Let's call it harm minimization. We'll both get a walk. I'll stand downwind from you in the parking lot to make sure you get fresh air. You can keep talking to me about the case, thereby fulfilling your obligations to me as a mentor!"

Shiloh laughs, saying, "OK, pack it up and let's take a stroll. Anyone one else want to join?" Ami and Evie agree, and the group head out of the lounge in the direction of the great outdoors, leaving Lauren and Craig behind.

Lauren finishes her final bite of apple, sitting with Craig in companionable silence. "So many important questions raised by the case."

Craig nods. "I don't even know what to think about the prof opening that can of worms in a first-year crim class. Is she going to give them answers, or just let those questions sit there? Quite the privilege to just throw the problem out there. Of course, there are Indigenous intellectual property laws out there, and maybe the students can even start to see those laws, but it can't just be about comparing different legal rules. It's not only about concepts of law but about legal structures and institutions."

Lauren nods, "It can be a challenge to get past an interest in Indigenous law generally to a commitment to deal with law in all its messy and very particular detail. Honestly, I kind of like it that she gave them something complicated to cut their teeth on. As you say, it does raise all the big questions. And I do mean *all*. How do we teach and learn law when issues cross boundaries – jurisdictions, ways of being and knowing, material and spiritual. And so many different legal questions are implicated: criminal, tortious, property, wills and estates, harm, remedies, ownership – alongside other ways of thinking about law – gender, power, privilege. Of course there will be answers to find, but I do like it that the students are at least grappling with the harder questions."

"And for us Indigenous folks?" Craig asks. "Don't you think we are also facing harder and harder questions about implementing Indigenous law in the ordinary spaces of daily life?" Craig shifted a bit in his seat and said, "So many difficult politics here. It is one thing to remind outsiders that Indigenous law continues to exist in the world, but it is another thing to do the hard work of actually using Indigenous law to solve problems in the world. One can't just talk about Indigenous intellectual property laws springing back into existence without taking institutions into account. This is going to mean the rebuilding of Indigenous IP institutions."

"Yes," Lauren says, "and it's going to require some work exploring how current Canadian and international institutions may need some re-engineering, and changes in policy, and operating assumptions." Her attention is caught by a swooping movement, as outside the window a pair of ravens land in a branch high in a tree. They caw back and forth, seemingly in the middle of an ongoing piece of storytelling. With a glint in her eye, Lauren continues, "And I suspect this will involve conversations and collaborations with our activists, artists, and intellectuals, old and young alike!"

* * *

And so we leave our imagined characters as they continue the work of learning law, whether in the spaces of the formal classroom or through engagements with others in the lounge, or indeed, conversations while walking, even if only to the designated smoking areas alongside the parking lot. I am left carrying forward a few thoughts. One is that it matters, when thinking about Indigenous intellectual property, to be specific about the legal orders from which the questions arise. This does not mean "knowing" everything about each Indigenous legal order in North America, but it does mean a change in the presumption that Canadian default understandings of property apply. Indigenous art and societal/cultural expressions take on meaning within the rich context of their legal orders, and these expressions require specific engagement with questions of governance, economy, and identity. Colonial inheritances and histories will remain a part of the conversation, as they often situate contemporary conflicts that continue to carry the legacy of the stories that are told about both Indigenous and settler state lawfulness and lawlessness. The conversations, especially intergenerational, and with spaces for interruption, are crucial to the work of unsettling our inherited colonial erasures, and engaging in the (perhaps messy and difficult but also more life-affirming) practices of learning law and acting lawfully in the multi-juridical world we have inherited. Part of the work that needs doing is being done within Indigenous communities, as they engage with (and in cases rebuild) the law around important societal and cultural expressions. Part of the work is also being done by non-Indigenous folks and institutions, as they exert themselves to learn about the legal regimes of others, in order to grapple with the questions that will enable respectful and practical engagements with the world of the real, both tangible and intangible. What lies ahead, we hope, are more conversations that open space for more questions. These are conversations worth having.

## BIBLIOGRAPHY


Bracken, Christopher. *The Potlatch Papers: A Colonial Case History* (Chicago: University of Chicago Press, 1997).

Calder, Gillian. "Embodied Law: Theatre of the Oppressed in the Law School Classroom" (2009) 1 Masks: Online J of L and Theatre 1.

Ceric, Irina. "Beyond Contempt: Injunctions, Land Defense, and the Criminalization of Indigenous Resistance" (2020) 119:2 South Atlantic Quarterly 353.

Claxton, Nicholas Xemtoltw & John Price. "Whose Land Is It? Rethinking Sovereignty in British Columbia" (2019–20) 204 BC Studies 125.

Cook, Peter et al, eds. *To Share, Not Surrender: Indigenous and Settler Visions of Treaty Making in the Colonies of Vancouver Island and British Columbia* (Vancouver: UBC Press, 2021).

Drews, Keven. "B.C. Families Search for Sacred Cedar Masks Sold at Auction," *Globe and Mail* (29 November 2012), online: <https://www.theglobeandmail.com/news/british-columbia/bc-families-search-for-sacred-cedar-masks-sold-at-auction/article5789775/>.

Drews, Keven. "Sale of Island Masks Sparks First Nations Concern over Preservation of Culture," *Times Colonist* (20 January 2013), online: <https://www.timescolonist.com/national-news/sale-of-island-masks-sparks-first-nations-concern-over-preservation-of-culture-4575445>.

Drews, Keven. "Woman Asks B.C. to Alter Heritage Law; Family to Punish Member over Masks' Sale." *Global News* (20 January 2013), online: <https://globalnews.ca/news/380655/woman-asks-b-c-to-alter-heritage-law-family-to-punish-member-over-masks-sale-3/>.

Johnson, Rebecca. "Questions about Questions: Law and Film Reflections on the Duty to Learn" (2020) 50 Northern Review 83, online: <https://doi.org/10.22584/nr50.2020.004>.

Kantorowicz, Ernst H. *The King's Two Bodies: A Study in Medieval Political Theology* (Princeton: Princeton University Press, 1957).

Lavoie, Judith. "Sale of First Nations Masks Sparks Call for Better Legal Protection." *Times Colonist* (21 January 2013), online: <https://www .timescolonist.com/local-news/sale-of-first-nations-masks-sparks-call-for -better-legal-protection-4575575>.

Louie, Ren "Wikinanish." "Persistent to Potlatch: The Continuity of Nuu-Chah-Nulth Potlatches through Covid-19." *Martlet* (1 February 2021), online: <https:// www.martlet.ca/potlach-nuu-chah-nulth-covid-19/>.

Morales, Sarah & Brian Thom. "The Principle of Sharing and the Shadow of Canadian Property Law" in Angela Cameron, Sari Graben & Val Napoleon, eds, *Creating Indigenous Property: Power, Rights and Relationships* (Toronto: University of Toronto Press, 2022) 120.

Napoleon, Val. "Behind the Blockade" (2010) 9:1 Indigenous L J 1.

Napoleon, Val. "Indigenous Women Talking: The Work of Indigenous Feminisms in the World" in Emily Snyder et al, eds, *Critical Indigenous Feminisms* (Toronto: University of Toronto Press, forthcoming).

Napoleon, Val. "Thinking about Indigenous Legal Orders" in René Provost & Colleen Sheppard, eds, *Dialogues on Human Rights and Legal Pluralism* (Dordrecht: Springer, 2013) 229.

Napoleon, Val, Rebecca Johnson, Debra McKenzie & Richard Overstall. *Indigenous Intellectual Property: An Interrupted Intergenerational Conversation.* Victoria: Indigenous Law Research Unit, 2021.

Pasternak, Shiri & Dayna Nadine Scott. "Introduction: Getting Back the Land" (2020) 119:2 South Atlantic Quarterly 205.

Rosen, Yereth. "Neiman Marcus Agrees to Settle in Landmark Indigenous Property Rights Case," Arctic Today (24 March 2021), online: <https://www .arctictoday.com/neiman-marcus-agrees-to-settle-in-landmark-indigenous -property-rights-case/?wallit_nosession=1>.

Scassa, Teresa. "Copying of Inuit Robe Highlights Gaps in Canadian Legal Framework" (26 November 2015), online (blog): Teressa Scassa <http:// www.teresascassa.ca/index.php?option=com_k2&view=item&id=200: copying-of-inuit-robe-highlights-gaps-in-canadian-legal-framework>.

Shylloin, Folarin. "Cultural Heritage and Intellectual Property: Convergence, Divergence, and Interface" in William Logan, Máiréad Nic Craith and Ullrich Kockel, eds, *A Companion to Heritage Studies* (Hoboken: John Wiley & Sons, 2016) 55.

Uerpmann-Wittzack, Robert. "Introduction: Cultural Heritage Law and the Quest for Human Identities" in Evelyne Lagrange, Stefam Oeter and Robert Uerpmann-Wittzack, eds, *Cultural Heritage and International Law: Objects, Means and Ends of International Protection* (Cham, Switzerland: Springer, 2018) 1.

Wiwchar, David. "Sacred First Nation Masks Sold to Highest Bidder," *Indian Country Today* (10 December 2012), online: <https://ictnews.org/archive/sacred-first-nation-masks-sold-to-highest-bidder>.

Zerehi, Sima Sahar. 2015. "Inuit Shaman Parka 'Copied' by KTZ Design Well-Studied by Anthropologists," *CBC News* (2 December 2015), online: <https://www.cbc.ca/news/canada/north/inuit-shaman-parka-design-history-1.3345968>.

# Index